...is stirring book is an account of ...the modern world have come to ...violence, and a specific program ...ho would put a halt to this trend. It is an analysis, based on Stowe's long experience as a foreign correspondent, of how doctrines of violence took root all over the world among both Communists and Fascists, and took the form of extreme nationalism, militarism, intolerance, and oppression. It shows how the average American today has become the last stronghold of moderation and tolerance, and how the totalitarians everywhere are trying to capture his mind and allegiance.

Against this attack Stowe proposes specific defenses. He reveals the degrading effects of blind partisanship and extremism. He exposes the subtle, beguiling arguments of the totalitarians, who seek to involve us in the vile tactics and expedients of power politics. He asserts that the crisis mentality is self-nourishing. He shows us how we can defend ourselves morally, intellectually, and emotionally; how we can destroy the power-seekers; and how we can bring into our daily lives the practical application of principles of justice, social welfare, peace, freedom, and security. Against the totalitarian crossfire, of which you are a target, Stowe raises boldly the banner of the decent citizen — the citizen who will fight *against* nationalism, *against* boom-and-bust, *against* the pathological quest for absolute military security, and *for* respect for the law, *for* civil liberties, *for* tolerance, and *for* a genuine world government that is not a jealous union of insecure nations.

Sigma Delta Chi, honorary journalistic fraternity, Leland Stowe has received honorary degrees from Harvard and Wesleyan, and has been decorated by the French and Greek governments. Other books by Stowe are *No Other Road to Freedom*, *They Shall Not Sleep*, and *While Time Remains*.

Also by Leland Stowe

NO OTHER ROAD TO FREEDOM

". . . he possesses all the qualities of a glamorous war correspondent. Among these are the gifts of vivid description and dramatization, warm emotional sympathy for the peoples whose struggles he is reporting, and a remarkable knack of being in the most exciting place at the right time."
—W. H. Chamberlin in the *Atlantic Monthly*

THEY SHALL NOT SLEEP

"One of the best of our war correspondents does one of the best pieces of reporting that has come out of the war."
—the *New Yorker*

WHILE TIME REMAINS

"In one of the most passionate, best informed and most readable books of our unhappy era, Leland Stowe writes as though he had been commissioned to draft mankind's final testament. It is the magnum opus of a great reporter."
—Sterling North in the New York *Post*

These are Borzoi Books, published by
ALFRED · A · KNOPF

TARGET: YOU

TARGET:

YOU

by Leland Stowe

ALFRED A. KNOPF

NEW YORK

1949

FOR

MY SISTERS

Rev. Elsie F. Stowe,

Myrtle S. Pease,

Hattie E. Stowe,

&

Fern E. Stowe

ACKNOWLEDGMENTS

These pages are concerned with Mr. and Mrs. John Between of the U.S.A. They were written by one John Between. They are addressed to as many John Betweens and Jane Betweens as may be interested in exploring the *what, where, why,* and *how* about themselves in a world society haunted by fear of totalitarianism, revolution, and war.

Since this is in no sense a simple project, it cannot possibly provide all the answers required; perhaps no more than a certain number of partial answers at best. This is why I wish to express my sincere thanks to Blanche Knopf and Edward R. Murrow for their early encouragement of a hazardous venture. I owe much to Vera Micheles Dean and Byron Dexter for their careful study of the original outline and for the many pertinent suggestions that they offered. In addition I am especially indebted to Harold Strauss, of Alfred A. Knopf, Inc., for his unusually perceptive and vital criticisms of the manuscript in its later stages.

Without these constructive counsels the limitations of this endeavor would be much greater than those which inevitably remain. Any kind of exploration imposes its own risks. If the exploration in these pages helps to provoke a more general and realistic examination of "the most important man in the world"—his situation and what he may do about it—the efforts here involved may be justified.

L. S.

BRONXVILLE, N. Y.
JANUARY 1949

CONTENTS

I· SPOTLIGHT ON A SADLY NEGLECTED
    CHARACTER   3

II· WHAT HAS HAPPENED TO AMERICANS?   16

III· AMERICANS AND EUROPEANS   38

IV· HOW FASCISM CAME TO EUROPE   65

V· WHAT THE SECOND WORLD WAR DID
    TO EUROPEANS   91

VI· AMERICANS AS THE MAJOR TARGET   121

VII· THE CROSSFIRES OF TOTALITARIANISM   137

VIII· BETWEEN BOOM AND BUST   165

IX· OUR FIRST DEFENSE IS THE LAW   185

X· THE PERILS OF "SECURITY"   207

XI· WHAT PRICE NATIONAL DEFENSE?   230

XII· THE OTHER DEFENSE—WORLD GOVERNMENT
     THROUGH WORLD LAW   258

INDEX   follows page 288

TARGET: YOU

Chapter I

SPOTLIGHT ON A
SADLY NEGLECTED CHARACTER

Who is the most important man in today's world?

No, he is not the President of the United States, nor even Generalissimo Joseph Stalin or whoever may succeed him.

Oddly enough, the most important man on our planet is one of the least-noticed as an individual. He has no real conception of his own significance. He assumes that the "big fellows" really decide things. Famous names and glaring headlines seem to vindicate that assumption. So he does not see himself as he is, or where he is.

He does not perceive the exact nature and various identities of the forces ganged up against him. He recognizes Communism for what it is, but like a bull hypnotized by anything red, he is distracted from other enemies equally dangerous. He tends to look in but one direction when in reality he needs to watch attentively in several.

This man is long accustomed to health, strength, and freedom of choice; and for this reason he is inclined to be careless, and sometimes reckless. His influence in the world is quite extraordinary—greater than he knows. His potential power can scarcely be measured. Yet he is also weaker than he should be. For one thing, his knowledge of both his friends and his foes is fragmentary and frequently superficial, and he does not see clearly the form and weapons of some of his greatest adversaries.

The man who is more important than presidents and dictators makes the mistake of assuming that they are

3

stronger than he. As a result he repeatedly ignores what he is capable of doing. And he ignores especially the consequences of what he fails to do. Many of the world's most powerful men, emperors and czars, have suffered from the same costly blindness. You might say, then, that he is just a drowsing, half-conscious Goliath, not much disposed to protect himself to the utmost of his ability or to exploit his talents, assets, and opportunities to the degree that his safety requires. But despite all this he is almost certain, one way or another, to determine very largely the future of most of the world's peoples as well as the future of the United States.

In the British Commonwealth, Scandinavia, France, and a few other countries this man has many cousins. Today they have much less power than a generation ago and they are also threatened; but they are much more conscious of their exposed situation than he. They belong to the outside world's embattled and fast-dwindling middle class, and their problems are strikingly similar to his own. But they are not the central figures in our universal drama. The man with many cousins is the central figure simply because he possesses the most power, because he is the most vigorous and most economically secure representative of the middle class now remaining anywhere in the world. As such he is peculiarly a symbol of our times. More than that, he is *the target of our times.*

The human target of a world revolution needs many things. Especially he needs self-knowledge, an accurate perception of his enemies, and an awareness of how to act in his defense. In actual fact his survival depends quite as much upon his mental and spiritual armor as upon physical weapons. What types of armor must he develop if he is to survive? How must he mobilize and use his inner resources? Will he perfect them and exploit them in time?

This is the true drama of the most important man in today's world. It has universal meaning. It reaches into the lives and destinies of people in all corners of the globe. It is a drama in which the principal actor must finally establish himself as either the hero or the dupe.

Obviously we need to see this man clearly and to know him well. We need to understand precisely what he is up against, how he may be expected to act, and how he may seal his fate by failing to act. With him our free societies and our democratic systems will gain renewed strength and thus prevail. Or with him they will ultimately perish. Without him they cannot possibly survive at all. In our time this middle-class American is the one man who is truly inexpendable. Curiously enough, and wherever he lives, his name is the same.

Who is this sadly neglected yet absolutely indispensable fellow?

His name is JOHN BETWEEN.

In its deepest possible meaning he is the middle man of the twentieth century's world revolution. In all recorded history no man has ever been caught so *in between* as he.

What the neighbors call John Between is really not important. You might think of him as Bill Smith down the street. You might call him Mr. American Middle Man. You might take a second look in the mirror and recognize him as yourself. That could be a little startling, but we are concerned here with all those who are generally known and classified as "average Americans." In reality we are investigating ourselves.

What is the American middle class?

Wherever I go in the U.S.A. I meet John Between at every turn. Behind the grocer's counter he says: "Well, what do you think of Truman winning the election?"—and of course he himself had something to do with that. At a gas station in New England he remarks: "That Berlin blockade is a nasty business." And of course John is involved in that. At a luncheon of Chicago executives he declares: "I don't know how we're going to do it, but those Russians have got to be stopped somehow." He is paying his portion for ERP and the rest, so Soviet pressures have become his personal concern. A professor in Mississippi says: "I guess it will be a long time before we get another salary increase around here." And he knows most of the reasons why, and particularly what it means to belong to the nonunionized white-collar class.

You meet John Between everywhere in the United States because our country is the greatest and perhaps the last stronghold of what Europeans know as the bourgeoisie. This is true because two World Wars have severely diminished the middle class in Great Britain and continental Europe. Our American system originated without a titled aristocracy such as exists in the Old World. It developed far fewer distinctions of class, while providing greater opportunities for individual betterment. With us barriers of birth and circumstance have always been much less obstructive and exclusive than in Europe or Asia.

As a result the American middle class embraces an astonishing variety of people and occupations. It includes shopkeepers, small businessmen, and some big ones; all so-called white-collar citizens, and also skilled and semi-skilled workers who belong to unions; salesmen and motor dealers, publicity men and real-estate agents; preachers, professors, and teachers; artists and writers; most doctors and lawyers; most engineers and scientists; independent farmers who own ten good acres, and others who may own five hundred or more; policemen and firemen; almost all politicians, and several million citizens who are federal or state civil employees.

The scope of New World opportunities and the elasticity of our democratic system combine to create an American middle class of remarkable breadth, and to keep it con

stantly renewed and broadened. After arriving almost il-
literate at Ellis Island, countless immigrants emerged as
prospering self-made men or women in fifteen or twenty
years. They are accepted according to what they have accomplished, not according to where they started. The same
applies to innumerable Americans of the humblest origins.
In our society the door is always open to membership in
U.S. Middle Men, *Unlimited.*

The yardstick of family income seems to be the only
fairly reasonable mechanism with which to identify the
American middle class. In 1947, for instance, the "middle
income" of our 42,000,000 families was $2,920.* In that
year 69 per cent—or nearly 29,000,000 U.S. families—had
joint incomes of $2,000 or more. Even the families of skilled
and semi-skilled workers averaged incomes of $3,000 per
year; those of sales clerks were just below that figure. On
the extremes about 31 per cent of our families are compelled to live in seriously reduced circumstances, with incomes of only $2,000 a year or considerably less than that.
A small percentage of Americans are ranked in the very
high income brackets.

But in between lives John Between, representing an impressive majority. His average income may be about $3,000
annually. On the other hand he may earn $10,000 a year,
or $25,000—or possibly considerably more than that—and
still be quite typically "middle-class" in his background
and habits, in his prejudices, his qualities, and his psychology. Although Mr. American Middle Man occasionally
evolves into a millionaire, he usually remains utterly incapable of assimilating the manners and code of an aristocrat or of competing with the Vanderbilts. Much of where
he started from sticks for life. This explains the American
phenomenon of gilt-edged bourgeoisie.

A vast number of middle-class Americans do not own
their own homes. Not all of them own automobiles. But

* Cf. Federal Reserve Board Report, *New York Times,* June 15, 1948.

virtually all of them have radios, and all of them have a typically middle-class outlook—a certain assurance about their place in society and a middle-class sense of values. They can be numbered roughly in several scores of millions, and that is why our great middle class constitutes the balance of power in the United States.

These middle citizens are the *governing* power in the U.S.A. They elect our Presidents and name the men who make our laws. They are the great central force that decides what kind of government the United States has; what kind of congressmen and senators will enact what kind of legislation; what kind of domestic and foreign policies the administration in Washington will feel authorized to adopt. Multiplied by many millions, John Between either determines the actions of the world's most powerful nation by his positive collective electoral mandates and by the pressures of his public opinion—or he determines them by default, through his negative inaction.

Unless we understand the influence of the American middle class we cannot grasp the essential meanings of our dilemma in today's revolutionary world. Nor can we strike through to many of the basic reasons for our perplexities, apprehensions, and fears. The decade of the 1950's may well be termed the Fearful Fifties. It can scarcely fail to be one of the most momentous and decisive decades in many centuries. The stakes are our civilization and survival itself. And what America's middle men do, or fail to do, in this decade will largely decide what the United States of America does, how it does it, and how these decisions affect and alter developments throughout the world. There is no other common man and common denominator of such pivotal dynamism as John Between.

Yet when I meet him, in Idaho or Oregon or any other state, John betrays no slightest hint of recognition that he really belongs to the most powerful group of human beings in any national society on earth. Usually he murmurs something like: "Of course, there's nothing I can do to prevent war"; or he ends a discussion by explaining with a frustrated air: "After all, I'm just an ordinary citizen." Suppose you replied by saying: "But you're a member of the greatest middle class in the world." John would look blank and probably answer: "So what?"

In this he is typically American. For as typical Americans we dislike thinking of ourselves as belonging to any particular class. It is American to nourish a kind of class-rejecting and inverted snobbism. It is part of our free and easy social conduct and our free-spoken, independent-minded habits. Unless we were born into certain racial or religious minorities, we are inclined to think there are no class distinctions of much importance in our society. But this is a reckless and dangerous illusion. Day in and day out the majority of Americans live middle-class and think in middle-class terms. We react consistently as members of this same class react in all parts of the world. We have the same deep attachment to property and material progress. We have the same veneration for individual effort and the homely virtues. We have similar privileges and prejudices; an identical aversion to instability and lawlessness. We also have the same personal interests and freedoms to defend. In addition we Americans exist as a people who are peculiarly marked in the eyes of the world.

We are marked by our unique well-being and the abundance of our privileges. We are further marked by our political philosophy and our unrestrained capitalist system; by the exceptional scope of our personal freedoms; even by the amazing number of radios and automobiles we possess. Perhaps we are equally marked, in other eyes, by our lack of awareness of precisely what we are and where we are. Foreign peoples, more conscious of the unprecedented collective power of the American people, have compelling reasons to measure us with a sharp and uncompromising realism. They see very clearly that their

own lives will be tremendously influenced for many years
to come, in little ways and big, by the United States government's actions and by the voters who determine those
actions. So today we are perpetually under an invisible
scrutiny from friends and foes alike.

The champions of the totalitarian police state—Communists and Fascists—have the great advantage of recognizing American democracy as their principal enemy and
of continually studying its weaknesses with searching care.
They attack the middle class wherever they can, and they
have conquered it, largely liquidated or enslaved it, in
many lands. To the totalitarians, therefore, America's
middle men are the last entrenched and powerful adver-
sary. It is their first necessity, then, to know our weaknesses as intimately as they know our strength.

Goliath drowses and doesn't quite know his own name.
But the totalitarians are wide awake, always on the aggressive, probing for chinks and crevices in the big fellow's
armor. Destroy or cripple the American middle class—and
the world is theirs.

Why are we the target?

We are the target because our free and numerous
middle-class society constitutes the only major barrier for
successful resistance to Communist and Fascist ideologies
and dictatorship.

Because a long chain of events has now pushed the
American people directly into the crossfires of the world-
wide revolution.

Because we are caught between the onslaughts of Red
totalitarianism on the Left and the reconsolidating forces
of Black totalitarianism on the Right.

Because, as free-enterprisers, we live between the challenge of Communist Marxism on one side and a dangerous
expansion of monopolistic Big Capitalism on the other.

Because we are also menaced by uncurbed inflation on one hand and by the possibility of a great depression on the other.

In short, because we in the United States are caught between all the major forces of dynamic change unleashed by the world political revolution and by the industrial-technological revolution. Even without the "liberated" atom these revolutionary forces were tremendously explosive. Then the United States itself superimposed upon these still untamed forces the shattering revolution of atomic fission and atomic weapons. Thus we are now compelled to exist in between the most incalculably volcanic and disruptive forces any generation has ever faced. They might well be called an unholy trinity of revolutionary change.

Today, then, three vast revolutionary pressures are intermingled. Where such profound pressures converge and intermingle is not exactly a pleasant place for a drowsing Goliath to be obliged to live and stand his ground. It's true that, as yet, John Between's hands and body remain free. But how free is his mind? Can he make it sufficiently free, perceptive, and informed to arm himself adequately against the shocks and eruptions ahead? This is where the decisive test of the world's last great middle class must come. In plain fact, its crucial test has already begun. Somewhere in the future a time-limit at present shadowy will one day draw sharp and near. Can the middle men and women of the United States meet the test before that deadline arrives?

It is realistic to admit that the odds against our safely meeting this test are very considerable. The American people must grow much more and achieve far more, in a much shorter period of time, than any other middle-class nation has ever done. It will not be easy or simple. Complacency and narrow self-interest and distorted conceptions can serve as deadly enemies. Yet the John Betweens of the U.S.A. have proved themselves capable of rising to a supreme challenge again and again. In our past, and very recently, they have been greatest when the issues and the stakes were greatest. Of itself this is reason for hope. Like many other human beings the American performs exceptionally when he understands that nothing less than exceptional performance will serve.

Since the second World War ended, the full extent to which John Between is a target has escaped him. But the most important man in today's world is infinitely more than a target. Without yielding to arrogance, he has the right and need to be conscious of his true worth, of his qualities and capacities. Even though he may be called the common man, our friend John, as an average American, has much in his make-up to inspire respect and admiration.

Wherever I meet him, John Between believes deeply in the essential dignity of man—and he lives this belief with conviction and fervor. He is fiercely attached to his personal freedom. More than that, he cherishes such freedom for others, whether neighbors or strangers in distant lands. He clings to independence of mind on most vital issues— and has been known to turn topsy-turvy the electoral weathervanes of Dr. Gallup and other presumed readers of the national mind. He ardently defends his right to speak out, and regularly practices that right with undeniable zest.

When a conflict or a controversy is obviously lopsided, John's sympathies instinctively go to the underdog. His sense of fair play cannot be stifled, and his desire for justice asserts itself constantly in his personal life. On the whole he is commendably law-abiding. His respect for law and order is profound. His abhorrence of tyranny is deep and strong. His belief in self-government and the democratic processes is basic to his entire philosophy. His neighborliness and his hospitality are truly remarkable. His natural generosity of spirit is often surprising. There is an openness and frankness about him that wins friends easily. Men with these qualities have become more and more rare in our kind of world. Yet these same qualities might almost be termed common to the common man in the United States.

If you do not relish having your back slapped by a total stranger, it is wise not to seek a quiet drink at an American bar. If you prefer to rest your eardrums, it is not prudent to expose yourself where more than five or six American citizens are assembled—nor sometimes even then. Americans as a rule are bumptious, boisterous, gregarious creatures endowed with slight regard for personal privacy. They are so well satisfied with their own way of life that they seldom show much interest, or a thoughtful respect, for the ways and customs of other peoples. They are born-and-bred equalitarians—as every U.S. taxi-driver unconsciously informs his customers as he opens up a conversation on domestic politics, the Russians, or the weather. They have no reticence about their prejudices, no matter how extreme or unworthy some of them may be. They flaunt their faults in the same unabashed, unreserved manner in which they usually demonstrate that their hearts are in the right place. Quite unconsciously they tend to assume that to be American is to be somewhat—or perhaps definitely—superior to any other sort of being. About most Americans, including their shortcomings, there is little moderation.

But as I observe John Between more closely, I am reminded that he is endowed generously with the qualities of his very faults. Taking John by the millions, he pays his bills and looks you in the eye and walks with the carriage of the free man he is. In most ways his horizons are big, and he loves few things more than to act big or be big. Although he may regard himself as just a little fellow, or an ordinary guy, the truth is that he likes enormously to do the big thing. Smallness is not a part of his nature, or so rarely as to be quite exceptional. He believes in himself, in *his* community and in *his* country; at least this has been his predominant and traditional outlook until recent years. He is equally capable of believing in *his* world and in One World. The American world, which he helps to shape, bears the imprint of his hand and spirit everywhere.

Such a man is John Between of American Middle Men, Unlimited. In his own right he is Somebody. Without his great qualities and the loyalties by which he lives he could never have become the most important man in the world. For despite his shortcomings, his lack of awareness, and his present confusions John Between possesses and represents a great deal that is universally magnetic. He is much more than the enormous power to which he has fallen heir. He is the symbol to men everywhere of how men can aspire to freedom and then remain free.

In reality John Between symbolizes the American people, as that term is used. It is we, as Americans, who share his qualities and faults and must also share his fate. As our middle class goes, so shall we all go in the turbulent reckoning of our times.

Perhaps, therefore, we should first look into ourselves to read the compass needle for our future, and then seek all pertinent lessons from what has happened to our middle-class cousins in Europe. If there now remains any hope for the European middle men's future, it lies chiefly in the hands of their American cousins. It depends upon the solidity, alertness, and comprehension of the U.S. middle class and upon whether or not it finally succumbs to the same forces that have liquidated or permanently crippled the same kind of people in the Old World.

But we cannot learn much from the experience and

fate of others until we have learned considerable about ourselves.

Why do we worry about tomorrow?

Why do we feel the way we do?

There is no fear so corrosive and debilitating as fear of the unknown. Yet there is a great deal within us and around us that need not be unknown. What we see and understand is what we can hope to master in the end.

Chapter II

WHAT HAS HAPPENED TO AMERICANS?

In the summer of 1947 something occurred that is without precedent in our history. More than one thousand young Americans, mostly veterans, decided to migrate *from* the United States. They rushed to accept the offer of a travel subsidy and good jobs in Australia. For the first time since the original colonists reached Massachusetts and Virginia an important group of Americans left our shores en masse to settle and adopt citizenship in another country. Could this be the first tiny ripple in the turning of a fabulous immigrant tide of more than three centuries' duration? Perhaps not. But it was certainly something utterly new, somehow shocking to American self-assurance and pride.

Why did they voluntarily abandon the unique and prized privilege of being Americans?

Before the first contingent sailed for a newer world various emigrant veterans gave their reasons quite frankly. They cited our high cost of living . . . the keen competition in our economy . . . the overcrowdedness in many fields of endeavor. They admitted that their incomes in Australia might be not much more than one third of what their prewar incomes in the United States had been, but they insisted they would spend much less down there, and live better. A Navy veteran from Los Angeles said he and his wife expected to have a more wholesome family life, with fewer automobiles and less reason "to be on the go." Others explained that America was in too much of a hurry.

16

When I devoted a newspaper column to this remarkable development I received an immediate appeal for more information from a veteran in Denver. He was married, aged thirty-one, and a journeyman steamfitter of ten years' experience. He wrote: "My wife and I are definitely interested in removing to Australia, or to any other young progressive country *in whose future we can have confidence. . . .* I will briefly give you my reasons. First and foremost, I am opposed to American policy, both foreign and domestic. Our middle of the road foreign policy is not aggressive participation [evidently meaning in the United Nations and international co-operation], nor are we meeting our domestic problems forcibly. Our leaders can change easily. But the public attitude that America is a satisfactorily-finished product, worth preserving as it is, will probably prevail during my lifetime. *I choose to be a part of a population which realizes that its homeland is far from completed and intends to move on toward that end.*" (Italics mine.)

The Denver veteran's statement is not one easily to be dismissed. Nor can we ignore the fact that even a relatively unimportant number of Americans are emigrating from the United States. For these incidents are merely a more dramatic illustration of something most unusual and significant that has happened to the American people. For some years now we have given increasing indications that our confidence in the American way and the American dream is beginning to fade.

You often hear it said that the United States was the only major belligerent to emerge "undamaged" from the two World Wars. In regard to strictly physical destruction this is true. But there remains the question of spiritual, moral, and psychological damage. There remains the equally pertinent problem of what wars and depression, unaccustomed strain and disillusionment have done to us inwardly.

This generation of Americans has made two tremendous armed sorties into a strange and once remote world. In between we paid a very heavy price for a great depression. These convulsive forces of change have brought their pressures to bear upon us ever since 1918. They compelled a stupendous increase in our productive might. Simultaneously they multiplied our national and international responsibilities enormously. In the process they also multiplied our federal debt, our taxes, our anxieties and uncertainties. Although our cities and homes escaped becoming physical victims of war, we ourselves have become in various degrees psychological casualties of the world-wide revolution. The old American "normalcy" has vanished. The house we live in has been changed profoundly, as well as the world around it. We too could not remain immune.

Some of our changes are definitely for the better. Collectively we have made great progress from the isolationist illusions of 1919 and 1920. As a nation we are considerably more mature and responsible than when Woodrow Wilson's fight for the League of Nations was rejected. The defeat of leading isolationist senators and congressmen in the November 1948 elections furnished further impressive evidence of the broadened outlook of American voters. While becoming more aware of our world responsibilities we have also become more realistic and in many ways more skeptical. Americans, in fact, have learned a good deal over the past thirty years. But in the process we have lost certain things as well.

It is probably too soon to estimate just how our change in attitudes will finally balance up, for better or worse. Already, however, you can perceive a few things that we have lost, or seem to be losing.

What is it that the people of the United States are losing?

There was a time when Americans talked buoyantly about tomorrow. Back in the 1920's many of us actually talked as if we had the world by the tail. In those days most of us felt certain we had the key to permanent prosperity; we knew the U.S. system was unbeatable. We had no qualms about America's security, or about our standard of living, and very few about the future.

Today the American speaks a different language: "Of course, nobody knows how long good times will last. . . . What's the use of planning, if there's going to be another war? . . . It's the Communists and the labor unions that are causing all the trouble. . . . How can a fellow live decently with prices like these? . . . What's the matter with Congress, anyhow? . . . I tell you there won't be any stability until we have it out with the Russians. . . . How are we going to make any profits with the cost of everything up and more taxes ahead? . . . If I knew when the slump would begin, I could tell you. . . . I don't see any hope until the Republicans get in. . . . Every time things begin to perk up, there's another crisis, in Berlin or China or somewhere."

Since the end of the late war remarks like these have become commonplace in almost every section of the United States. The old typically American self-confidence seems almost to have vanished. The overtones of American speech have become overtones of dissatisfaction and complaint, and especially of doubt. Even while we express our loyalty to American democracy and the free-enterprise system, we voice fear of the Soviet-Communist menace. And those who publicly laud the American way rarely venture to speak boldly about its being bigger and better tomorrow. Those who listen most carefully have reached the same conclusion—a loss of faith on the part of the American people, lack of belief in our way of life, fear of tomorrow.

To be afraid of the future, and particularly to doubt the future of the United States, has been utterly alien to previous generations of our citizens. Is this change primarily a spiritual deterioration? Is it caused by a crisis in religion? Or by a general decline in morality as well as morale? Is it, perhaps, essentially an "illness of American culture"? Are our machines and gadgets in this super-mechanized civilization destroying our faith? . . . For present purposes it is sufficient to recognize the nature of the disease. Listen and observe with a little care and you will notice its manifestations among friends and people whom you meet.

Postwar visitors from overseas have been astonished and deeply perturbed to hear Americans saying things they never dreamed that citizens of our uniquely favored land could say. Barbara Ward, the foreign editor of the *Economist* of London, summed it up in this way: *

> Every hand seemed to be on the wrist of business, waiting for the first fluctuation which would herald the inevitable slump. It was curious to hear aggressive defenses of the "American way of life," since that way of life appeared to be capable of arousing only negative responses—anti-Communist, anti-labor, anti-liberal—or alternatively, anti-management, anti-reactionary, anti-Fascist. . . . The visitor from abroad could hardly fail to ask: "But is this the richest, the most powerful, the most dynamic country the world has ever seen? Is this the nation with an industrial structure unrivaled in human history? . . . Do these men have the atom bomb?"
>
> For if all these things were true, how could there be this gray pervasive disquiet on the subject of war-smashed Russia? And if the disquiet sprang from fear of Russia's ideas, not of Russia's armed forces, what should be said of the effectiveness of an "American way of life" that gave its adherents so little confidence? . . . Indecision, fear, a hankering for the past—what

* Cf. *New York Times Magazine,* December 28, 1947.

sort of guides were these for the most powerful nation not only on earth but in the history of man? I left America puzzled and discouraged.

The words of Franklin D. Roosevelt come immediately to mind: "The only thing we have to fear is fear itself."

In the black spring of 1933, with the nation's banks closed and the banking system completely paralyzed, the American people listened and learned that this is true. Have we forgotten so soon?

Is there anything more un-American than for Americans to be dominated by fear of tomorrow?

We must grant that a world in revolutionary upheaval naturally spawns uncertainty and anxiety. An international society in which frightful atomic weapons exist uncontrolled is inevitably poisoned by fear. Yet Miss Ward and other foreign observers are justified in being dismayed by the dimensions of American postwar doubts and fears. We in the United States still possess infinitely greater weapons, power, and geographical protection than any other nation. Compared with that of all other countries, our relative security is most exceptional. Ours is still incomparably the richest, most fortunate land on earth. It remains a land of tremendous opportunities—for continued prosperity, for personal initiative, for tolerable economic compromises; and equally for hope, for peace and security through international co-operation.

Perhaps we need to remind ourselves of some of the things we have just recently done. Between Pearl Harbor and V-J Day the collective achievements of the American people were little short of astonishing. This was true in governmental and industrial planning; in industrial organization and expansion; in global strategy; in aerial and marine transportation; in scientific research; in the building of tremendous armed forces from scratch; in the fi-

nancing of this entire vast effort; and in the performance
of our armed forces under all sorts of conditions around
the world. In all these respects no single nation has ever
met such stupendous wartime requirements with such
conspicuous and often such startling success.

You might have expected that American citizens would
emerge from this remarkable collective performance suf-
fering from an extreme affliction of self-confidence; possibly even of national arrogance. Yet we proceeded quite
generally to resign ourselves to fear. We began telling
ourselves, and others, that we really do not believe in our
demonstrated capacities. Although we can achieve near
miracles through national planning and united effort in
wartime, we do not believe that we can plan and act with
a similar success and unity when the spurs of national
danger are lacking. Instead of being overconfident about
preventing depression, maintaining prosperity, and building an organized peace, we speculate about an "unavoidable" economic slump or an "inevitable" war. We appear
no longer convinced that the United States can remain
strong and highly productive. This, of course, is a denial
of the American way as we have always lived it.

What does the average American fear,
or think he fears?

If the American middle class becomes defeatist or betrays its ideals and yields to the totalitarian crossfires, it
will collapse as other middle classes have done. Our great
epoch of freedom would vanish, possibly for several generations. Meanwhile self-government in many other countries would be left too weakened to endure.

In a fundamental sense, then, far more depends upon
the morale and actions of our millions of John Betweens
than upon any other single group of people anywhere in
the world. We are the strategic center, the keystone of all

the forces of freedom. If we face this fact, we can afford to tremble somewhat at the responsibility of being average Americans. We live in a period when Americans cannot do less than lead; when Americans cannot be less than big. All other peoples who seek to preserve or to attain freedom look to us for confidence, for faith and new hope. Yet in many ways we are hesitant, self-doubting, and unsure.

This has been chiefly true because the average American is beset by three dominant fears: fear of another war, fear of the Soviet Union and the Communists, and fear of another economic depression.

Are these fears completely justified? Or are they exaggerated?

It seems to me most Americans have exaggerated at least the first two fears, either through lack of perspective or insufficient consideration of all the facts involved or through emotional reactions. The immediate question is not whether there will ever be another major conflict. The immediate question is whether we still have some time in which to work to prevent war. In the same manner the immediate question is not whether the Communists can win electoral control in western European countries or in the United States. It is already demonstrated that the Communists cannot win anywhere in western Europe without active intervention by the Red Army; nor can they possibly seize power in the United States with their present reduced strength. The immediate question, then, is simply how effectively we take steps to curb the spread of Communism in Europe and to deprive it of fertilizer on our home soil.

Is fear of an early war with the Soviet Union justified? What are the probabilities?

Far too many Americans have accepted the assumption that such a war is to be expected almost any time within the next two or three years. Of course, war is like auto accidents, pneumonia, and sudden death: it is always possible. I would certainly not be so reckless as to say that a major conflict cannot conceivably happen between now and 1970, or even within twelve months. But it is my firm and measured conviction that any war with the Soviets is at least decidedly *improbable* during the next several years. There are strong and impressive factual reasons for this belief. The odds against an early war ought to remain against it into 1954, and possibly considerably beyond that date. Virtually all of the best-informed European and American authorities have consistently refused to regard any early East-West major conflict as highly probable. Here is one example well worth remembering.

My friend Paul Scott Mowrer is more thoroughly acquainted with Europe than anyone I know in our present diplomatic service, from ambassadors down. He has spent most of the past thirty-eight years as a foreign correspondent and trained observer in Europe. When he was home on leave in the autumn of 1948 the first thing I said to Paul Mowrer was this: "You've heard all the talk about an early war. What do you think about the Soviets starting a war with us?" Paul's swift and reflective reply cut through the superficial alarmist speculation like a razor. "The Russians couldn't beat the Germans alone," he said quietly. "Who thinks they could possibly lick the United States? I don't think Stalin and the Politburo are fools."

Paul Mowrer proceeded to cite the identical facts that had governed my own reasoning for many months. The United States possesses the most gigantic industrial plant in the world; the largest Navy; the greatest Air Force and the most formidable long-range bombers on earth; scientific brains and laboratories far exceeding those available in any other nation; an unrivaled technological know-how; bacterial weapons of unknown but terrible propensities, plus an undisclosed number of atomic bombs.

That list of brutal realities ought to dispose of any early likelihood of a Soviet-launched effort at world domination through force of arms—unless the men in the Kremlin are idiots rather than the hard-boiled realists their actions have with remarkable consistency portrayed them to be. The all-round *inferiority* of Soviet war-waging potentials cannot be diminished appreciably within ten years or considerably more. There are serious reasons, then, to regard this as a minimum margin of time, probably available, in which we can strive to consolidate peace. Within this period, it is true, a great depression might come in the United States. If so, that might radically alter some aspects of American predominance of power. It might release dangerous pressures toward an adventurous gamble with war, inside both the Soviet Union and the U.S.A. But aside from this contingency the odds should remain measurably against an early war. Here in America we have had far too much alarmist conjecture and far too little responsible weighing of the factors that should provide a fair margin of time in which to pursue peace.

The American's immediate fear of Communism in the United States, or in western Europe, is also exaggerated. The Communists won their revolution in Russia under most exceptional circumstances. But they have won power in eastern Europe only through the active presence of powerful Red Army forces, aided by direct Soviet intervention. The Communists have been soundly defeated in Italy. They cannot win a civil war in France, even though they may try it eventually. Beyond these facts we tend to forget that Communists have never yet won power in any highly industrialized nation. And they have never won in any country whose people have a strong democratic tradition and experience.

These hard facts cut the Communists down to their proper stature. They indicate clearly that the Lenin-Stalin

Marxists should not be able to win power in western Europe during these next decisive years. They show emphatically that the Communists face tremendous obstacles and handicaps in the United States. Short of an atomic war, with widespread destruction and hunger across our land, only an extreme economic collapse could create conditions in which Communist proselyting could thrive in America. Without another depression, as bad as that of 1929–32 or worse, such conditions cannot possibly exist here.

Rather than indulge in nightmares about a domestic Red menace we Americans should recognize that the one surest way to defeat our native Communists is to take practical steps to prevent another economic paralysis. By 1951, or some time thereafter, the danger of such a depression is likely to become acute. Certainly we cannot afford to ignore what some twenty million or more permanently unemployed would do to the political thinking of our people. It would almost inevitably create grave pressures toward some form of totalitarianism—probably both toward Communist radicalism and also toward Fascist extremism, thinly disguised.

As of today, however, Mr. American Middle Man greatly overestimates what 75,000 American Communist party members can achieve, or hope to achieve, under existing circumstances. We have very important influences in our favor. Our press and our people are aroused and alert against Communism. Our FBI has the Reds' leadership and party organization most efficiently documented and watched. In no country are such vast private funds available to combat the Communist ideology. Our labor unions, both in the A.F.L. and the C.I.O., are strongly anti-Communist by a large majority. In the past two years most of them have purged their leadership of Communists and taken strict measures against infiltration. American churches, and especially the Roman Catholic Church, bring pronounced influence against Communist activities and propaganda. All the organizations of American capitalists, highly efficient and strongly financed, are mobilized against the Communists and their doctrine. On this one issue America's powerful conservatism stands united with the important force of American liberals and progressives. With such an extraordinary array of organized influence, wealth, and public sentiment against them are we still afraid of some 75,000 U.S. Communists? Why?

The third prevalent American fear, that of another depression, is more realistic in many ways. Anxiety over continued inflation precipitating an economic slump springs from more than over-accentuation of a possibility. In the minds of some economists and other technicians this apprehension may be concerned with a *probability*. Our people are fundamentally sound when they recognize that we are in a boom, and that—by all past experience—a bust is likely to follow it. This fear can only be dissipated when both government and business join in positive preventive actions on a broad scale. It might be said, then, that our economic fear has been created in considerable degree by the failure of U.S. democracy's representatives to act constructively, and by failure of U.S. capitalism's policy-makers to demand prompt action and to co-operate in it.

In reality the problems of war, Communism, and depression are all lifetime problems for our generation. They require a long view even more than a short one. They require long-term planning and co-ordinated efforts rather than glandular explosions and impetuous improvisations. It might be possible for Americans to place the blame for another war on somebody else; but if Communism—or Fascism—ever takes over the United States, the responsibility must rest solely upon the American people. Should another boom lead to another bust, that, too, would have to be charged solely against the United States government, its people, and its system.

What are the deeper implications behind our fears?

At the end of a lecture at a preparatory school in Vermont a serious-faced youth of about sixteen waited on the fringes of a group until he could at last ask a question. It came like a thunderbolt out of the blue.

"But, Mr. Stowe," he said, "do you really believe that our civilization is worth saving?"

With due acknowledgment of its bleak and vulgar and frothy aspects, I tried to explain why I most certainly do. I learned afterward that the lad who turned the howitzer straight on me happened to be a grandson of Thomas A. Edison. Even if he had not been, he was certainly no ordinary American boy. Yet there was something in his sharply questioning, skeptical mind that I have found quite typical among American youths with whom I have talked at dozens of our colleges and universities from coast to coast since 1945. A similar skepticism was strongly present in the somewhat older Americans I met in uniform overseas.

It is probably no accident that the most skeptical Americans, proportionately speaking, are those who are roughly within the age limits of eighteen to forty-five. Either they were shunted out into the vicissitudes of our great depression or directly into World War II, or they reached their late teens just in time to be confronted by its bewildering aftermath. These have not been schools calculated to promote an easy optimism about life in general. Nor have they been training courses designed to foster an unthinking assumption that all aspects of the American way, or even most of them, are beyond need of improvement.

There is a wonderfully healthy attitude of "You've got to show me" about most American youth, young men and young women, today. It can be a notable long-term asset—

if it does not degenerate too frequently into defeatism, re-stricted ambitions, and loss of enthusiasm. But has there not also been rather too much defeatism seeping down from our middle, depression-conditioned generation of late? And even from our older generation? When one listens to unsupported or superficially expressed assumptions of "inevitable" war and "unavoidable" depression, one is compelled to wonder. Somehow the rightful dignity of any American citizen shrivels tragically when he winds up his declamation on the dark future by saying: "But what can *I* do? I'm just an ordinary guy." Confronted by Hitler, and then under Nazism, millions of Germans begged off with "I am only a little man." It was not that they could do nothing. The truth was that *they made no real effort to find out what they could do, and most of them did nothing at all.*

If the United States is phenomenally big and strong, then it is big enough and strong enough to lead the world —away from war, away from Communism, and away from serious breakdowns in production and employment. Yet when you listen to the John Betweens in your community, they seem to indicate far too often that they are incapable of bringing their opinions to bear on Washington; incapable of electing more intelligent and responsible members of both houses of Congress; incapable of making the preferences of free men felt in our national life. (On November 2, 1948 they seemed highly capable of making their preferences felt!) But when average Americans talk they often seem to be resigning themselves to regarding U.S. prosperity as an uncontrollable will-o'-the-wisp. If our youth are becoming increasingly skeptical of many things, including the American dream, could it be that they have acquired too many excuses for skepticism from their elders? The least they might expect from us is some convincing demonstration of faith that it is possible to control adequately our huge, industrialized machine—a demand by citizens that concerted action be taken by government and industry well in advance of breakdown and serious trouble.

Another implication behind our fears is that a perilously large percentage of Americans, however gloomy about their country's prospects and the world going to the bow-wows, do not care sufficiently to do something about it themselves. The most obvious thing every American citizen can do is to go to the polls. Yet close to fifty million American voters, or approximately half of all those qualified, failed to register their choices in the Presidential elections of 1948. But the American way is based upon a mandate from the people. Confusion and defeatism are spread by inertia and indifference.

The implication behind our fears is that there is little the average citizen can do about our great domestic and foreign problems; at any rate, that John Between himself is powerless to act. Yet it is precisely the active majority—or even the active majority of the active minority—that determines which men and which policies will prevail in Washington. And almost every citizen belongs, or can belong, to some group that makes its influence felt politically —the farmers' agencies, the Chamber of Commerce, the National League of Women Voters, the United World Federalists, the labor unions, the National Federation of Women's Clubs are merely a few among scores. Opportunity for civic action through organizations of an extraordinary variety is unquestionably much greater in our American democracy than in any other country. To ask what we can do is to ignore and deny the most effective mechanisms for the expression of citizens' opinions that have been created under any democratic system. For Americans the opportunity to participate is fabulous. It is only the *will to participate,* the will to do something toward shaping our future, that is lacking or generally limited to responsible minorities.

Does it seem strange, then, that skepticism and frustration have made wide conquests in postwar America? "Fear itself" is a dangerous thing to let loose in any society. When it also percolates downward from "depression-conscious" men of great power who are the very top in industry or trade, it poisons minds already uncertain and harassed. For the general public can scarcely be expected to have more faith in the American way and the future of free enterprise than those who control our productive apparatus.

Why is the contemporary American confused and afraid?

First, because he can no longer take much or most of his personal security for granted, as in the past.

After the last depression his security remained seriously impaired. The recovery of the thirties was only superficial. Production for the second World War merely supplied artificial respiration. Profits and wages soared upward again. All that this proved was that U.S. capitalism can make lots of money out of war, providing all the fighting and destruction occurs in other peoples' lands—something that probably can never be true hereafter. But wartime and postwar prosperity did not for a moment prove that our American economy, as now constituted and operating, can maintain a high level of income for all *without* war. Even today, twenty years after 1929, we have not yet established a normal recovery based on peacetime production. Our existing multi-billion-dollar annual production for ERP or of arms for western Europe and the Far East creates another highly abnormal and artificial activity. It probably cannot be prolonged for more than a few years. Then what?

It may be assumed that most Americans sense the fact that our exceptional pre-1929 peacetime prosperity left us with no reliable assurances of when, or if, it can be recaptured. In any event, our postwar insecurity has become triple-edged: economic, political, and scientific. All three edges exert pressure simultaneously today. Most that we once took for granted cannot be taken for granted again.

John Between's anxiety is further heightened because he attempts to face in two directions at once. Grudgingly or not, he accepts the necessity of living in the world, of U.S. world leadership for peace; yet he clings ardently to his nostalgia for the pleasanter, much more carefree ways of our recently isolationist past.

Our middle man looks longingly backward toward many traditional American blessings: the easier life, the lusty and adolescent irresponsibilities, the relative unconcern with national and world problems, the lower taxes and lower prices. Even the fat and succulent roadside hamburger has become a fond memory. Remember when sirloin steak was thirty-five cents a pound and pork chops were twenty-nine? That was true in most American cities as recently as 1939. Remember when you could buy quite a nice house for six thousand dollars, and apartments were easily within reach for most people? Remember when income taxes really weren't very bad? Remember. . . . What's the matter with this country, anyhow?

Does somebody ask: "What's the matter with *us*?"

Somehow you rarely hear that question. It's easier to blame someone else, or the depression and the war and nothing more. Yet Paul Porter, Chester Bowles, and others warned the American people precisely what punishing high prices would result if OPA controls were abolished in June 1946. The U.S. electorate predominantly swallowed the nonsensical assurances of business groups, such as the National Association of Manufacturers, that prices would shortly "level off." No public pressure of note was brought to bear on Congress to stick to price-controls. John Between refused to see as far as the end of his nose. Quite as much as Republicans, Democrats, and business lobbyists, the American people asked for madly spiraling high prices, and got them—squarely in the stomach as well as in the pocketbook. The good old days can also be what we casually toss out the window.

Perhaps we Americans are also haunted by accentuated apprehensions because of old and rather slipshod habits that we cling to from our much simpler past. In this and in many previous generations most of us have been negligently casual about direct political action. Ours seemed to be a pretty comfortable, fairly effective system—not at all hard on the thought-processes in the normal electoral year, and pretty much ignored in between. We had no strong Socialist Party challenging the basic premises of our economic pattern. Until very recently, no Communists worth mentioning. Our two-party system simplified everything and usually made it possible for political thinking to be quite simple. No isms to compel a voter to concentrate. Rarely a "foreign" idea. In fact, not too many new ideas of any kind. The good old days—and Warren G. Harding, then Coolidge, and Hoover for the pay-off.

It was not surprising that the American voter felt slight need to develop a critical political sense, or to bother to go to the polls in resounding numbers except on rare occasions. He could take his political security for granted as easily as his economic security. His democratic system, "the best in the world," did not seem to require much personal supervision, or to be in need of constant watching or persistent improvement.

Then the 1929 depression knocked him off his feet economically, and incidentally knocked a new measure of political awareness into his head. That brought the Roosevelt landslides, and also an unaccustomed amount of political and economic thinking on the part of many U.S. voters. The controversial Roosevelt reforms and successive

administrations had the constructive by-product of prodding Americans of both parties into greater consideration
of national problems and governmental policies. But somehow the postwar letdown seemed to find John Between
more worried, yet less interested personally. Apparently a
large proportion of America's middle class has not yet
abandoned its habit of being listless about individual political action and responsibilities. Inevitably this indifference or abstention serves to increase greatly their feelings
of insecurity. Congress is usually interested only in those
questions about which impressive numbers of voters
register some notable concern. The American who has pronounced fears for his future and his country's security lets
them prey upon his mind, nourishing resignation or defeatism, precisely because he exercises his own political influence far too little. Because he refuses to make his opinion
felt, he underestimates what can be done.

A Denver steamfitter, probably with no more than a high-
school education, can discern a "public attitude that
America is a satisfactorily-finished product" and reject that
Narcissan assumption by seeking a more challenging attitude in Australia or elsewhere. But the challenges to the
future of the United States remain in our system and in
our collective state of mind. It is John Between's problem
quite as much as a problem of the nation or the capitalist
system.

He assumes there is little he himself can do that would
really matter. But in this he is absolutely mistaken. There
are many things that any literate, responsible American
can do to assure wiser or stronger policies for preventing
war, or to reduce the chances of an ultimate dictatorship in
the United States, or effectively to demand constructive
steps against another depression. When it came to price-
curbs, labor legislation, housing, old-age pensions, and
other matters some twenty-two million Americans—less
than one fourth of our total electorate—stubbornly went

out and voted for Harry S. Truman, the man who presumably didn't have a chance. They did not stay home and nurse their frustrations—and before the Eighty-first Congress is finished, it looks as if they will get a lot of what they want. It was accomplished by the old and simple democratic process, by having ideas about certain issues and insecurities and demanding that something be done about them.

John Between of U.S. Middle Men, Unlimited, can reduce the causes of his predominant fears very considerably in the next few years if he is sufficiently concerned to make an intelligent and persistent effort to do so. His most harassing anxiety is due to his failure to make a serious and consistent effort to inform himself—to get all possible facts—and then to do something about them. He does not yet understand what two World Wars have done to the political thinking and social aspirations of the European and Asiatic peoples. He has not interested himself in the *basic reasons* for the world-wide popular demand for new and greater economic rights. He is not much concerned about what the Communists have to offer that appeals very strongly, and understandably, to underprivileged peoples. He does not see that the struggle in Europe between democratic and totalitarian forces is being fought out over the weakened remnants of the same middle class to which he belongs. He does not grasp clearly the great and vital distinctions between Socialism in Britain or Scandinavia and Communism in Russia or Yugoslavia.

He also fails to understand that capitalism, wherever it exists, is in an acute crisis. This means that what has happened to Europe's industrialized nations and their peoples over the past thirty years *can* happen to the superindustrialized United States; that much of it may well happen within another ten or twenty years.

If only twenty or thirty million American voters clearly understood the reasons behind these revolutionary facts and forces and would bring their comprehension to bear electorally upon Congress and upon the White House and the State Department, we should be far on the way toward winning peace and preserving the American way. The place to begin to overcome our fears is not outside us but within. The way to diminish our fears is through responsible participation and informed action as citizens.

But informed action by average Americans requires ample and accurate knowledge of what has happened to Europe's middle men and women. Where they turned to Fascism or to Communism we must understand *why* they turned. *What* influences and habits led them into self-deception? *Why* do other middle-class Europeans demand partial socialism? *Why* do the world's underprivileged demand radical and revolutionary changes? *Where* and *how* have some of our closest cousins sought to find more justice for all, and *how* have they lost opportunities that will never come again? These are all matters of immediate and personal meaning for the future of every American. For if democracy is threatened and capitalism is widely repudiated, there are reasons for it other than strictly physical. There are also causes created by human conduct and psychology.

Americans and Europeans are now bound together in a common, uncertain struggle for survival. In this struggle we have much more in common, and far more that is communally at stake, than any other peoples. It is now clear that we shall stand together or that we shall eventually fall together. This fact dictates a clearer and deeper knowledge of each other, Europeans and Americans, than we have ever had until now. Not only must we know ourselves with greater realism. *We must also know our closest of kin, and those nearest to us in experience, much better in order to know ourselves adequately.*

It is in this Europe, too, that a weakened middle class struggles to hold the barriers and still find a middle course of effective compromise. From the experience of these Europeans in particular we can learn much. They are the true veterans of freedom's seesawing battles in this century. If we are wise enough to learn from their dilemmas and mistakes, we shall forge new weapons against fear and create a new strength in our own democratic institutions.

Chapter III

AMERICANS AND EUROPEANS

As I travel around the U.S.A. John Between rather frequently asks: "What's the matter with those people over in Europe? Why can't they stop fussing and fighting among themselves?" John really doesn't mean it so, but his remark reveals an unconscious feeling of superiority. His implication is that we Americans are more peaceable by nature; that we know how to get along much better with one another, or even with foreigners; that somehow we Americans are different.

But are we in reality very different from "those Europeans"? If so, in what ways and how much? And in how many ways are we decidedly alike? When it comes to members of the middle class in various countries, certainly their interests, habits, and mentalities are remarkably similar.

Perhaps we tend to forget or ignore how exceptionally fortunate the people of the United States are; and undoubtedly we pay scant attention to some of the basic causes of our major blessings. We enjoy extraordinarily favorable circumstances of geography, resources, and opportunities. Yet we incline to overlook their great influence and to attribute our remarkable good fortune, past and present, chiefly to personal qualities of our own. We also tend to disregard what a tremendous lot we owe to the incredible American cocktail of intermingled races and peoples. The sinews of American expansion and power have been largely supplied, generation after generation, by constantly renewed influxes of immigrants from overseas, most of them from Europe.

Through its entire history the United States has benefited immeasurably from the richest blood transfusions any nation has ever known. New blood from the Old World brought us a large proportion of Europe's boldest spirits, her best energies and highest ambitions, together with a profuse variety of European talent. Thus the contributions of older Americans and more recent immigrants to our progress can rarely be separated. It is enough to take sober pride in the fact that Americans are the greatest human cocktail of widely assorted elements the world has ever seen. Our American experiment has proved that literally all kinds of people can live together in relative peace and harmony. That is one of its most significant achievements.

Even so we in the United States have thought of ourselves for decades and generations as pretty much "on our own," with a minimum of credit to outside influences or nature's. We were doing things "our way," and our American way was quite different in many respects from any other. Because we had fewer wars and much more success materially, perhaps it was inevitable to put particular stress upon those respects in which we were different, and upon others in which we thought we were different. While doing this, however, we have consistently underestimated those deep and indestructible links which bind us to Europe and its peoples.

Many of us now remember rather ruefully the unconscious arrogance and aggressive self-confidence that were so articulate during the boom years of the 1920's. Most U.S. citizens appeared to accept the abundance of our great boom as due chiefly to inherent superiority in the American system and its people. President Calvin Coolidge embraced this conviction wholeheartedly, and self-righteously informed the world that Americans had discovered the secret of permanent prosperity. In Europe, where I then worked, many good people felt that their less fortunate lands were being disdained if not scorned. Europe's ablest economists refused to believe that even "the world's highest standard of living" could remain immune to economic storms. In the end their soberer judgment proved to be correct.

Shortly before the great market crash in 1929 I happened to have André Citroen, then famous as "the Henry Ford of France," as my dinner guest. Because he was an outstandingly successful European industrialist I asked a simple question:

"Monsieur Citroen, how do you explain the extraordinary prosperity in the United States?"

His answer was swift and sharp: "American prosperity is chiefly due to the tremendous size of your internal domestic market. Give Europe a single market—from London to Istanbul—and you Americans would be astonished at what Europe would produce, and embarrassed by the prices at which we could sell. From Britain to Turkey is but fifteen hundred miles—a distance only half the width of the United States. But within this comparatively short distance Europe has twenty-seven different nations. That means twenty-seven different tariff walls, and people who speak more than thirty different languages. What would twenty-seven different tariff barriers between New York and Kansas City do to your American profits, wages, and living-standards? Did you ever think what these barriers of nationality, language, and tariffs do to Europe's possibilities for real prosperity?"

I confessed that I never had.

"Your prosperity is not all, or even predominantly, an 'American secret,' " said M. Citroen, smiling ironically. "Give us all Europe without national frontiers and tariff walls, and Europe would enjoy an unprecedented prosperity."

For the first time I saw some of the unique economic

advantages of the United States in their true perspective. I also understood for the first time some of Europe's most serious obstacles to well-being and peace. On our side we benefit enormously by geographical, ethnic, and political good luck. Size and resources and national unity on a continent-wide basis have been largely due to unique opportunities. On their side the Europeans have always lacked these priceless assets.

There are, then, very important differences in the inherited situations of Americans and Europeans. Nature itself has condemned the Old World's peoples to be the victims of a pronounced amount of "fussing and fighting." In all fairness we must remember the fact that—

Europeans are space-poor while Americans are still exceptionally space-rich.

In European countries the density of populations and the narrow limits of land on which to live force their peoples into much more reduced circumstances of livelihood than most Americans have ever experienced. The contrasts with our extremely favorable circumstances are very great.

In the late thirties the United States had approximately 132,000,000 people living in our continental area of 3,000,-000 square miles. That meant only 44 Americans per square mile. At that same time some 540,000,000 people lived in Europe (including European Russia) in a total area of 3,773,000 square miles. This constituted an average of 143 persons per square mile. More surprisingly, it indicates that some parts of Europe are almost as overcrowded as is China, a notoriously familiar example. China's seething population actually works out to 157 persons per square mile. Europe's compression of populations gave prewar Germany 341 persons per square mile; prewar Italy, 372; Great Britain and Northern Ireland, 495; Belgium, 711. Even France, with unusual agricultural space, had 197 persons per square mile—more than four times the population density of the United States. As of today and in the same all-European areas, more than 500,000,000 people are obliged to live in a total land space only a little greater than that occupied by 148,000,000 Americans.

Space-poverty, or what the Germans call the need of room for living, is a revolutionary force alien to our North American experience. Together with Europe's shortage of arable land, it goes far to explain why "those Europeans" have been the victims of continual controversies and frequent wars. They have been perpetually subjected to far more revolutionary and explosive forces than we have known until now. Like ourselves, they are the creatures of their environment. Yet the more advanced European countries have produced a middle class that faithfully resembles the American middle class in most essential ways. Europe's John Between is no longer so numerous, nor nearly so fortunate, as his American near relative. But he occupies the same central place in the social structure of the main Continental nations. His interests are identical, and in countries that have known real freedom and self-government he is as attached to them as our American John. But Europe's middle man has had to travel a much longer and more painful route, from original conditions utterly different.

Why have western Europeans taken so long to liberate themselves? Why have the Spaniards, the Portuguese, and the eastern Europeans still failed to achieve both political freedom and economic well-being?

If the average American seriously investigates these questions, he will have at once a greater compassion for the prolonged struggles of the European peoples and a deepened appreciation of the exceptional good fortune of his own country and people. The United States could produce a mighty middle class, numbered today in scores of millions, because our nation started from basic foundations utterly different and inestimably more propitious. In addition to virtually unlimited space for expansion and land cultivation North Americans have long enjoyed other truly exceptional advantages.

From the very beginning American colonists established freedom of worship and separation of state and church.

From their first settlements American colonists were able to practice a considerable degree of self-government; and United States citizens have now had more than one hundred and seventy years of freely elected and democratic government—not once stifled by the introduction of an autocratic regime and dictatorial controls.

The white majority of Americans have never known serfdom or slavery. Unlike almost all European peoples they have never been subjugated and rendered helpless by the ball and chain of land feudalism, nor by feudalistic hierarchies.

Europeans have had to struggle for generations and for centuries, and have had to fight countless revolutions and wars, in an unrelaxed effort to obtain basic privileges that Americans have always enjoyed. Among other things the Old World's middle class was compelled to wage a prolonged and bitter struggle before it could establish itself in western Europe. In eastern Europe the middle class was never able to become large, strong, and politically powerful. In comparison the American middle class had no serious brakes upon it from the outset.

Now that American middle men and Europe's much-weakened middle men occupy the same tempest-tossed boat, they have a common role to play, common perils, and a common destiny. But these facts make the basic differences in their background and experience all the more significant. We need to understand the different historical and psychological conditioning of western Europe's John Between.

Perhaps none of the Europeans' liabilities is of greater

importance than their heritage of land feudalism and its oppressive consequences as a barrier to political freedom and social progress. For—

Land feudalism has barred scores of millions of Europeans from entry into the middle class, where land availability has opened the door to middle-class independence for as many more Americans.

Europeans, like ourselves, are molded by the foundations and structures of the house in which they live; and the foundations of Europe's house were laid by feudalism. After centuries of struggle most of feudalism's medieval containing walls have been battered down in western Europe through revolutions and wars, just as a terrible war was required to abolish feudal enslavement of the Negroes in the United States. But in southern and eastern Europe land feudalism and its governing hierarchy proved to be much too deeply entrenched, even in this century. As late as 1936 they were the major causes for the tragic and ruthless civil war in Spain. Throughout eastern Europe land feudalism remained unaltered until 1945; and it still remains dominant in Spain and Portugal.

To most of us in the United States feudalism is something vaguely related to the time "when knighthood was in flower." Quite generally we assume it must have vanished with medieval times. Some of our between-the-wars tourists were lavishly entertained on the magnificent estates of a Spanish marquis, a Polish count, or a Hungarian baron. Yet the fact that it was feudalism which wined and dined them seldom entered their flattered heads. Even their hospitable and charming hosts had conveniently forgotten what their feudal wealth and privileges were based upon. Only the landless peasants, tilling the aristocrats' broad acres for a bare existence, understood the meaning of feudalism. They waited darkly for the day of reckoning and liberation. The average American is far removed from the shacks and shanties of our own similarly exploited sharecroppers. How, then, can John Between adequately envisage the lifelong oppression of overseas victims of land feudalism, numbering hundreds of millions?

In China alone the feudal land system has converted scores of millions of peasants into ardent supporters of the Chinese Reds. And wherever landed aristocrats have defended their extreme feudal powers and privileges without compromise or conscience they have served as unwitting agents of the Kremlin. In reality they have promoted social revolution. In this way those who fear Communism most have often served as its actual allies. To a notable degree this happened in Poland, East Prussia, Hungary, and Spain between the World Wars. Almost invariably feudal landlordism first became a partner of military or Fascist dictatorships, trying to hold on to every inherited power. Finally it served to promote another war; and throughout eastern Europe the feudal landlords inadvertently helped Red totalitarianism to triumph—while they lost everything. This is one reason why we cannot understand today's revolutionary Europe unless we understand the socially destructive role of land feudalism. Europe is only now in the final stage of liberation from its feudalistic straitjacket.

Wherever land feudalism hung on into World War II or beyond it, the growth of a strong middle class was impossible. For when millions of peasants cannot become economically independent, as American farmers can, they have no real chance to become politically free or to establish democratic processes in their homelands. Neither they nor their children, however intelligent and ambitious, can move upward into the middle class. This constitutes one of the great distinctions between the peoples in eastern and western Europe.

The feudal barrier to a strong middle class was first

cracked by the British, with their Magna Charta, some six hundred years ago. The Scandinavians were also in the vanguard, likewise liberating themselves from feudalism step by step. In France feudalism was dealt a knockout blow by the French Revolution. In all these countries, as in Belgium and the Netherlands, the masses gained the opportunity for greater economic independence than Europeans had ever known before. As a consequence they developed a middle class capable of winning an increasing measure of self-government and democratic liberties. These same middle-class western Europeans brought their new ideas and their new loyalties to a free society to the American colonies; later on, to the young Republic of the United States.

But the twentieth century found the *majority* of European peoples still imprisoned by land feudalism and controlled by feudal hierarchies. Kaiser Wilhelm's Imperial Germany rose to supreme power on the unshaken foundations of Prussian feudalism. The vast and sprawling Austro-Hungarian Empire and Czarist Russia were deeply feudalistic. Germany's middle class was large, Russia's negligible. But the German middle class lacked any inspiring counterpart of the democratic traditions of the Cromwellian and French revolutions. It proved incapable of bodily eliminating Prussian feudalism and militarism. The states that succeeded the Austro-Hungarian Empire possessed no middle class of size and strength, and few democratic traditions. Thus 1918 left a terrific amount of social dynamite strewn across Europe.

That dynamite has been exploding ever since. Yet the convulsions and dictatorships of the period between the wars failed to destroy feudalism or to build a healthy, expanding middle class in eastern Europe. Even after World War I more than 120,000,000 European peasants (nearly as many people as the population of the United States at that time) remained landless and land-starved. They were constrained tenants or sharecroppers on big landowners' estates. These estates included all the richest land in the feudal countries. Some of them totaled between 100,000 and 200,000 acres owned by a single titled family. The peasants had to work for whatever share of the crops their masters permitted them to retain. In sections of the United States many Americans are compelled to do the same thing today. That, too, could contribute to future revolution.

At this point you may ask:

How are Europe's land feudalism and its consequences related to the average American and his future?

As the Marshall Plan eloquently testifies, John Between has a new awareness that he needs friends and allies who believe in democracy and will support our concepts of freedom. The only place he can find the most important of these friends and allies is in Europe. But he can find them there in only two categories: among those nations which have had a strong middle class for a long time, or among those less-privileged Europeans who are fervently pro-democratic because they have suffered the oppressions of land feudalism for so many generations. In other words, we Americans can only get our greatest support either from Europeans who have institutions similar to our own or from other Europeans who sincerely want the kind of liberties that we possess.

You can say this quite simply in another fashion. John Between's personal interest in Europe is to help European democracy to survive and grow, as most of us recognize. But to do that we must actively support Europe's middle men, without whom democratic practices cannot persist. And to do that successfully Americans must interest themselves in helping other Europeans *to become middle men.* This is the only way that the peasant masses in Iron Curtain countries can eventually throw off tyranny and enslavement. They can only do so by being encouraged to become more like the John Betweens of western Europe and the United States. They can never do this by remaining either in feudalistic or in communistic chains.

This means that in order to become free, Europe's dominated people must be revolutionary—but revolutionary in the anti-totalitarian sense.

That is where the consequences of feudalism enter the picture. The widespread peasant revolt against feudalism has been exploited by the Communists with promises of "land and justice," which they betray at their convenience. As yet western democracy has promised these same peasants little or nothing at all by way of specific reforms. Yet the consuming objective of some 120,000,000 Europeans today is to obtain a few acres of land, or to obtain just enough more land to provide a decent living—with freedom. Eastern Europe accordingly offers us *120,000,000 potential allies* of democracy for the wooing and the winning. Their collective weight will ultimately have a profound influence upon the issue of freedom or Communism throughout the world, not merely in Europe alone.

The average European, whether of the middle class or the peasantry, has a common understanding of what "freedom to own land" means. On the other hand the average American can only comprehend its deep significance with great difficulty. For nowhere on the face of the earth have millions of ordinary citizens obtained large quantities of land so easily and so cheaply as in the United States. The American colonist, pioneer or immigrant, enjoyed a priceless privilege. Up to the 1860's he could move west and purchase a *required minimum* (a phrase quite unheard-of in Europe) of 80 acres for $100, or not much more. By 1860 "free land" became the slogan. Any citizen, or any person who intended to become one, became eligible for a quarter section of 160 acres under the Homestead Act of

1862. All that was required was the initiative to go where
the land was.* Meanwhile in Europe countless persons
died or half-starved in a vain, lifelong struggle to obtain
ownership of a mere five or ten acres. The doorway to a
predominant, prospering, ever broadening middle class
was locked and barred by feudalism.

It has not been that "those Europeans" and their peasant masses "just can't get along with each other." Only the
grossly uninformed could indulge in such a distorted and
oversimplified judgment. Under the yoke and chains of
land feudalism scores of millions of honest, hard-working
Europeans simply could not "get along" at all. This enormous gap between the experience of Europeans and Americans handicaps us greatly in understanding the revolutionary motivations for change—for a new and better deal
—in contemporary Europe.

There also exists:

A *basic difference between U.S. citizens' and Europeans' experience of religion in politics.*

John Between takes the separation of state and church
so much for granted that he rarely thinks of this natural
American state of affairs as something to be jealously preserved. We have never known a state religion whose leaders played a dominant part in politics and government.
We have never had our elementary schools and our entire
educational system controlled by any religious sect. Yet
these and similar practices dominated most of Europe for
centuries; and they persist in many countries today. Americans have been spared one of Europe's chief causes of
bitter dissension and bloodshed.

Western Europeans have had to fight for generations
before attaining freedom of worship and secular education.

* Cf. Duncan Aikman: *The Turning Stream* (New York: Doubleday &
Company; 1948), pp. 105–6.

Religious wars and inquisitions are a major part of the Old World's tragic history. The church, of one sect or another, has repeatedly interfered in state affairs. Even after centuries of such conflicts numerous European nations have not yet achieved any real separation of church and state. In other countries they have done so but partially and inconclusively. In a considerable part of Europe liberation from religion in politics seems no nearer today than when the United States Constitution was adopted in 1787.

This constitutes another great and basic distinction between the heritage of Americans and Europeans. American citizens have escaped the great misfortune of religion in politics. Our political parties are not based upon membership in a certain religious sect; but this is commonly the case in much of Europe. Pastors, priests, and bishops have never directed one or another of our political parties, have rarely sought election to Congress, and have never held high office in a national administration in Washington. But religious politicians in the national government have never been unusual in many European lands, while the church has held a monopoly of religion in many of them, with few or no limitations, for centuries.

The absence of these circumstances has enormously reduced internal political tensions in the United States. We cannot accurately envision, for instance, the lifelong political influence and power of Monsignor Ignaz Seipel both as the leader of Austria's Christian Socialist Party and for some years as Chancellor of Austria. Between the wars Father Hlinka played an equally decisive political role in Slovakia, and he was later succeeded by another prominent cleric under Hitler. In the free Czechoslovak Republic the Catholic People's Party distinguished itself for being the most liberal and progressive church-supported political organization on a continent where other such parties were usually conservative or outrightly reactionary. As a result anticlericalism never became an inflamed issue in Czechoslovakia as it has often been in Italy, Hungary, Spain, and some other countries, and as it repeatedly flares up with disastrous effect even in present-day France. In Communist-controlled Hungary I encountered, in 1946, an impressive example of the church's representative in national politics. Father Balogh, when I interviewed him, still managed to retain his position as Under-Secretary of Foreign Affairs under the Reds. Like many other Hungarian church leaders he was a remarkably adroit politician.

Europe's church leaders have made both good records and bad in national politics; they usually tended, of course, to defend their sectarian interests very strongly. This is why the issues of clericalism and of state-controlled or church-controlled education remain highly explosive in much of Europe. This also explains why anticlericalism has a pronounced and often bitter hold on large masses in countries like Italy or Spain, even though they are overwhelmingly Catholic. A great many Europeans feel compelled to wage a continual struggle against excessive religious interference or influence in their political systems. Americans have thus far remained providentially free from most of the complications and animosities that result from such a situation.

There is another broad differentiation between political practices in Europe and the U.S.A. It is—

The important difference between the U.S. two-party system and Europe's multi-party system.

The average American votes either Republican or Democratic because we have never had more than two major parties. A third party with any real mass support has been very rare in our history, nor has Henry Wallace made the permanence of such a party any more likely. Most Americans think in terms of two parties and no more. It is also an American phenomenon that neither Republicans nor Democrats have ever been forced to share their victories by forming a national administration based upon a coalition of parties.

The average European, on the other hand, is accustomed to coalition governments at frequent intervals or much of the time. This is because of the multi-party system and because European politics are more diverse in form. Most nations have a minimum of three or four strong parties; sometimes more than that. In prewar France at least a dozen different parties and groups fought for some degree of representation in parliament. Despite the war's upheaval France today still has five major parties, plus several lesser ones. The same situation exists in postwar Italy. In fact, totalitarian Spain and Portugal and the Red-dominated satellites are the only Continental countries where the multi-party system has been abolished or reduced to mere camouflage.

The existence of many political parties has given Europeans an entirely different political experience from our own. It has made them much more conscious of distinctions in political philosophies, and more precise in what the members of any particular party demand as an electoral program. But the multi-party system also tends to weaken seriously the authority of the French, Italian, and other European governments. Coalitions of several parties are subject to uncertain lives, often short and disruptive. Ever since her liberation France has suffered greatly from unstable government due to this one cause. We in the United States can scarcely conceive how much more involved and precarious our problems of government would be if Republicans and Democrats had to form a coalition in Washington in order to keep a strong Socialist, Communist, or Nationalist-Fascist party from assuming power.

European politics are also much more complicated than our own because Europe was the birthplace and original laboratory of an astonishing assortment of ideologies and political theories. These range from the church state to the separation of church and state; from absolute monarchies to modern parliamentary monarchies, as in Great Britain and Scandinavia; from anarchism and syndicalism to Marxian Socialism; from democratic Socialism to authoritarian Communism; from Fascism to Nazism and Falangism—and not a single one of these highly conflicting political and economic concepts has yet existed as a major threat, backed by a powerful party, in the United States. Alongside the above-mentioned ideologies there has sprouted in Europe a wide variety of republican parties, moderate Nationalists and extreme Nationalists, Christian Democrats linked closely to the church, and other categories of democrats or republicans who oppose clericalism.

To our own Mr. American Middle Man these extraordinary variations are understandably bewildering and mystifying. Under the far more tolerable circumstances of our vigorous, unhampered, and constantly expanding economy even the partisans of democratic Socialism have not yet become appreciably strong in the United States.

The uncounted and generally ignored political blessings of American citizens are as great as they are rare in many parts of Europe. Once slavery was abolished, our nation had no feudal abuses and no feudal hierarchy of aristocrats, Army, and church. The numbers of our seriously exploited workers have always been very much less than in most European countries; therefore anarchist organizations have been almost unknown here, while syndicalism and Communism have made little progress numerically. Our middle-class country has also had no constant fears of outside aggression, and until today no excessive drainage of our national wealth by the obligatory maintenance of large armed forces. Finally, because the United States was so big in space, so rich in resources, and so relatively underdeveloped, its people had slight occasion to feel prolonged economic insecurity. That is something entirely new to us, while it has been a constant problem and menace to a legion of Europeans. Not until 1929, in fact, did American citizens have reason to become seriously concerned about abuses and contradictions within their free-enterprise system.

On most counts the exact opposite was true for most Europeans. They were exposed to far greater insecurities. They could not win a rich and wonderful array of basic freedoms in the space of a single decade, as happened in the American colonies by the grace of Providence. Europe's racial and national groups were compelled to fight for generations, often for centuries, to achieve even a few of our essential freedoms. Here and there they won a bit, and lost again; and then lost more. In more than half of the Old World they have now lost out once more. And even in western Europe none of the citizens of any country possess opportunities and privileges remotely comparable to ours.

European politics have accordingly become more intense as well as more diverse. They have also become more subtle, and in some ways and in some nations they have reached a higher intellectual plane. The result is that Americans can learn much from the political distinctions in Europe, while Europeans can likewise learn much from our own unbroken experience in self-government.

Some of the differences between the American's political position and practices and those of the European have narrowed decidedly over the past thirty or forty years. In some respects our political actions, as well as our greatest problems, are becoming increasingly similar. Even the emergence of the Communist-supported, so-called "Progressive" party of Henry Wallace strongly resembles the "Unity" or "Democratic Bloc" improvisations recently in vogue in eastern Europe. But a much more profound, newly developed similarity concerns:

The role of organized labor
in European and American politics.

In the Europe of 1914, labor unions were much more highly organized than in the United States when Franklin D. Roosevelt inaugurated the New Deal. The pronounced growth of European Socialism was largely responsible. In Great Britain a tightly knit, aggressive Labour Party had existed for several decades; and this was equally true in Scandinavia. Throughout industrialized western Europe confederations of labor or labor syndicates had millions of members. Europe's trade unions were not confined to the upper bracket of skilled workers, as was the American Federation of Labor. They embraced the mass of ordinary workers. Socialist unions were especially strong in 1914 in Britain, Germany, France, and Italy. At that time Communist unions were much weaker. In some countries Catholic-sponsored unions also existed.

The trade-union movement first gathered notable strength in western Europe because workers there had the greatest need to organize. Their wages and living-conditions generally were far lower than in the rapidly expanding U.S.A.; and they could not "go west" or find available farming land as an alternative existence. Their only choice was to unite and fight for better conditions. The ideas of Marx and Engels gave them an incentive toward united action, an objective of their own, and a new awareness of their potential political strength. Thus Europe's factory workers became politically conscious long before American workers began to organize in large numbers. As a consequence unions in western Europe first emerged as an established and recognized participant in national politics, while American labor advanced at a decidedly slower pace.

Actually, it was not until the mid-1930's that the Congress of Industrial Organizations mushroomed into a national force and rather horrified conservatives by forming Political Action committees. The average middle-class American had not been educated to see much justification for this step. It seemed rather radical, even though it was clearly democratic in its practices. Yet this same sort of political action by unions had long been accepted by western Europeans, including those of the middle class, as a natural and inevitable phase of representative government in modern industrialized nations.

It was less shocking to Europeans because unions had been strong among them for a longer time. At the very outset of the Industrial Revolution the industrialists themselves had appropriated exceptional political powers and used them to further their own interests. As industrialization increased, thereby steadily swelling the ranks of the workers, European labor could no longer be denied political expression. The C.I.O.—a late-comer in the United States—took organized American labor much nearer the universally accepted European pattern. Just as in western Europe, our own industrialists, businessmen, bankers, and farmers could no longer enjoy a virtual monopoly of powerful political pressures.

As Lincoln said, we cannot escape history; nor can we escape evolution. Whether or not it may seem socialistic, Americans cannot avoid much longer a great deal more planning by our government. This, it seems to me, is dictated both by our nation's great physical size and by the dimensions of our problems. Much more extensive governmental planning is unavoidable also simply because our enormous industrial machine threatens, more and more, to run out of control. No tremendous machine can maintain a safe degree of stability without an adequate measure of controls and guidance. Nor is there any single group in our society—whether industry, business, farmers, or trade unions—that is notably endowed with a capacity for self-discipline on its own initiative, without the mediation and authority of personalities and instruments that represent the general welfare of the nation. Finally, we—like the Europeans—are no longer immune to either Communist or Fascist ideas and political organizations.

Thus the shrinking world, the Industrial Revolution, the universality of political ideologies, and other factors have brought American citizens into a situation which increasingly resembles that of Europe's peoples. Our central problems, our greatest uncertainties, and our chief dangers are strikingly similar to theirs. But in general political awareness, in precise political thinking, and in a personal appreciation of the privileges of freedom a considerable time-lag still persists for most Americans.

Europeans suffer from numerous divisions of opinion over ways and means in which to improve their social and economic systems. We in the United States are handicapped by having felt less urgency to study the causes of economic instability, and by having virtually no experience with Fascist or Communist police-state tactics and methods. But we have now reached a point where we can no longer dally with these problems. We have also reached the point where neither our freedoms nor our security from attack can be taken for granted.

The ideal of One World may yet be far removed from practical attainment; but there has been a steady, almost startling growth in the *community* of European-American interests ever since 1917. At the midway turning-point of this fateful century what the Old World and the New have in common, despite their important differences, is of truly great significance. For together with the Europeans we face common physical dangers, common ideological challenges, common scientific and technological unknowns, a common urgency to evolve economic systems that provide more, and more justly, for all, a common menace to our civil liberties and to our processes of self-government.

America's John Between undoubtedly has more in common and shares more similarities with his European middle-class cousins than he is likely to have taken into account. For the affinity or kinship side of the *Euro-American* ledger is indeed impressive. Its meaning for our own future may well prove to be decisive. In our present world situation we have a peculiarly urgent need to understand:

The common denominators of average Europeans and average American citizens.

We belong, first of all, to the European family. We have an intimate relationship with Europe that we do not have with the people of any other continent. Three centuries of our separate New World existence have not broken this relationship; in many ways it has been intensified. European civilization is the origin and controlling influence in our own. Either a North American or a Latin American can travel across Europe and discover in many countries an astonishing number of things that are familiar. Whether in London or Paris, Stockholm or Rome, Budapest or Athens, the essentials of life are expressed in ways much more similar than dissimilar to those in American cities.

To begin to feel and sense Europe you must reach Moscow, as I have, fresh from China, Burma, and India. Moscow is partly Oriental, of course, but its dominant flavor is European. It also has a touch of American influence, in its modern buildings, its movie theaters and industrial development, in the lustiness and self-confidence of its youth. In recent decades all of Europe has been transformed by American products and processes. But all of the United States has been shaped for three centuries by European infiltrations—cultural, philosophical, and spiritual. More and more the mother civilization and the offspring civilization tend to intermingle and to merge into what might more accurately be called the *Euro-American* or the Inter-Atlantic civilization.

Western Europeans are especially close to all North Americans. They are part of our immediate family—British or Scandinavian, German or Dutch, French or Italian, makes slight difference. Yet it required even more than two World Wars to make United States citizens begin to become truly conscious of their intimate relationship with western Europe. The threat of Communist domination of the entire European continent has aroused a new sense of our kinship, although that American die-hard minority known as isolationists still seeks to avoid recognizing this fact. Actually we had unwittingly admitted our kinship with Europe when we joined in battle against the Kaiser's imperialism, and again against Hitler's. But western Europe only achieved a special identification in our speech and thoughts when Soviet Communism suddenly controlled the other half of the Old World. When Congress overwhelmingly adopted the Marshall plan, "Western civilization" assumed a new and more personal meaning for the people of the United States.

Under the Marshall Plan we may invest up to $20,000,-000,000 or even more to preserve free and democratic societies in western Europe. We find this not merely prudent or expedient. We recognize that the huge expenditures for ERP are essential for the security of the U.S.A.; they are an investment for our own protection. Basically we are striving to save everything that western Europeans have in common with ourselves. That is our stake in western Europe, and their stake in the United States. Our common bonds now require joint support and a common defense.

What are the bonds between
western Europeans and U.S. citizens?

We think immediately of the common denominator of individual freedoms and democratic, representative government. But our bonds are woven of a much greater variety of strands than one might hastily suppose. Some date from the origins of Christianity, others from the Greek and Roman civilizations; still others from more recent times. When we consider even a few of these ties the term Euro-American takes on a deeper meaning.

Western Europeans and North Americans have a common cultural inheritance.

Our systems of law are founded upon the same basic principles.

Our philosophy and ethics are branches from the same trunk of European knowledge.

Our New World universities were founded and developed upon the experience and learning of the much older European universities.

Both western European and American science have common foundations. They share the legacy of Galileo and his successors as they share the contributions of Einstein and all other modern scientists today.

Western Europeans and North Americans alike are beneficiaries of the Renaissance, of Martin Luther and the Reformation; of an imposing series of explorations and theories that have increasingly liberated the minds of Western men and have gradually improved their material lot. We are alike in the governing charts of the mind and in the deepest expressions of the spirit.

These similarities of formation, experience, and outlook are so enormous they can scarcely be summarized adequately. Certainly they are more powerful and more profound than the nationalistic and other differences that still persist between western Europeans and American citizens. The interflow and intermingling of Europe and America never ends. Without the daring contentions of European thinkers of the same and earlier generations our Declaration of Independence could not have become an immortal expression. Within a few years Jefferson's lofty words and noble ideas recrossed the Atlantic to share in influencing the French Revolution. It is in the mind and the spirit—in the things by which men live—that the peoples of western Europe and the United States have forged forward, by common inspiration and toward common goals. From early colonial days we have all been much more together than we have realized. What have we been doing? Aside from our immediate nationalistic interests we have also been building an inter-Atlantic, European-American civilization. Now that its survival is seriously open to question we begin to grasp the enormousness of its meaning. But do we in the United States yet comprehend adequately that—

Western Europe is the center of decision for the survival of democracy everywhere?

The balance of power between the Soviet-Communist East and the democratic West lies in the industrialized and progressive nations of western Europe. Nowhere in Asia do the decisive elements of modern power exist to a degree even remotely comparable. Nowhere outside the United States itself are these same elements so remarkably developed. It is only in some future generation that we can expect them to be developed on a pronounced scale in China and India, whose potentials of power are great indeed. The Soviet Union has made notable industrial progress since 1917, and is capable of very impressive modernization over the next thirty years. But the industrialized power of western Europe is already an accomplished fact. In the great East-West crisis and rivalry western Europe constitutes the center of decision. But to understand how crucially important western Europe is to the United States, we must first distinguish its particular elements of power.

More than 250,000,000 people live west of the Stettin-Vienna-Trieste line. When we speak of western Europe as the natural and foremost ally of our New World, we refer to these 250,000,000 people and what they represent. As yet, however, probably no more than a small fraction of American citizens have a clear idea of what these western Europeans represent. We merely apprehend, in a general way, that our own future would be gravely menaced if these peoples were engulfed by any form of totalitarian dictatorship.

Western Europe's industrial power is a first and major factor. The combined industrial plants and equipment of Great Britain, France, the Low Countries, Scandinavia, western Germany, Austria, and Italy are tremendous in productive capacity. No other region outside the United States can rival this area in this respect. Among the Soviet satellite countries only Czechoslovakia and Poland possess an important industrial potential. Thus Europe's industrial balance of power lies in her free and advanced nations.

An associated factor has equal historical meaning, but can too easily be overlooked. For western Europe also possesses the greatest reservoir of skilled and semi-skilled workers anywhere outside the North American continent. Tens of millions of the world's most experienced industrial workers live in the countries west of the Iron Curtain. They have an exceptional training with modern machinery and industrial techniques. In this they are very much superior to the average worker in Soviet factories. If Moscow and Communism could control western Europe's machines *and* skilled labor, the world's greatest productive capacity would lie in the hands of the Kremlin's leaders. The powerful position of the United States would be radically reduced. Both productively and militarily the United States would be thrown on the defensive. Our total strength thus depends even more upon the other Western democracies than upon ourselves.

But western Europe also constitutes a tremendously rich center of scientific skills and equipment. Its combined laboratories are the closest rivals to those in the United States. In pure science and its basic discoveries Europeans have consistently led the world until now. They again demonstrated this emphatically by their fundamental trail-blazing in atomic fission. We must recognize, then, that western Europe represents a great and irreplaceable force in this age of technological progress. Under Communist or Fascist control its laboratories and scientists might drastically alter the balance of world power against the U.S.A. and other outlying democracies. So long as they are on our side they serve to strengthen inestimably the forces of free societies.

To this list must be added all the intangibles of western European knowledge, culture, and spiritual inheritance. These factors, too, must be considered together with the manpower of some 250,000,000 people. It becomes abundantly clear why western Europe, topped by its civil liberties and democratic tradition, is nothing less than the center of decision between the Soviet East and the free West. China, India, and other Eastern nations have their own importance as well. But theirs is notable chiefly in terms of manpower, resources as yet undeveloped, and strategic geographical positions. On the other hand western Europe's combined assets are of skill and quality, and they are of immediate weight and effectiveness. For the United States, caught in a world struggle for power, western European nations and their people are truly inexpendable. They cannot be replaced because no other large group of the outside world's population possesses such vital and varied elements of developed power as they possess in exceptional measure. Suddenly the New World's future depends upon the peoples of the Old World almost as much as the other way round.

We have been trying to get a more specific blueprint of the unique and extraordinary community of interests between U.S. Americans and Europeans; particularly between western Europeans and ourselves. For if we do not understand what has already happened to Europeans in this century, we have slight chance of understanding what may yet happen to the people of the United States in the remainder of this century.

Our societies stand exposed to the same revolutionary forces. We cherish the same great heritage. We cling to identical civil liberties. We are compelled to defend closely related systems of government and free enterprise. The ramparts we watch cannot be guarded separately—not without mortal danger to our way of life.

Thus our common denominators as "Westerners" have now brought us to a common defense of our European-American civilization; in reality, to a common destiny for our Euro-American family. This defense centers upon the middle class in western Europe, and even with greater intensity upon the great middle class in the United States. For only where the middle class persists as a central bastion against extremism from Left and Right can democratic practices still remain strong. In Europe the people in the middle have been subjected to vicious assaults from both extremes for the past thirty years. Our middle class has as yet been spared this cruel experience. That is why we have particular need today of knowing exactly what has happened to our kind of people over there. We have need to know because the central target of the totalitarians has moved from them to us.

Chapter IV

HOW FASCISM CAME TO EUROPE

Those of us who were sent abroad as foreign correspondents in the 1920's were probably as innocent about
what was really happening in Europe as most of our fellow
countrymen were. This was certainly true when my turn
came in the summer of 1926. Not only were there a multitude of things to learn in the slow, hard way. There was
also the fact that to report governmental crises, international conferences, and the speeches of big politicians is
not nearly enough. In those first years I began to see that
all Europe was in the grip of deep and explosive revolutionary forces created by World War I. Somewhere I also
began to perceive that politics are more than conflicting
parties and slogans; that politics are *people*.

Simple as this fact may seem, most of us tend to dismiss
or ignore it. Yet people do make their politics and their
politicians; and having made them, people fall for what they
themselves helped to create.

It is necessary to be clear about this before considering
the question: what happened to the Europeans between
the wars? For the greatest seductions of our times have not
been achieved by beautiful and conniving women. The
greatest seductions of this century have been perpetrated
upon millions of credulous "push-overs" by political demagogues who substituted totalitarianism and enslavement
for rape. Perhaps no form of immorality is so frightfully
destructive to human society as the seductive techniques of
dictatorial propagandists. I had presumed that I went to

65

Europe merely to report on world affairs, but what I saw,
and what I have been compelled to evaluate on five continents ever since, has been nothing less than the processes
and perils of political seduction.

This is where the common people of Europe come into
our story; and especially those in-between Europeans who
belong or once belonged to the middle class. For what has
happened to any European nation's middle class during
the past thirty years of the world revolution *can* happen
to citizens in any other country, including the United
States. There can be no slightest doubt about this. I have
seen it happen in Germany and Spain. I have seen its entrenched consequences in Italy and elsewhere. I have
watched the steady undermining of the strongly democratic French people, their integrity and their unity, between the wars. Since the last war I have seen impotent
though unwilling peoples again being dominated by police-
state methods in several eastern European lands. Even
though they did not accept political seduction they could
not escape it. And nowhere, not even in neutral Sweden or
Switzerland, have the people been able to remain immune
to the persistent pressures of the totalitarian revolution.

At the point where my own personal exposure com-
menced, Europe's middle man, virtually all of her ordinary
citizens, had already become the victims of Kaiser Wilhelm's dreams of conquest. In Russia the seductive slogan
of "Peace and bread! Peace and land!" had won a decisive
mass support for the Bolshevik revolutionaries. The Germans had gone from defeat into immediate mass uprisings
and bloodshed, with a Red republic proclaimed briefly in
Bavaria and a Communist dictatorship set up in Dresden.

What was perhaps most significant of all about World
War I was its aftermath. Popular revolutions swept all the
defeated countries. Béla Kun's Red regime and terror were
followed in Hungary by a "White Terror," which was

equally brutal and much more extensive. Street rioting and violence swept the cities of Italy. The Prussian war lords had sown wildly, and most of Europe reaped the whirlwind. When the German Socialists, backed by thirty-eight per cent of the popular vote, restored relative order, the German people were hungry, destitute, and an early prey to a devastating inflation. The plight of most Europeans was identical, save in degree. Through war and revolution Europe's middle class was bankrupt and subjected to wholesale liquidation. When currency inflation reduces a man's lifetime savings to a spending value of one cent or even ten cents on every dollar, revolution has occurred. A currency revolution plays very few favorites. It blankets almost all of a nation's population, and it makes its victims revolutionary in many other ways. In a word, the first World War exposed Europe's ordinary men and women completely to demagogic political seduction.

What was the attitude of Europe's middle class as a consequence?

Even in the middle or late 1920's you could walk the workers' districts in British, French, German, Italian, and other cities and listen to the results of World War I. Even though these European workers had never belonged to the better-off bourgeoisie, what they said was of tremendous importance to the seriously impoverished middle class. In unprecedented millions Europe's workers now demanded far-reaching economic reforms, with outright Socialism and state ownership of key industries in their national economies. The Communists still lagged far behind in converts (save in Germany where their voting strength was notably great), but the Socialists and the Left in general had never been so strong.

I remember how they talked in the Clichy and Saint-Antoine districts of Paris. "Who made money out of the war?" a short and gesticulating factory employee demanded. "Only the Krupps and Schneider-Creusot, the steel-owners and their bankers. Then why not nationalize the arms plants and steel and other big industries? Then they can't arrange with the Germans to pad their pockets in another war."

The armament-makers and the Comité des Forges, which controlled some two hundred and fifty producers of steel in France, had become highly suspect to French workers. Krupp, Thyssen, Stinnes, and I.G.Farben, among others, had become equally so to Germans, who maintained their Social Democratic Party as the largest in Germany for nearly eleven years. The Pirellis and similar big industrialists bore the brunt of the Italian laborers' condemnations. In Vienna, too, Socialism was stronger than ever before. In Britain the Labour Party was expanding steadily.

But the pronounced growth of Europe's Marxists, paced by the Socialists, had merely increased the dilemma and uncertainty of all those middle people who had always avoided the extremes of Left or Right.

In the 1920's what were the predicament and state of mind of Europe's John Betweens?

When I talked with Jean, who owned the café and zinc-covered little bar at the corner of our street in Paris, he might well have been speaking for most of the small café proprietors or most of the white-collar class in France. (A little later a small restaurant-owner in Berlin expressed almost identical worries and complaints.)

"What can one do? Prices are too high. Always taxes and more taxes. There is no stability for business. The politicians, they are only busy taking care of themselves. It was better while we had Poincaré. But now things are going from bad to worse again. I tell you, monsieur, what we need is a strong man."

When I paid the rent our landlord usually harked back

to the losses he had sustained in government bonds and other savings as a result of inflation. He became more of a nationalist and more anti-labor with each passing year. He had once thought he possessed a solid nest-egg for his wife's and his own old age; but war and inflation had reduced it to a robin's egg size, or perhaps less.

We took regular lessons in conversational French from a wonderful, white-mustached aristocrat of nearly eighty, the Baron de la Touche de Pellerin. He and his wife had enjoyed a very comfortable income from *rentes* and other securities in 1914. Now they were obliged to scrape along in a poor cramped apartment, living almost entirely on the few francs per hour that the courageous old baron eked out from his teaching. Although he belonged to a distinguished family of the French nobility, and so to the prewar upper class, he was now as badly off as the poorest of the middle class.

Throughout continental Europe millions upon millions of families had suffered this brutal economic constriction and leveling-down process. Its sharpest force struck members of the bourgeoisie: shopkeepers and minor business executives; salesmen, clerks, and stenographers; professors and teachers; garage-owners and small farmers; doctors and lawyers; and the legion of men and women who were employed by federal or municipal governments. After losing three fourths or nine tenths of their savings, mounting high prices further deprived large numbers of these people of adequate necessities and minor luxuries for years. Since the Office of Price Administration was abolished in June 1946, U.S. citizens have had a hint of inflation's vicious effects. Our dollar rapidly became worth less than fifty cents in terms of 1944 prices. But this is mild indeed compared with the inflationary impoverishment that afflicted Europeans after both World Wars.

In London, Brussels, or Paris, and in Rome, Vienna, or Berlin I met the same kind of middle-class people upon whom the same deprivations and retrenchments had been imposed by the folly of modern war. For nearly ten years they had struggled desperately either to make ends meet or to win back a portion of the better life they had been accustomed to and felt rightly theirs. Everywhere these European middle men were confused, and often they were as resentful as the Socialist or Communist workers on the Left. Where the French bourgeois was highly critical of his government a similarly placed Austrian or Italian was more so, while the middle-class German seethed inwardly over what he regarded as the extreme injustice of his personal fate and that of his country. Europe's middle men were rebellious, frustrated, and in many respects lost souls. They had a deadly fear of Communism. They were afraid of the Socialists' greatly increased strength. In Italy and Germany especially they were exasperated by a sense of helplessness and hopelessness. That was why many of them had little faith in their government and talked about the need of a "strong man." As I remember it this was pretty much how some millions of jobless and other depression-hit Americans felt when they went to the polls in 1932 and voted for Franklin D. Roosevelt. But Europeans never had such a simple choice, nor one that would prove to be comparatively so moderate.

By the late 1920's, however, economic conditions had improved very considerably in France and Italy, even if for very different reasons. Although the Germans were worse off than most other Europeans, U.S. loans and the Dawes Plan had begun to ease their plight a good deal. Then came the great market crash in the United States—and within two years our depression had spread with disastrous consequences across all of Europe.

This is something for Americans to keep clearly in mind today. It was the U.S. depression that killed all hope of European recovery in 1929. It served largely and directly to plunge scores of millions of Europeans—first of all, their

middle men—back into renewed unemployment, impoverishment, and despair. Without an economically strong
and stable United States, and without a healthy trade with
us, neither Britain, France, nor Germany could keep their
economies out of a paralyzing slump. I was in Geneva
when the proud and previously unshakable British pound
sterling was forced to abandon the gold standard. A cold
chill of fright shook all Europe. Europeans knew that the
ravages of depression could no longer be escaped. They
were sliding into the pit with us, the world's dominant industrial and financial influence. A similar U.S. crash in the
1950's could not fail to affect Europe in precisely the same
way, but probably more disastrously and with irreparable
political consequences.

If the economic slump in the United States was primarily
and largely responsible for Europe's severe depression in
the 1930's, it was also in large measure accountable for the
European peoples' being pushed into totalitarian extremism politically. That, too, is where Europe's middle class
assumed a central role in the tragic developments that led
straight to Hitler and to World War II.

We who were foreign correspondents had far too much
political drama to report in those days. Perhaps we concerned ourselves to an exaggerated degree with the higher
and official drama; with the bitter struggle for power of
political leaders and parties. In retrospect I confess that this
was a failing of mine. When Mussolini was indulging in
his histrionic balcony act and Hitler was roaring vengeance
and even little Dollfuss was strutting like a peacock in
Vienna it was too easy to forget for considerable stretches
that politics are also people—the common people. And the
dictators or would-be dictators monopolized so much news
space in our home newspapers that our editors had little
room for simple pieces about Johann Schmidt or Giuseppe
Martinelli. But in each European country Johann and
Giuseppe and Jan and Jacques really represented the bal-

ance of power, the deciding factor, simply because they lived in the middle of their nation's society. If they were to seize power, either the Fascists or the Communists would have to win a great number or most of these middle men.

It was a terribly costly trick of fate, then, that once more plunged Europe's middle class back into unemployment, tightened belts, hopelessness, and rebellious resentment. It happened just when they had finally begun to pull themselves up the ladder again, at the end of the 1920's. And nowhere was this second collapse and downward plunge of such deadly and universal consequence as in Germany. Yet almost everywhere on the Continent it ushered in a decade of political extremism and political assassinations, of moral and social disintegration, of violence and of political seduction based upon incredible lies and distortions.

What happened to Europe's middle men as a result of inflation and depression?

Between the filing of dispatches about governmental crises and abortive international conferences and the vindictive harangues of the new demagogues, we witnessed the degradation and final abdication of the European middle class. I say abdication rather than conquest because the middle men of western Europe actually had an opportunity to choose. The French people had a choice, but they tolerated corrupt politicians and a venal press and other self-destructive abuses throughout the entire period between the wars. The Italians had a brief few years in which they could choose. Until Pilsudski imposed a dictatorial regime of generals and landed nobility in 1926, the Poles had a choice. The Germans had nearly twelve years of free electoral choice—and ended, in 1932, by giving Hitler's Nazis greatest strength. The decisive millions of these votes came from Germany's frustrated, Red-fearing middle class. Germany's men between were seduced wholesale. It was the costliest and most catastrophic mass political rape in human history. Of course it can happen again—in any industrialized nation whose middle citizens yield to similar emotionalism, blindness and disregard for personal and parliamentary liberties.

As the Nazis fought their way to power we watched the persistent and diabolically adroit seduction of Johann Schmidt, typical representative of Germany's great middle-class mass of the disinherited.

Talk to a small German shopkeeper in any city or town and he was almost certain to be another Johann. Whether in Cologne, Leipzig, or elsewhere he said much the same things. "What we need is somebody to put the Communists and the Jews in their place. What kind of life does a real German have these days? And how can Germany live under the dictate of Versailles? *Lieber Gott,* we have a right for room to live in. Why should the French, the British and the others have armies and air forces while we have none? In much that he says Hitler is right."

This was where Hitler, Goebbels & Company made their most telling appeal. They exploited systematically every dominant fear, resentment, and aspiration of Germany's embittered and economically prostrate middle men. The Nazis appealed to their sense of injustice, knowing this to be justified in some respects. They exploited the prevalent feeling of inferiority among middle-class Germans. By blaming their present plight on the war-defeat "stab in the back" story, on the Jews and the Communists, the average German—Johann Schmidt—could salve his shattered self-respect. The Nazis shouted that Germany's sovereignty and power—and military might—would be restored. Hitler knew that this intense nationalism was irresistibly strong in the highly emotional make-up of the average German.

I saw extremely intelligent German journalists, men of great ability and international experience, swallow the Nazis' propaganda bait as easily and completely as a thwarted, underpaid schoolteacher in Bonn am Rhein. One of these was Dr. Friedrich Sieburg, Paris correspondent of the *Frankfurter Zeitung* and author of a penetrating analysis of French character called, *Is God French?* I admired Sieburg for his marked professional talents and regarded him as an enlightened European. But at heart he was a German, with all the fierce nationalism and resentment of the average middle-class Teuton. These things were more important to him than individual freedom, democratic self-government, the basic moralities, or humanitarian principles. Like countless other German intellectuals he went along with the Nazis. Today, if he is living, Sieburg might aptly write a companion volume to his deft portrayal of the French, entitled "Is the Devil German?" Such a suggestion could not be made today if Sieburg and Germany's middle class had not abdicated into servitude, if they had not become ardent partners of Nazism in its immeasurable crimes.

On the streets of Berlin in 1933 I saw ordinary German citizens who were appalled and distressed by Nazi beatings and outrages against their Jewish fellow citizens. But they were in a helpless minority, and more and more they hid their true feelings. Germany's long-submerged "little man" and "little woman" had been swept off their feet by Hitler's wooing, and almost completely out of their minds. When *der Führer* or Goebbels addressed huge assemblies in the elaborately festooned Sports Palace, I studied the faces on all sides. Most of these people were as middle-class as German frankfurters and beer. The number of women was extraordinary. They leaned forward breathlessly, with fanatically gleaming eyes fixed on Hitler. When he promised to "wipe out the Bolsheviks and the Jews forever," their faces registered such intense hatred as I had never seen and hope never to see again. They shrieked in a mass frenzy. You left the Sports Palace limp as a dishrag and trembling for the future of Europe—yes, and of America.

Where could this madness be stopped now? Where and how?

Germany's "little men" had abandoned themselves to madness. They had done so because a madman told them that Germany would be great and mighty again; that they belonged to a master race and were superior to all other peoples; that they were the innocent and faultless victims of international plotters and racial connivers; that their economic distress was due to a mere handful of Jewish citizens, to labor unions, to socialistic government—to anything except to the fact that the Kaiser and his German war lords had deliberately launched a war in which 37,-508,000 persons had died, been wounded, or were listed as missing. This was all extremely comforting to middle-class Johann Schmidt. He had suffered much. He had very little self-confidence left and no more self-respect. He deeply resented all people who were somewhat or much better off than he. He was in no mood to blame himself for any portion of his unhappy lot—and he was too German to blame much of it on those who had misruled Germany. Hitler and the Nazis would put the "little men" up where they belonged, and tell the world where to get off—a most pleasurable feeling for a middle-class German.

With the exception of anti-Semitism most of these blandishments had long before been employed with startling success by Mussolini and his Blackshirt Fascists. They had seduced Italy's middle men with the same rabid nationalism, the same gangster tactics and street fighting against all political opponents, with the same promises to "save the country from the Communists," with similar denunciations of all Socialists, pacifists, sincere democrats and moderates. As in Germany, the chief supporters and party members of Fascism came from the Italian center—middle-class people who were as anxious to be saved from thinking and civic responsibilities as from their economic miseries.

But while Nazism (and Fascism) won their decisive mass

support in the middle and lower middle classes their shrewdly calculated courtship was equally successful on an entirely different and upper level. As American correspondents watched the skillful operations of Hitler and his brain trust we wondered where the Nazis got the tremendous funds they spent so lavishly on party propaganda, on mass demonstrations and spectacles, on "Strength through Joy" excursions for the German workers, and on hundreds of other ambitious projects. These expenditures were running into a great many millions of dollars, all of which could not possibly come from dues and special levies extracted from the financially pressed average German. Little by little the evidence leaked out, and we learned—

How the Nazis were subsidized
by rich and powerful German industrialists.

It is not especially surprising that many of Germany's most influential capitalists and industrial magnates should have secretly contributed large sums to help Hitler establish a Nazi dictatorship. They had been reared in an autocratic Teutonic tradition and had been spiritual partners of the Kaiser. They did not hate totalitarianism, but merely Communists and the kind of totalitarianism (of the proletariat) that the Reds espoused. They had a deadly fear of Communism, and many scores to settle with the governing German Socialists. They were militarists at heart, congenitally so. Most of them despised democracy, and particularly its equalitarian aspects. A militaristic and nationalistic dictatorship, with huge orders for war production, seemed attractive to them—on the assumption that these kings of the Ruhr's great factories could continue to direct an upstart "front man" like Hitler. This is how many powerful Italian industrialists had reasoned about Mussolini, and this is how their German colleagues reasoned about Hitler.

If Joseph Stalin had had a twin brother of German citizenship, and if this Germanized Stalin had clipped his mustache and vehemently denounced all categories of Marxists, and had changed his tune slightly here and there —as Adolf did—the Ruhr magnates would have called him their man. This, in reality, is what they did—and what they got.

But any American reporter who had been around Europe a good deal in the 1920's had already been tipped off what to expect. He had received numerous warning intimations from men of wealth and high position of a fact that Americans may have serious need to remember in the years ahead. The fact is this: *in any industrialized nation where fear of Communism (or even of Socialism) becomes a phobia a certain percentage of important industrialists and other capitalists will always support a Fascist dictatorial movement,* without regard for the destruction of democracy and other peoples' liberties. For such as these, their profits and personal ambition and power override all other considerations. Because money ordinarily means power and they have much of it such men always think they can keep the real power for themselves.

Between 1926 and 1933 I had become personally acquainted with a large number of Europe's leading industrialists, bankers, and other businessmen. In those years a vast proportion of Europe's news concerned economic questions and controversies, from war debts and German reparations to monetary crises, and finally to the causes and proposed cures for the world-wide depression. It was almost as easy for a correspondent to get on friendly terms with finance ministers, industrial tycoons, and Europe's J. P. Morgans as with the proprietors of his favorite restaurants in any Continental capital.

During the four-month Paris conference on reparations that formulated the Young Plan in 1929, some of us saw a great deal of Dr. Schacht and Dr. Vögler, who were the

chiefs of the German delegation. We also saw much of
Owen D. Young, Thomas W. Lamont, Jeremiah Smith,
and other notable American delegates, although very little
of the illusive J. P. Morgan himself. But Schacht and Vögler proved to be exceptionally educational. One night,
while Ralph Barnes and I were trying to interview him,
Dr. Schacht came as near to voluntary, staged-for-the-
impression apoplexy as anyone except Adolf Hitler could
come. He almost shrieked his defiance. "The German
people," he exploded, "will fight another war rather than
permit their children or grandchildren to pay for the last
one." In less than three years Hjalmar Horace Greeley
Schacht was secretly helping Hitler to power. He soon became the financial wizard of the Nazi dictatorship—and
eventually squirmed successfully out of a guilty verdict at
the Nuremberg trials. From what I observed of Dr.
Schacht, there is nothing surprising about any part of his
record.

But the tip-off did not come only from Germans like
Schacht and Vögler. It came equally from various other
capitalists or industrialists whose mentality, regardless of
their nationality, in many ways resembled that of these
outstanding German financiers. As France became more
deeply divided between Left and Right, and strikes and
public demonstrations seriously diminished production, I
heard a number of important French capitalists begin to
speak a pro-Fascist language: "If only we had a strong government, as in Germany and Italy—" . . . "Of course I
have no use for the Nazis' racial policies, but they have
got rid of the Communists—and they've fixed their unions
so they can't strike." One said quite frankly: "What we
need is a French Hitler." The ignominious capitulation of
France in June 1940 was the logical fruit of that attitude.
Although middle-class Frenchmen were deeply poisoned
by it in the immediate years before the war, at least they
had more excuse than industrialists and businessmen who

were the most influential and most privileged in their society.

An important number of European capitalists—British, French, Belgian, Dutch, Scandinavian, Greek, and others— thought they could "do business with Hitler" and that "the Nazis, after all, are not too bad." I met a good many American industrialists, exporters and the like, who felt the same way. Their profit motives quite obscured their professed political and humanitarian principles. Those Americans who had large plants and big investments in Germany took great pains not to offend the Nazis and to get along with them. It is not a pleasant spectacle to see a key executive of a great U.S. corporation play ball with a dictatorial and bloody regime like Hitler's. If such men will play ball with foreign Fascists out of business expediency, what would you expect them to do if a star-spangled brand of American Fascism should ever make a serious bid for power in the United States? Just as there are all kinds of human beings, there are all kinds of capitalists.

Hitler knew that when he found sufficient popular and middle-class support he could get all the cash he needed from the wealthy industrialists and Junker aristocrats and feudal landowners. Fritz Thyssen and Albert Vögler became early contributors to the Nazis' party chest; and in 1931 Thyssen introduced Hitler to a large meeting of the Ruhr's topmost industrialists as "the savior of Germany." Stinnes, Krupp, and many other magnates fell in line. The financial worries of the Nazis were over. The deepening depression made seduction of most of the great German middle class a simple matter of hate-appeal, extreme nationalism, and flattery of the "little man." Hitler, Göring, Goebbels, and Himmler were in.

*What Germany's befuddled and mesmerized
middle class asked for—and how they got it.*

During the first months of the Nazi regime I was sent to
Germany by the *New York Herald Tribune*. By that time
there was no more need for political seduction inside
Europe's largest country. The mask was off. Highly organized intimidation had replaced dupery. So many millions of Johann Schmidts had been duped by Nazi propaganda and Hitler's ravings that German cities echoed day
and night to their parades and *"Heils!"* and frenzied mass
activities. Now the Nazis' main concern was to intimidate,
utterly and completely, that large minority of the population which feared them or hated them. It could be done
most effectively, of course, by transforming the Hitler regime into an ironclad dictatorship with the utmost speed.
In speed and ruthlessness this transformation was breath-
taking.

A seemingly endless succession of drastic Nazi decrees
placed shackle after shackle upon the German people. In
his first month of power Hitler forced all workers into the
so-called German Labor Front. The Nazis did exactly as
the Fascists had done in Italy. The workers were deprived
of all their hard-won rights. No more labor councils and
arbitration commissions; no more labor courts and col-
lective-bargaining privileges. They paid their dues to the
Nazis, who controlled the German Labor Front, and the
Nazis used their money as they saw fit. By 1938 the Labor
Front had 25,000,000 dues-paying members, and they were
forced to pay at an annual rate of $153,000,000.* There
were no more "labor problems" in Germany, and that was
what Fritz Thyssen and other industrialists who had subsidized Hitler had hoped for.

* Cf. Albert C. Grzesinski: *Inside Germany* (New York: E. P. Dutton
& Co.; 1939), pp. 185–7.

If private congratulatory dinners were held among high executives and free-enterprisers in the Ruhr, they did not continue for long. For the Nazis had been in power only a year when they demonstrated that those who hold the big moneybags in a totalitarian nation do *not* hold the guns. The Nazi Ministry of Economics arrogated to itself almost unlimited authority over German industry and business. No fewer than twenty-six different control bureaus were set up for various economic and trade groups, each in the firm hands of a Nazi commissioner. German capitalists could still do business, but they could do business only under Hitler and the Nazis—and on their terms. At this point Fritz Thyssen and many others began to learn what an incredible fool a supposedly smart businessman can sometimes be. As for Thyssen, his flight into exile became merely a question of time. His colleagues, who had invested their hard cash in a totalitarian movement they thought they could control, were bossed around by Nazi bureaucrats, and paid through the nose whenever party leaders decided it was time for them to be "patriotic" again. They were "patriotic" to the end, and the ruins of thousands of German factories are today a monument to their cupidity.

But how were the middle-class Germans getting along? When I saw them in the first flush of Nazi triumph and their own presumably restored importance, they believed all their troubles were over. They—and Adolf—ruled Germany. They had uniforms and badges and party insignia galore. They also had the Gestapo and block spies in every street, wherever they lived and wherever they worked. But they were Germany's new elite, her Teutonic "chosen people," so they didn't seem to mind.

When you looked around, however, you saw that the cost of Nazi circuses and defiance of the world came extremely high. All white-collar and salaried persons had a variety of Nazi taxes automatically levied against their pay envelopes; in fact, so did everyone. When Dr. Goebbels thought up a Winter Help Fund, allegedly for the poor, Johann Schmidt found his weekly salary automatically reduced; or if he was an independent shopkeeper, an arrogant young Nazi collector bluntly let him understand that he had better be generous if he wished to keep many customers. Under the Nazis' totalitarian system what the Germans got was steady work, with increasing taxes and constant special assessments—intensified work for less money, and the suppression of all personal freedoms. Even the right to voice a protest or to express a free opinion no longer existed.

In Berlin I saw fear tyrannize the lives of all kinds of people. Fear clamped down its ironclad rule most effectively through a swift succession of Nazi decress that perverted the previous laws of the German nation. Because the Nazis had blackmailed their way to supreme power through violence, bloodshed, and crime they took immediate steps to "legalize" all past or future violations of normal laws. Confirmed Nazis replaced democratic or moderate judges in all the courts. Special tribunals were set up to punish opponents of the regime. Death sentences and life imprisonment were inaugurated for a long list of relatively secondary offenses, usually without appeal.

Under the rigid and brutally extreme Nazi decrees what was Johann Schmidt to do? That, in fact, was his incessant excuse: "What can a little man do?" Even though he might disapprove secretly of certain Nazi policies or actions, he usually approved of some of them. He was a conformist by nature. He had an exaggerated respect for any and all higher authority. He was accustomed to take orders and to click his heels when obeying them. Now he had a further most compelling motive for doing so—a deadly fear of punishment and of getting into trouble. In Berlin or elsewhere you rarely encountered Germans who dared to criticize Nazi oppressions or brutalities in open fashion. High-pressured intimidation proved as devastatingly efficient as demagogic seduction. It transformed into conformists or involuntary collaborators millions of Germans who had previously refused to vote for Hitler. And what happened to Germany's middle men had happened in similar manner to Italy's middle class.

The great majority of Johann Schmidts lost their personal integrity along with their civic and political freedoms. They were swamped, stifled, and coerced by the one-party system of dictatorship and police terror. Even in the Germany of Hitler's first year a frightening percentage of them did not seem to mind at all. Those who objected, in some respects or many, walked a tightrope day and night and flung up their hands in the Nazi salute at the slightest provocation.

In either Italy or Germany you could go back to the Fascist beginnings and see how this degrading, disastrous conformity had been imposed successfully on those bourgeois middle citizens who should have been capable of resisting it. It was imposed both by the tactics of the Communists and by those of the Fascists and Nazis. The extremists of Left and Right had deliberately destroyed law and order. While fighting for power they defied the police and violated the laws with increasing impunity. The Italian and the German middle classes never organized in defense of freedom of speech and political assembly. Red mobs and Blackshirt or Brownshirt mobs invaded and broke up opposition party meetings. More and more citizens were beaten up or killed. Leftist and Rightist hoodlum gangs ran rampant. *But the center majority of law-abiding people failed to demand that the authorities rigidly enforce freedom of assembly and other civil rights at all costs.* Because Italian and German middle men never took a bold, firm, and united stand against wholesale abuse of the basic rights of all citizens, they sacrificed their own chief weapons for defense against tyranny. By their neglect they opened the door to violence, political gangsterism, and intimidation—and soon became their major victims. When it was too late it was utterly too late.

Between the wars we saw the Fascist-Nazi strategy of violence overwhelm the similar strategy of the Communists and completely overwhelm the middle class in the process. But how did the center majority in Italy and Germany permit this to happen? It was accomplished by—

The spread and exploitation of a "crisis mentality" among the people, backed by a Fascist-Communist application of the "Big Squeeze."

The first World War provoked a series of great crises throughout Europe. These crises were social, economic, and political in nature. In various countries they were strongly revolutionary at first; but they were tempered by the establishment of partial political stability, and in some lands by a gradual economic improvement. Neither the Communists nor the Fascist-Nazis had any interest in progress toward recovery and stability. They could only thrive and build a greater following among the masses in an atmosphere of acute national crisis. What the totalitarian extremists wanted was power, and they could not hope to hold power except through prolongation of the crisis.

This is not to say that Reds and Fascists were alone responsible for the severe and persistent crises that bedeviled continental Europe from 1919 to 1939. Although these crises usually had common economic causes, there were other contributing influences, which were often strictly national, and they differed according to the country concerned. The degree of democratic experience among the people—as in Britain, France, or Belgium—also enabled some nations to reduce considerably the menacing effects of recurrent crises. The democratic and moral resistances of the French were slowly ground down during twenty years of crisis, but they were never pushed into outright totalitarianism.

The dictatorial Leftists and Rightists, however, deliberately aggravated the national crisis in France and in every European country where they could possibly do so. To the eternal credit of the level-headed British and Scandinavians, the extremists had no real success and gained no important mass following in these strongholds of self-government. In these lands an entrenched, intelligent, and politically adult middle class held its ground firmly. In France a similar middle class yielded slowly but repeatedly under heavy attacks from the extremists. In the central countries of Europe—Italy, Austria, and Germany—the middle class had far fewer democratic traditions and loyalties. Its members were much less politically aware and politically experienced, and also much more emotional.

What we stepped into from the quays of Cherbourg in 1926 was not merely the Old World. It was a continent obsessed by the "crisis mentality." The European peoples had survived the first World War, but they could not subsequently escape an atmosphere deeply poisoned by political instability and economic uncertainty. Only in Scandinavia or in countries like Hungary, Italy, and Poland (where semi-Fascist or Fascist military dictatorships already had absolute power) were governments stable. And under military dictators oppressive government brought with it an atmosphere of intense psychological strain. Wherever Fascists and Communists still struggled for power, the aggravation of internal crises was one of their chief weapons.

Since the close of the shooting phase of World War II Americans have been living in an atmosphere of permanent crisis somewhat similar to that which most Europeans have known for some thirty years. Under the complexities of our postwar problems, and particularly because of our unsolved and frustrating controversies with the Soviet

Union, we have also become victims of the "crisis mentality." We too are now generally afflicted with the same disruptive and dangerous disease that has plagued Europeans, confused them, and misled them for many years.

The middle men of prewar Europe wanted security from attack and security from inflation, depression, and want even more avidly than we want them today. Quite humanly, they wanted these first essentials of a tolerably good life as quickly and fully as possible. But some sort of crisis always stood in the way. "I can't plan. I can't be sure of anything," declared Jean at our Paris corner café. Then, as the great depression spread from the United States across Europe, the Jeans and Jans and Johanns talked with mounting explosiveness. They talked about "drastic measures" and "decisive action"; and more and more they talked *against* other and presumably more favored groups in their own national community. The "crisis mentality" blinded them and unbalanced their judgment. They were increasingly in the mood for something "drastic" or "radical."

This is where the big squeeze of the totalitarians, Communists and Fascists, came into play—and into its own.

The crisis mentality is self-nourishing. So it proved to be at the terrible and prolonged expense of Europe's multitude of men between. For the experts of the Big Squeeze exploited economic depression and political confusion and disunity to convince Germans, Austrians, Frenchmen, and others that no middle and moderate solutions were possible. In this Fascists and Communists became partners. They dinned and thundered into all ears the false claim that only a greater crisis—a totalitarian and revolutionary prescription—could dissipate the prevailing crisis. There was no choice, they asserted, except between Rightist and Leftist extremism. There was no solution except through violence and abdication of all personal freedoms, of multiparty systems, and of self-government. To end the crisis, frustrated ordinary citizens must embrace the Permanent Crisis of dictatorship.

Hitler promised to end the crisis of Germany's physical defeat and spiritual inferiority and that closely related crisis of thwarted German nationalism. But for this restricted crisis Hitler merely substituted the infinitely greater and more destructive crisis of Nazism, which was dependent upon and determined upon world conquest. If the Communists had won out in Germany at that time, they would simply have created another much intensified and enlarged crisis of their own kind.

It is vital for us to understand how the Big Squeeze worked and with what tactics in many parts of Europe. From Right wing and Left wing the Big Squeeze destroyed large sections of the middle class in France. It mesmerized and swallowed up the middle men completely in Italy, Germany, Austria, Spain, and elsewhere. Yet it could have achieved such disintegration and destruction only in an atmosphere created by the crisis mentality. For wherever average citizens are persuaded that a crisis exists, they lose their capacity for calm reflection. Their justified or justifiable desire for reforms is deliberately inflamed by totalitarian agitators, who seek in this manner to obscure their own vicious practices and lying propaganda.

While the Communists exploited the noble ideal of international brotherhood, the Blackshirts and Brownshirts championed a restored, robust, and rabid nationalism. The totalitarians always have certain positive values to offer, and one or more of these are worth-while values. They are real values—until they have been perverted and until the cost paid for them, or to be paid for them, has been carefully added up. When the Reds demanded the abolition of land feudalism they had justice and morality on their side. When Mussolini promised the restoration of "law and order" he voiced an urgent need of Italy. When Hitler insisted that Germany must have equality among nations he was saying what all Germans profoundly believed to be right. But in each case these and similar constructive values were wrapped up in one take-it-or-leave-it bundle with other aims and practices which were vicious and debasing. The trick of the totalitarians was—and is—to dupe average people into seeing nothing except a few isolated values (reforms or objectives) that in themselves are commendable and respectable.

If Europe's middle men could be beguiled into thinking only about a better livelihood and more justice in economic terms, they would pay scant attention to what Fascists or Communists did to human liberties. If Germany's bourgeoisie could become infatuated with a promised restoration of German nationalism and military might, they would turn their eyes away from racial extermination, concentration camps, and Gestapo tortures for others. National aggrandizement at the expense of systematized robbery and murder, economic security at the expense of self-government, stability of government at the expense of the right to dissent, a position of pronounced power in European or world affairs at the expense of freedom of speech and the sanctity of the individual and the home—these were the baits of the dictatorial parties; and because they were well-spiced and tempting baits, ever larger portions of Europe's distressed, confused middle class swallowed them. Under ruthless Nazi-Fascist direction the Big Squeeze compressed the predominant human forces of the Old World within its smothering grasp.

The great mistake of Italy's and Germany's men between was to believe that Mussolini and Hitler could give them permanent security by suppressing their liberties, their margins of choice in earning a living, and their political rights. Their great illusion was to imagine that law and order can ever be created by organized political gangsters. Their supreme hallucination was to suppose that systems dedicated to armed might will not lead a nation eventually into war. Their final error was to think that the leaders of a dictatorial party can be given absolute power and still be controlled.

This is what we saw happen in Europe between the wars. We saw political seduction employed by the totalitarian demagogues with greater success than ever before, and with infinitely greater cost to human beings and their moral values. We saw political seduction replaced by calculated and vicious intimidation. We saw the strategy of violence dominate many nations through organized violation of law and suppression of civil liberties. We saw the cultivation and intensification of the crisis mentality, so that these other degrading political methods would be tolerated and finally embraced by millions of frustrated, exasperated people. Year by year and country by country we witnessed the abdication and the capitulation of a major portion of continental Europe's men between.

They had not intended to be "taken" by the Fascists and Nazis; nor to sell themselves to military dictators who were close kin to the Fascists at heart. In most of Europe the middle men had lost *themselves*. They had not known how to protect themselves by holding in the center and making their middle ground impregnable. They had been weakened psychologically, physically, and spiritually by war, by inflation, and then by depression. They had wanted the bright baubles offered by Fascists, Nazis, and nationalists more than they had cherished vital rights and privileges that they already possessed or were still free to struggle to attain. In such manner we saw Europe's men between abandon the great reality and the potential promise of that political way which lies *between*. We saw them lose themselves—and in doing that they lost the peace, and immeasurably more than peace itself. They lost,

even in today's Britain and France, the possibility of leading a tolerably good and a tolerably improving existence
through the remainder of their lives.

When Prime Minister Neville Chamberlain went to
Munich in September 1938 he carried an umbrella. It was
an appropriate symbol of Europe's abdicated middle class.
In the face of mightily armed and brutal dictatorships
Europe's middle men now had little left save an umbrella
—and the tornado of history's most punishing and widespread retribution was closing in blackly overhead. The
rights they had not defended, the freedoms they had betrayed, the truths they had abandoned, the moral values
they had contaminated or rejected—all had gone for nothing more than a frail umbrella in mankind's greatest
storm.

Where Europe's John Betweens had failed would there
still survive, somewhere, another great middle class capable
of awareness and vision, of integrity and unity?

Chapter V

WHAT THE SECOND WORLD WAR
DID TO EUROPEANS

Every war correspondent who had known Europe between the wars received ample warning of what war and
human misery, enemy occupation, and the betrayals of
collaborators were doing to the political thinking of the
European peoples.

As the Nazis took over Norway I saw the beginnings of
popular disillusionment and resentment, to be swiftly followed by a resurgence of individual integrity and devotion
to freedom. Through the summer and autumn of 1940 I
watched Hitler's totalitarian conspirators and militarists
close their steel trap upon the proud and brave peoples of
the Danubian-Balkan countries, again betrayed by their
politicians and others greedy for personal profits.

During the Greek-Italian war, and later in Burma, I
heard common British soldiers and well-educated British
airmen speak with an unaccustomed and utterly un-British
vehemence. They knew they were paying a terrible price
for the blunders and blindnesses of their past leaders. As
their closest comrades died, one after another, they were
filled with such acid bitterness as only the young and the
betrayed can experience. But they were also possessed by
an ever deepening resolve. Never again, in their own land,
would they resign themselves fatalistically to the abuses,
ineptitudes, and callous assumptions of the past.

I remember the cruel agonies of R.A.F. Pilot Sammy
Cooper before he died that night in the mountains of Al-

bania, and how the men of his squadron—men of such great and noble gallantry—looked and spoke afterward. I remember the silence of desperately wounded Greek soldiers and the look in their eyes. I remember the Finns, and, later on, the Russians, saying and believing the same kind of things. I remember recently liberated Italians who talked of a "new day." I remember the first members of the French Resistance whom I met, and the sharpness of their insistence that those who had sold France must never be permitted to do so again. I remember, shortly after the liberation of Paris, the booming words of a French workman in a little café in the Saint-Antoine quarter: "The French people, monsieur, will vote *well to the Left.*" He might have spoken for most of Europe.

For what we encountered everywhere in the combatant or occupied countries of the Continent was the ground-out grist of protracted bombings, bloodshed, tortures, and enslavement. And what we heard was the new voice of Europe. Her middle class had now been ground down almost to the level of her peasants and workers, save that they too had been further stripped and impoverished. Even the Paris that I had known and loved, although virtually unscarred, was scarcely recognizable. Its street scenes had altered profoundly. The Champs-Élysées and the rue de la Paix were no longer thronged with well-dressed persons. The chic and elegantly attired Parisiennes had vanished almost completely. However neat they managed to be, people's clothes were unmistakably old. From more than one café terrace I watched hundreds pass by without being able to observe a single pair of new or relatively new shoes. But the expression on Frenchmen's faces had changed even more than the quality of their attire. They had lost much of their former effervescence. There was a new restraint, sometimes sullenness, sometimes a sharpened purposefulness in their features, sometimes a groping something that could not quite be defined.

Everywhere in Europe, as the war neared its close, we found a slow and painful reawakening of long-imprisoned minds and long-tortured spirits. But the reawakening was prodded and accelerated by a large minority who clamored for restoration of national respect, for a radically changed political life, and for social reforms. The Resistance had produced energetic and youthful new leaders, and the Communists had played an impressive and effective role in resistance everywhere. By their unfailing zeal and frequent heroism in the face of Gestapo barbarities they had won many converts among those who normally would never have joined their ranks. This, too, I had seen happen during the civil war in Spain.

Both Mussolini and Hitler had sought to justify the suppression of all freedoms in their countries by the promise to "wipe out the Communists." When Hitler plunged the Old World into unprecedented destruction he first made a pact with Moscow—and then proclaimed the struggle as a war "to save Europe from Communism." For years Hitler shrieked assurances that he and the Nazis would "destroy Bolshevism forever." Now, in Europe's ashes and debris, we had an opportunity to judge the effectiveness of bombs, bullets, and shells in exterminating an idea. The method had been quite as effective as attempting to extinguish a roaring brush fire with a broom. The Fascists' anti-Red broom of armed violence had spread glowing Marxist embers across the entire Continent. Once the uneasy postwar truce had replaced massed destruction, the masses began to express themselves. The early results can soberly be described as a revelation. They swiftly showed—

*How World War II tremendously increased
the strength of European Leftist ideas
and parties; especially of the Communists.*

In the crippled and bomb-shocked Europe that American correspondents explored, the institution of orthodox, laissez-faire capitalism was indeed a major casualty. To anyone familiar with prewar Europe it was not surprising that both Communism and Socialism had registered notable gains among the workers. But a remarkable proportion of western Europe's middle class had also lost faith in the kind of unrestricted capitalism that exists in the United States. Even though the bulk of these middle men still refused to join Marxist parties, a great many of them insisted that curbs be placed upon key capitalistic enterprises, which, they felt, had exercised "too much power" in the past and had abused that power. They sought a safer economic solution through compromise and reform, while the Reds clamored for another model of the Soviet and Lenin-inspired experiment.

In this Europe we saw the fruits of Hitler's demagogic promise and the stupidity of his formula for "destroying Bolshevism" through police dictatorship and war. For Europe's Communists had never been so numerous, so thoroughly organized, and so ably led as now. As the facts became available they were both emphatic and startlingly plain.

Where Italy's Communists had less than 100,000 party members before Mussolini, they have a present strength of more than 2,200,000. The prewar party membership in France had been approximately 350,000, but by 1947 it had approached or passed the 1,000,000 mark. In Czechoslovakia the Communists' growth, starting from 85,000 in 1935, was nearing 1,500,000 by 1948. Where Yugoslavia had had a small Communist nucleus of perhaps 20,000 under prewar regimes, it had now swollen to somewhere between 500,000 and 600,000. In Poland Moscow claimed the Communist jump to be from 20,000 to nearly 800,000; and with due allowance for exaggeration, the increase had certainly been tremendous. Even in Catholic Belgium the Lenin-Marxists had multiplied to an approximate 100,000.

But European Communists had not made notable progress everywhere. Where had their gains been lowest or nonexistent? Precisely where democratic Socialist parties had long been strongest. Throughout the period between the wars Socialist governments had predominated in the Scandinavian countries. They had inaugurated a considerable amount of state ownership. This meant that their economies had already begun to merge socialistic and capitalistic enterprises, operating peacefully and successfully side by side. The Scandinavians remained loyal to democratic processes in a mixed and socialistic-tinged economy. Moscow itself did not dare to claim more than 48,000 Communist party members in progressive Sweden in 1948. Great Britain also remained impressively immune to Red ideology. Its Socialist Labour Party had been the great gainer from the war and enjoyed such powerful mass support that the Communists of Britain remained at somewhat less than 50,000.

This does not mean for a moment that war and bombings had failed to have a revolutionary effect upon the British people. They had simply become more radical in their own British way, a way that has a genius for avoiding whatever is extreme and whatever is destructive of personal liberties. But the record of Conservative governments between the wars had soured the British on the wisdom or infallibility of their rich and powerful. By their smashing victory in 1945 the British Socialists achieved an electoral revolution that was a mandate for revolutionary economic reforms. The people who stayed at home and took the bombings had undergone the same sharp change in political thinking as the embittered and determined Tommies I had known on foreign fields.

When I talked with young Frenchmen and French-women, including many from aristocratic and traditionally conservative families, I found most of them surprisingly progressive in their attitude. Perhaps some of that has worn off with time, but the prevailing mood of French youth was by no means conservative. French Catholics did not hesitate to champion a considerable measure of socialistic state ownership. In fact, their chief party—the Popular Republican Movement—along with the Socialists and Communists, firmly supported state ownership of certain key industries.

What the second World War had done to a majority of Europeans was to make them both more radical (more Leftist) and more precise in their political thinking, and also much more insistent. The average European had lost whatever apathy or political indifference he might previously have had. The average member of the middle class had lost so much, he was compelled to defend his position in society and so to demand reforms that had real meaning. And again, as after 1918, war spread the ravages of inflation in its wake. Inflation decimated and reduced the middle class as never before.

In the summer of 1946 I reached Hungary just after the final spasm of the most fantastic inflationary destruction of a currency that any nation has yet suffered in all the records of history. I still carry in my wallet a bank-note of the largest denomination ever printed. It is a note for *one quintrillion* pengös. Eighteen zeros are required to formulate that astronomic figure. During my last previous visit to Budapest, in 1940, five pengös had been worth one dollar. Less than six years later one quintrillion pengös had become worth less than one dollar—and then worth nothing at all. Hungary's currency had disappeared in a blizzard of meaningless paper—and with the pengö the wealth or the life savings of almost all Hungarians had also disappeared.

This, of course, is the absolute extreme among the currency inflations that afflicted all of Europe's combatant or occupied countries. But throughout the Continent postwar inflations have taken a devastating toll, greatly inflaming the fires of social change. Millions among the remaining middle class were reduced to near bankruptcy or to outright impoverishment. In eastern Europe's satellite nations this harmonized conveniently with the long-term designs of the ruling Communists. It was not uncommon to be told by a dispossessed white-collar citizen down the Danube: "It suits their purposes to have us weak and impotent." But this also happened to the same kind of people in western Europe by the *force majeure* of the extreme costliness and destructiveness of modern war. Inevitably the middle class lost the most because it had the least means of protecting itself—neither the means of the wealthy and the experienced market operators nor the unity and organization of labor-union members.

Along with inflation-bred resentment there are other reasons—

Why postwar Europeans are both more radical and more Marxist in their politics.

"Those are the people who sold us to Hitler," said my French friend Jean in a voice to remember.

He was talking about the collaborators, the Vichy politicians, and also about certain big French industrialists and bankers. If anything, he had a more intense hatred for capitalists who had worked with and for the Nazis—and reaped handsome profits while their country was enslaved —than he had for Pierre Laval and his ignominious associates. You had no difficulty in finding Belgians and Dutchmen, Italians and Greeks, who spoke in exactly the same way about similarly placed and prominent people in their own countries. The collaborators had lived well and usually padded both their pockets and their stomachs while true patriots went hungry and hunted. The betrayals and the betrayers could never be forgiven. But those collaborators who had long enjoyed exceptional influence in their nation's economy and governmental affairs discredited capitalism quite as much as they besmirched themselves. Industrialists, bankers, and others who accepted the idea that "Hitler is our best defense against the Reds and the labor unions" in reality invited revolutionary reforms quite as much as war. The end of the war found a majority of the people, including Europe's middle men, with an aroused desire for positive reforms and sweeping measures that would prevent the possibility of repetition.

The major reasons for the postwar gains of Communists, Socialists, and pronounced "progressivism" in Europe can be summarized in this fashion:

1. The principal supporters and collaborators of Fascism had come from the ranks of industrialists, bankers, big landowners, and others among the wealthy conservatives.

2. Industrial monopolists, arms-manufacturers, and other outstanding capitalists were those who profited most as a class, or profited most exorbitantly, during the war—unless their particular plants and properties happened to be bombed out. Italian and German industrialists profited greatly from the war-production booms launched early by the Fascists and Nazis. They were proportionately by far the most privileged under Mussolini and Hitler, save for Fascist and Nazi party leaders themselves. In the occupied countries the big industrialists had little choice but to work for their conquerors. None the less, too many of them had collaborated willingly and gained handsome returns as long as the Nazis called the tune. By their actions they provoked widespread opposition not only to the

power they had enjoyed, but equally to certain capitalistic practices that had permitted them such power.

3. The forces for radical change were greatly intensified wherever land feudalism had resisted even moderate reforms between the wars. Europe's millions of land-starved peasants remained revolutionary, or became more so, because the monopoly of the big landowners and titled aristocrats had not been broken or even reduced.

4. Meanwhile Fascism and Nazism, and the wartime forced-labor methods of the Nazis, had convinced the great mass of Europe's workers that they must recover their lost rights, and that their only security lay in building new postwar unions of increased strength.

5. Finally, the dispossessed middle class was forced into greater and more radical political action by its extreme economic plight. Because they had made the most serious errors in the prewar past, Europe's men between had the powerful incentive of lessons learned through bitterness and disillusionment.

The motivations for political and economic change were consequently as profound in Europe as the war's destruction and dislocation had been great. This is why—

Socialistic reforms placed new curbs on capitalism in Great Britain and France.

Two World War calamities within twenty-five years had convinced an extraordinary number of Britishers that major and key industries would be much safer (whether or not they were more profitable) if their exceptional powers were not in private hands. As true Socialists the British Labour Party submitted its program to free, democratic debate and acted only upon the approval of a majority in Parliament. With the overwhelming approval of the British electorate the coal mines, electric utilities, railroads and transport, cable and commercial wireless, civil aviation, and the austere Bank of England were transferred to state ownership. To us that sounds like Socialism in a big way. Yet some *four fifths* of British private enterprise remained untouched, and large compensation was paid to former shareholders in all the above-mentioned enterprises. Capitalism is still, and by far, the major economic force in the United Kingdom.

The French had made strikingly similar demands for reform. State ownership was accordingly extended to the coal mines and large electric power combines, to the Bank of France and several of the largest private banks, to most of the airplane factories, and to the Renault automobile plant. In both Britain and France, however, immediate postwar nationalization stopped just short of the steel industries, which had been the subject of much popular agitation and denunciation. Big Steel appeared to have escaped state ownership in France, largely owing to the weakness of swift-changing governments in Paris. In Great Britain Premier Attlee and the Labour party leaders hesitated for more than three years before deciding to move frontally against the powerful steel interests. Top U.S. administrators of the Marshall Plan were reported as strongly opposed to such a step. But in October 1948 the Attlee government decided to carry out its campaign platform by nationalizing 107 steel concerns employing about 300,000 workers.

Under the proposed plan about sixty per cent of Britain's iron and steel industry will be transferred to state ownership, although the old managements would remain. The companies involved have a total issued capital of about $780,000,000. The Labour government counts on its steel reform being passed by Parliament before the summer of 1950. In other words the British Socialists determined to put Big Steel in government hands before their party must again face national elections. Without a major part of the steel industry being nationalized, they

believed their earlier Socialist measures might be jeopardized.

Here, however, we are concerned primarily with the
fact that the average Britisher and the average Frenchman
strongly demanded a considerable amount of Socialist state
ownership. They had lost all confidence in considerable
sections of big industry and big business. Two World Wars
had convinced them that the people, through the state,
should have greater controls over the key industries and
dominant banking organs of their nation. Rightly or
wrongly, they wanted the vast economic and political
powers that were gathered in relatively few private hands
to be curbed and moderated. The only kind of capitalism
they were still prepared to trust was that which could be
spelled with a small *c*. The embarrassing thing was this:
although two great global conflicts had demonstrated in
Europe that you cannot destroy the idea of Communism
or Socialism (or any idea, including Fascism) with bombs,
they had demonstrated quite conclusively that you *can*
destroy capitalism through war. Let any modern war be
sufficiently destructive in any single country, and capitalism cannot survive it.

It was the British middle class—not the workers—that
gave British Socialism the wide margin of its thumping
electoral triumph in 1945. It was bourgeois Frenchmen—
shopkeepers, café-owners, teachers, and other white-collar
people—whose active support made the considerable extension of state ownership certain in France. Large numbers
of these men and women in between had shifted from prewar conservatism to the new political center, or slightly to
left of center. War and inflation had transformed them
into progressives—and European progressives today are
very much more progressive than those Americans who
supported Roosevelt's New Deal. Thus a predominant
pattern was set in western Europe. This pattern is a combination of capitalist free enterprise and Socialist state

ownership, with the former still functioning throughout
the major proportion of the national economy.

When I returned to eastern Europe in 1946, I found a
decidely different pattern. Six years earlier I had watched
the Nazis setting up puppet governments in Hungary,
Rumania, Bulgaria, and Yugoslavia. Now the Soviet
Marxists had done the same thing. Six years earlier the
Nazis were appropriating major economic interests in
these lands and draining their production for Berlin's
exclusive benefit. Now the Soviet Communists had become
the economic monopolists along the Danube, for Moscow's exclusive benefit. Here there was no large middle
class to oppose foreign domination, and the minority of
middle citizens had been rendered impotent by inflation.
The Communists had concentrated quite as much on paralyzing the white-collar people as upon liquidating the
wealth and power of the aristocracy. As a first step toward
controlling the peasant majorities in eastern Europe—

The Soviet Communists obliterated land feudalism in the satellite countries.

Wherever feudalism persists, this is one of the smartest
moves in the Soviet program. It is smart because it can be
based upon social justice; because agrarian reform answers
the deepest and most urgent desire of the long-exploited
peasants. If our western democracies are not interested in
justice and land for 120,000,000 European peasants, we are
really not interested in promoting democracy itself in lands
where the peasants *are* the people.

But the Soviets were far more realistic. Long before the
war ended, Moscow had a drastic land-reform program for
Poland, East Prussia, and Hungary, where landless peasants
had been oppressed for centuries. The new Red-controlled
regimes launched an immediate frontal assault on feudal

landlordism and put sweeping land reforms into effect. The great feudal estates were at last cut up and small parcels of land distributed to hundreds of thousands of peasants. There was an urgent need for this fundamental change. But what was done in the name of justice for the majority of the people also served conveniently to destroy the political power, once and for all, of the landed aristocrats who had blindly refused to make long-overdue compromises between the wars.

In 1940 I had gathered a good many shocking facts about Hungary's land feudalism on the spot. Now, in 1946, I devoted a month to investigating the methods and results of the Communists' agrarian reform. I did this because, as an American, I hate tyranny—and feudal landlordism is still one of the most brutal forms of economic tyranny in our world; witness China and many Latin-American countries, as well as Spain and Portugal. I did it also because Hungary's peasant millions should and could have become the middle men and the great central democratic bastion of that beautiful country—if Count Károlyi's courageous efforts toward land reform in 1919 had not been thwarted and suppressed by the opposition of feudal reactionaries. Would the Communists dare to make genuine middle men of the Hungarian peasants? Or was this distribution of long-sought acres merely a hoodwinking device?

In Hungary alone I learned that some thirty-four per cent of that country's present territory had been redistributed. That was the measure of the peasants' crying need. Now a total of 7,962,000 acres had been expropriated, including a major portion of some 1,422,000 acres that had been owned for many generations by various Roman Catholic orders and organizations. An average of seven acres was allotted to 584,000 landless peasants and farm laborers. Yet there remained another 750,000 peasants who needed land, or more land, desperately. But they could not get it. Again overpopulation—there simply was not enough land to go round, even in small parcels.*

Hungary offered a typical example of how the Soviets had destroyed the foundations of land feudalism throughout eastern Europe. These revolutionary agrarian reforms permitted the Communists to pose at the outset as "champions of the oppressed masses"—something that the democracies could well afford to learn to do. But where the peasants themselves had always dreamed of ownership of a few acres as spelling economic independence and political freedom, Moscow's Marxist strategists had entirely different motives. After the Bolshevik Revolution they had given the Russian peasants land, but only as a first step toward collectivization.

The Hungarian agrarian specialists with whom I talked in Budapest had no more illusions than the Communists had. They pointed out that twelve acres or more were an absolute minimum to support the average peasant family. Five, seven, or ten acres would still prove insufficient for minimum subsistence—and there still remained 750,000 peasants who could get no land whatever. Even those 584,-000 who had obtained some land would eventually discover that they could not make ends meet. What then?

Within a few years, said the experts, the Communists would use the peasants' insufficiency of land as an excuse to establish collective farms on the Soviet model. When the Cominform denounced Marshal Tito and Yugoslav Communist leaders in June 1948, it declared frankly that collectivization of the land was its ultimate goal for the Iron Curtain countries. "Justice and land" for the peasants had merely served as attractive bait. By this means the Communists had appropriated the political power and privileges of the Polish, East Prussian, and Hungarian feudal barons. These gentlemen had refused to eliminate the medieval

* Cf. Leland Stowe: "Hungary's Agrarian Revolution," *Foreign Affairs*, April 1947.

abuses of their land system while they had a last, golden opportunity. By their obstinacy they had handed the Communists a revolutionary ace card. But the peasant millions had simply gone from one tyranny into another.

Meanwhile I was discovering:

How the Communists lost all chance for broad popular support among the people of the satellite countries.

You did not have to talk long with a Hungarian or Rumanian to learn how much the people, as a whole, hated their Soviet and local Communist leaders. They had not been fooled by perpetual talk about "the will of the people." They had a cynical appreciation of the emptiness of such Red-concocted phrases as the "Democratic Bloc" or the "Fatherland Front." They had had far too much experience with previous oppressive and dictatorial regimes. They had suffered too much from secret-police abuses not to be bitterly antagonistic to the perpetual surveillance and interference of local prototypes of the Soviets' M.V.D. After five months along the Danube it was clear to me that the Soviets had lost a great, a unique opportunity in eastern Europe. They could have won the sympathy, or at least the tolerance, of a majority in each of the satellite countries. Instead a considerable majority of the people had become bitterly anti-Soviet and anti-Communist.

"We had no choice but to get along with the Russians, if it were at all possible," a Hungarian professor remarked sadly. "With a certain amount of reasonableness it might have worked, at least not too badly. But in many ways it is harder to get along with the Soviets and Communists than it was with the Nazis. The Germans were more particular about appearances. They had much more finesse."

I had seen how effectively the Nazis employed political seduction in these same countries. They had inserted large chunks of molasses, exploiting local anti-Semitism and every other prejudice or aspiration. But the Soviet Communists much more often used political seduction as a bludgeon. They had established Soviet monopolies of all major productive resources in Hungary and Rumania—in Danubian shipping companies, in oil, bauxite, commercial aviation, timber, and banking. Through these monopolies they were draining the economies of these satellite countries, yet their propagandists rabidly denounced western or American "imperialism." The average Danubian was not so stupid as to fail to see and understand what was going on. He resented with equal vehemence both the Communists' actions and their double-tongued propaganda. Although he had never known real and complete democracy, he knew that it meant all the things that he was denied: independence of political parties, freedom of speech and of the press, civil liberties and individual security against arrest without warrant. The blatant mockery of the Soviet Communists' "new democracy" antagonized and alienated the majority of Hungarians, Rumanians, and other peoples. Where more clever totalitarians might have seduced them, they were outraged—and inwardly committed to the cause of the West.

The Red totalitarians also employed the tactics of intimidation quite as ruthlessly as the Nazis had done. It served to consolidate their power, but it drove a large majority of the Danubian peoples into silent and most stubborn opposition. These people had known intimidation from their various rulers over many generations. They had learned how to bide their time, but their fierce desire for independence had never been broken—neither by the Turks nor by any of their successors. By their extreme dictatorial methods the Soviets and Communists simply created many millions of potential allies of the western democracies. The men between of eastern Europe are indeed caught in the Red vise. But in no sense have they abandoned their principles or abdicated to that disastrous moral compliance which characterized the Germans.

As promoters of Lenin's Marxism the Soviets and Communists had failed utterly down the Danube, as I learned from evidence that mounted impressively on every side. Through agrarian reforms they had made an adroit bid for popular mass support, but they had killed its possible effects through economic exploitation and police-state oppression. Even as they clamped down the Iron Curtain they had lost most of the people behind it.

But curiously enough, the foremost exponents of western democracy—the British and United States governments —had also proved to be recklessly inadequate salesmen and promoters of their own political doctrine. Where the Soviet Communists prattled fine idealistic phrases and offered something entirely opposite in practice, the Anglo-Americans (in the first postwar years) performed in an almost equally contradictory manner. It is most important to understand:

How the U.S. and British governments failed to win the support of postwar Europe's masses.

Both in Europe and in Asia the Anglo-American democracies revealed an amazing disregard or fear of what the Europeans and Asiatics most vociferously were demanding. London had the excuse, such as it was, of striving desperately to hold the remnants of the British Empire together. Washington had none short of ignorance—or fear of the people and what they demand in the way of economic reforms. Obviously we cannot promote democracy anywhere in the world if we are motivated by fear of the desires of the majority. While the Soviet Communists were overplaying their hand the Anglo-Americans, heedlessly and dangerously, underplayed their own best hand—which was a natural.

We had done it before. After the first World War Wilson

talked noble phrases like "self-determination." But Washington never offered the slightest hope of freedom from feudal exploitation to Europe's vast legion of landless peasants. For any class of people freedom begins *where they live*. The policy-makers of the U.S. government were not interested in liberating European peasants from their economic chains. Nor were they any more interested in what price-fixing, market-dividing international monopolies did to the living-standards of average Europeans, workers or members of the middle class. Our representatives talked splendid Jeffersonian abstractions, and continued to do so between the wars. "Life, liberty, and the pursuit of happiness" do not automatically put a crust of bread into any citizen's mouth. They have to be applied, both politically and economically.

The measure of the Anglo-American postwar governments' shortsightedness and timidity has been starkly illuminated in Greece and Italy; in China, Indonesia, Indo-China, and many other places as well. In Greece Winston Churchill's pro-monarchist and British imperialist prejudices prevailed. Upon liberation Athens might have made at least an attempt at a broad coalition regime. But the Churchill government distrusted Greek republicans and Socialists in the E.A.M. resistance movement as much as its small minority of Communists. It supported the Greek royalists and anti-republican elements. Churchill and his advisers were chiefly interested in the strategic position of the crumbling British Empire in the eastern Mediterranean. They revealed no genuine concern about establishing a truly representative, democratic government in Greece. Their policies and connivings were largely responsible for the shockingly brutal civil war that ravaged Athens in December 1944 and January 1945.*

---

* For further documentation of these facts see Leland Stowe: *While Time Remains* (New York: Alfred A. Knopf; 1946), Chapter xiv, "Mr. Churchill Brings 'Democracy' to Greece."

What were the Anglo-American democracies offering the brave, hungry, and despairing Greek people? All that London's actions and Washington's silence combined to offer was triumph for a blackly reactionary regime and the certainty of years of bloody civil strife in Greece. Like the Fascists and Nazis the Churchill government claimed that the "Greek Reds" were being destroyed. Those of us who, as correspondents, witnessed the beginnings of the Greek tragedy in those heartbreaking days in Athens reported frankly that Right-wing oppression would drive many thousands of Greeks into Communism. It did this so emphatically that the civil war soon became permanent. In March 1947 President Truman felt obliged to demand American intervention in Greece. Four years after the first outbreak in Athens, Communist-led guerrillas were still fighting in the mountains. The most terrible and inexcusable bloodshed in postwar Europe had not occurred anywhere under Red dictatorships behind the Iron Curtain. It must be charged, in Greece, to the deplorable shortsightedness and ineptness of the Anglo-American governments. In the liberation period of greatest opportunity the two most powerful western democracies had offered the Greek people nothing whatever in the realms of justice, more freedoms, and social reforms.

Italy provides an even clearer example of British-American negligence and bankruptcy in political vision. The Italian peninsula was the first part of continental Europe to be liberated by British and United States armed forces. Italy was also under complete Anglo-American administration, military and civilian, for the longest period of time. It was therefore possible for our representatives and governments to support and encourage whatever elements they regarded as most important to establishment of democracy in Italy. But—

*British-American policies consistently ignored
the majority of the Italian people and the reforms they demanded.*

The only beachhead that the Anglo-Americans created
and successfully developed in Italy was strictly military.
Politically they had neither a program nor fixed objectives.
From the very outset British and American officers and
officials accepted the social overtures of Italian industrialists and aristocrats, former Fascists or close collaborators of
the Blackshirts. These people "spoke such perfect English."
Their good manners and luxurious entertainment were
more important than their anti-democratic, reactionary
records.

Italy's workers and a portion of the peasants had supplied the only real resistance as Mussolini was overthrown.
Save for a few intellectual leaders they were the only Italians who fought for their freedom, and fought on our side.
The workers clamored for a return of their long-suppressed
rights under free trade unions. Once again the peasants
demanded land on which to live. The Communists supported them and promised the moon. Most of the Anglo-
American policy-makers remained completely aloof from
both workers and peasants.

During the next three years Italy's postwar unemployment rose dangerously, to as much as two million workers.
The great majority of Italians were shockingly destitute,
underfed and underclothed; a great many without homes.
Yet the Italian upper classes reveled in the costliest of
foods, indulged in the most elaborate champagne parties
anywhere in Europe, and lived on a scale of unconcerned
extravagance. Many of them had made large fortunes as
Fascists or collaborators. Others had retained all their properties and most of their great wealth. The Allied-sponsored
Italian government accepted nearly two billion dollars in

aid from the United States. Yet American officials even failed to demand that luxury and other taxes be imposed on all Italian citizens who could afford to pay them. Rich Italians, in fact, paid taxes that were ridiculously small, while Americans of equivalent incomes or possessions were helping support Italy's most notorious playboys. American journalists and other observers were both shocked and alarmed by the startling, indefensible gap between wealthy Italians and the rest of the people. This gap had persisted for four full years. The British and U.S. governments blindly left the field wide open in Italy to exploitation by Palmiro Togliatti's energetic Communist organization.

What was the western democracies' major objective in postwar Italy?

Presumably, it was to win the people to free and representative government. But *who* were the people in Italy?

The Italian people, of course, are the workers and peasants. Together they constitute approximately 80 per cent of the electorate. Of 29,000,000 registered voters of both sexes, more than 40 per cent depend directly on agriculture for their livelihood. Some 7,500,000 of these actually till the soil, and a majority of these work on land that does not belong to them.* In addition there are millions of industrial workers.

Between 1944 and the crucial Italian elections of April 1948 neither the American nor the British government championed important political and economic rights for Italy's workers and peasants. Although some 2,000,000 landless farm laborers were desperately impoverished, and another 1,500,000 were exploited sharecroppers, the Anglo-American democracies offered nothing better to these victims of Italian feudal landlordism. Communist propagandists offered several acres "and a cow." But no pressures for fundamental reforms, for either peasants or workers, were

* Cf. *New York Times,* April 4, 1948, dispatch from Rome by Arnaldo Cortesi.

ever made by Washington or London on successive regimes
in Rome. The western democracies offered nothing con-
crete to the very people they claimed to be most anxious
to preserve from totalitarianism and Communism.

In the weeks and months directly preceding Italy's 1948
elections the United States and British governments suddenly became panicky about the menace of a Red victory
at the polls. For the first time in history the American public also became extremely concerned about the outcome of
a national election in a single European country. For four
years our government and we ourselves had acted as if what
happened to the Italian people was no immediate concern
of ours. We talked loudly about believing in representative
government and the will of the people. Yet we had consistently ignored the most essential interests of the Italian
people. Now, suddenly, we woke up to the long-obvious
fact that *the Italian people are those who have the most
votes.* Without the ballots of a majority of its ordinary
citizens democracy would be done in and Communism
would triumph in Italy.

If the situation were not so grave, Washington's last-min-
ute actions of desperation would have been highly amus-
ing. Our government rushed more grain, food, and cash
into Italy. We made a gift of ships and offered new concessions regarding Trieste. The whole performance was as
undignified as a septuagenarian would-be wolf showering
silks and diamonds upon a night-club blonde. No more
humiliating demonstration of the fantastic bankruptcy and
blindness of the great democracies' postwar policies has as
yet been given anywhere. Until the fifty-ninth minute they
had done everything possible—by all that they had failed
to do—to help the Reds take over Italy through an electoral
majority.

The more moderate and conservative Italian parties
were equally alarmed, and so was the Catholic hierarchy.
At last Premier Alcide de Gasperi and other Christian

Democratic leaders began to talk of "needed social reforms," even including some degree of redistribution of land to the peasants. They also accepted the principle that labor should share in the management of industrial enterprises.

Less than a month before the Italian elections Pope Pius XII delivered an address of exceptional significance. He attributed "a deplorable lack of reflection" to those who were waiting for a return of rugged individualism. Men's right to liberty, he said, "cannot be the fascinating but deceptive formula of one hundred years ago." The Pope also declared that "some supporters of the right of private property" were so abusing this right that they were doing more to destroy it "than its enemies." * Even after the Christian Democrats' notable electoral victory Pope Pius reiterated his concern over "the solution of the fundamental problems growing out of the ruin and revolution of war." At the heart of these, he warned, "lie the just and necessary social reforms; particularly the urgent need to provide the poorer classes with housing, bread and work. . . . But if [increasing] productivity is attained as a result of unbridled competition and of unprincipled expenditure of wealth, or by oppression and despotic exploitation of labor . . . it cannot be sound and natural." †

It is fair to credit the Vatican with a realistic understanding of the postwar mood and demands, as well as the needs, of the Italian people. But the Anglo-American democracies showed no foresight whatever, and pitifully little comprehension. They did not seek to defend the people. They did not demand "just and necessary social reforms." Predominantly they left such extremely practical actions to such forces as might be conscious of the revolutionary conditions of our times.

* Cf. *New York Herald Tribune,* March 8, 1948; Rome dispatch by Barrett McGurn.
† Cf. Address of Pope Pius XII to a group of cardinals on June 2, 1948.

In Italy's 1948 elections the Catholic Christian Democrats won 12,751,000 ballots, or 48.7 per cent of the total vote. The Communists and Left-wing Socialists obtained 8,025,000 votes, or 30.7 per cent. The Right-wing and democratic Socialists, with some 1,860,000 votes (or 7.1 per cent), emerged as the third largest party. The Nationalists, Monarchists, and small pro-Fascist groups combined gained only some 8 per cent of the total vote. Thus the Italian people, voting in unprecedented numbers, overwhelmingly showed that they favored drastic social changes. De Gasperi had promised heavy taxes on the wealthy and land for the peasant victims of feudalism. Months after the Christian Socialists received their popular mandate it remained to be seen how many fundamental reforms they would enact. If they refused to fulfill their promises boldly and adequately, the Italian people would turn eventually either to a Right-wing or a Left-wing dictatorship, probably through civil war.

Italy, then, has provided a precise and illuminating example of—

Western Europe's radically revised concepts of democracy.

Postwar Europeans are much more advanced in their political and economic thinking than Americans have yet found it necessary, under the harsh force of circumstances, to be. By a large majority the Europeans favor important reforms along these lines:

1. The restoration and extension of the rights of labor.

2. Greater economic security for citizens of the middle and lower classes.

3. More curbs and controls on the operation of the capitalist system, with various degrees of state ownership and Socialism in key branches of the economy.

4. Limitation and reduction of monopolist corporations and abolishing of international cartels or trusts.

5. An end to feudal landlordism, and distribution of land to the peasants.

6. A greater direct participation of the people in the management of both government and industry.

In these and other respects the Europeans seek both a liquidation of feudalism and fundamental changes in the old laissez-faire, let-things-go-as-they-will system of capitalism. They do not believe that all forms of economic controls by the state are bad; rather, a majority of Europeans insist that certain controls—in our highly industrialized age —are absolutely necessary. They do not regard all forms of planning by the state as dangerous and destructive of liberty; rather, they insist that a certain amount of planning by the government is required for both national and individual welfare. They believe that today's massive industrialization must be met by radical revision of our concepts of democracy. Free and representative government must concern itself as greatly with the economic rights of individual citizens as with their political rights. This is where socialistic ideas and methods come into play. The Europeans have rejected the "rugged individualism" of U.S. capitalism in its unrestricted form. They maintain that capitalism's more glaring inequities and abuses must be removed; that greater checks and balances must be provided if recurrent depressions are to be avoided. In short, by their repeated electoral verdicts *Europeans envisage modern democracy as an intermixing and merging of capitalistic and socialistic practices.* They are justified in this view by all that happened between the wars. Nowhere in postwar Europe has the old-style absolute capitalism of free-for-all, do-as-you-please competition survived.

But, most notably and remarkably, the idea and practice of democracy have survived Europe's great convulsions.

Thus the American government and people still have potentially powerful allies in western Europe. Although Europeans have made and feel forced to make compromises between capitalism and socialism, they have somehow retained their faith in freely elected, parliamentary government. So long as the United States does not try to deny their right to make compromises of their own free choice, they will be with us—as a first barricade against Communism. But Europeans will not tolerate being asked to unlearn what they have paid a fearful price for learning. They will not undo reforms that they now regard as essential to the freedom they have preserved at such stupendous cost. They regard it as the first right of victims of oppression to determine, for themselves and by themselves, what were the chief causes of their recent sufferings and disasters. In this sense the Europeans are far from being backward. They are more experimental and more boldly progressive on political-economic questions than the American people because repeated national catastrophes have compelled them to be so.

Nevertheless there remain in Europe powerful forces of reaction as well as of conservatism in general. If the events that brought Fascism to dominance after World War I have any meaning at all, we in the United States must remain especially conscious of the fact that—

The European reaction merely waits to seize power by all possible means, including Right dictatorship.

In Italy the extreme nationalist and pro-Fascist elements may have received no more than some 2,500,000 votes in 1948. Mussolini, however, started with only a small fraction of that number.

In France the moderate Republicans and democratic Socialists form a weak, indecisive center between the two extremes. They are under constant attack from Communists and from the Right-wing authoritarian followers of General Charles de Gaulle. There are serious grounds for fear that de Gaulle may not shun establishment of a dictatorship if conditions of acute national disunity should present such an opportunity. He himself has said as much.

Germany remains a great interrogation point of menacing possibilities. It appears certain that a majority of Germans do not, as yet in any case, want a Communist state. But the Germans have never been exposed to a successful and prospering democracy. They have known only a few years of democratic experience of any kind. The Germans are accustomed to highly autocratic and totalitarian government. They long to be told what to do. Dictatorship is what they best understand. To democratize western Germany will be a long and uncertain task. It is supervised by Anglo-Americans, who thus far have shown an extraordinary incapacity to promote democratic elements anywhere in postwar Europe. So long as the western powers permit the vast industrial powerhouse of the Ruhr to be owned and managed by the same German industrialists who managed it for Hitler, we shall need to keep our fingers crossed about the future prospects of democracy in Germany. Sooner or later a Nazi type of nationalist reaction will come out into the open again.

The Communists have proved incapable of winning a majority of the people anywhere in Europe. They could only seize power where the Red Army was near at hand, or where Marshal Tito had formed his own Communist-controlled army and police under Nazi occupation in Yugoslavia. It is little short of amazing that not a single European people voluntarily embraced Communism after World War II. That is the measure of the Europeans' deep and instinctive loyalty to the concept of democracy. But their loyalty, however great today, can once again be betrayed as recklessly as it was by Fascists between the wars.

Especially it can be betrayed by fear-inspired and negative policies of the Anglo-American governments, and by indifference and wishful thinking on the part of the public in Britain and the United States.

While in Italy in 1947, James Reston of the *New York Times* observed that, although Communism might be losing its political appeal, its "economic appeal" remains extremely magnetic to millions of Europe's impoverished and underprivileged. Mr. Reston asked two very pertinent questions: "How can the United States revive Europe economically without at the same time reviving or maintaining a privileged class that does not share United States ideals or objectives? . . . How can the United States block the expansion of totalitarian Communism without sustaining the very kind of privilege that contributes to the success of Communism?"

These will be the great uncertainties and risks of the years immediately ahead. They will be determined by the clarity or the contradictions in U.S. policy in Europe. They will be decided also by whether the Marshall Plan is administered uniquely to restore European economy or to re-establish at all costs an unreformed capitalism in Europe. Until now Washington's postwar policies have shown far more consideration for the "privileged class" of Europeans than for the underprivileged majority. For the United States to repudiate and reject those social and economic reforms which the European majority demands could only result eventually in the loss of that majority by U.S. democracy. Only Right-wing European elements, anti-democratic and pro-Fascist, could benefit in the end.

The real danger in western Europe is no longer that the Communists will gain power. Short of another major conflict, it is impossible for them to do so. The real danger, as Walter Lippmann has said, "is that constitutional governments—unable to govern well and to cure the discontent which the Communists exploit—will collapse as between the wars they collapsed in Italy, Hungary, Poland, Germany and elsewhere." If this is permitted to happen in the countries of western Europe, Fascist dictatorships would again replace one democratic government after another. We Americans would find ourselves with the direct heirs and descendants of Mussolini and Hitler as our supposed allies again—merely another color of totalitarianism.

Who and what are the only possible European allies of American democracy?

It should be clear by now that our only allies in Europe are the mixed masses of people who live and struggle in between; between the Left-wing and Right-wing forces of totalitarianism. As of 1949 they constitute the electoral majority in their respective countries, although seriously divided on how radical social reforms should be. Everywhere in Europe our allies belong to the broad middle group. They range from conservative or moderate republicans to the democratic, anti-Communist Socialists. In terms of U.S. politics most of these people are quite radical; certainly more "progressive" than F.D.R.'s New Deal. Nevertheless they are the only champions and practitioners of democratic freedoms and representative government now remaining in the Old World. *American democracy has the choice of working with them or of inviting ultimate and certain disaster by trying to get along without them.*

In France and elsewhere the parties of the democratic Left and Center have been described as the third force. That is another way of emphasizing their "in between" status. The French third force has already been whittled down seriously by the Communists and de Gaullists. Without the anti-Communist Socialists it could not exist. Without the support of the embattled middle class it would also be doomed. The survival of French democracy depends chiefly upon this uneasy working alliance between the middle class and the Socialists. It is well to remember that whenever Fascism comes it wins its mass following from a discontented, impoverished, and wavering middle class.

If the Marshall Plan accomplishes its announced purposes, it will put the western European nations back on their feet economically. That means it must give renewed strength and economic stability to the popular majorities, which are now pro-democratic. It means, too, that Europe's middle class and middle men must be restored to positions of security and expanded political influence in their society. In no sense does it mean that a majority of Europeans will ignore or repudiate the cruel lessons they have learned from nearly forty years of war, revolution, and dictatorship. They cannot abandon, or be expected to abandon, their deepest convictions about the necessity of rebuilding a better human existence in an improved and reformed political-economic system. They will be what harsh circumstance and bitter experience have made them—insistent upon change, and upon certain changes that are bold and fundamental.

These are the Europeans with whom Americans of the U.S.A. have so much in common, without having shared the extreme vicissitudes which have sharpened the thinking and immeasurably intensified the aspirations of Europe's men between. Until World War II the European peoples, and particularly their middle class, were the central target of Right and Left totalitarians. Today these same forces have shifted their crossfires across the Atlantic. The middle class of the United States is their last powerful enemy. When we Americans understand our community of interests with the European peoples, and when we comprehend that their tragic and costly lessons are also applicable to us, we shall know what any adequate defense of free government and individual freedoms requires in a doubly revolutionary world.

Chapter VI

AMERICANS AS THE MAJOR TARGET

United States citizens of our generation are on the spot.
We live in the only important nation in which traditional
capitalism remains unrevised and unhampered. We are
accustomed to a standard of living so exceptional that it
cannot decline very far without serious social and political
repercussions. Simultaneously Americans, and particularly
our middle class majority, are the chief target of both the
Left-wing and the Right-wing totalitarians.

The great question, then, is one that developments well
within our lifetime will not permit to be sidestepped: Can
the broad central group of the population of the United
States remain successfully united against the powerful combination of pressures that are aligned against it? Can we
find and steer a middle way that will preserve both our
domestic freedoms and our free-enterprise system?

In the light of the drastically changed conditions and
outlook of postwar European peoples perhaps we need an
up-to-date inventory of the present situation of American
citizens. Since we are human targets, what armor do we
wear? Are there notable chinks and crevices that may make
us vulnerable to various revolutionary forces, foreign and
domestic?

Since the major features of our strength are widely appreciated, it would be prudent to examine the negative
side more closely. In a general way we realize now that our
government and public opinion were far from ready to
assume the heavy responsibilities of world leadership in

1945. We have also become even more aware that American security depends very largely upon the maintenance of democracy in western Europe. Thus the American people have been thrust into an entirely new and significant relationship with Europeans. Both our physical safety and the stability of our institutions are closely linked to the future of our European first cousins. Somehow we must understand them better. Somehow we must cooperate with them much more effectively. Yet our past experience makes us ill-prepared to resist, ably and persistently, the same destructive forces against which our nearest and greatest European allies stubbornly struggle in the face of more formidable odds.

As Americans we are ill-prepared for the critical difficulties directly ahead of us, for several understandable reasons. We have had no first-hand experience of that extreme social, economic, and moral destructiveness which has been inflicted upon the European peoples by nearly forty years of war, dictatorship, and inflation. We have had, as yet, very slight personal exposure to the complex forces of the world revolution. We have had no experience whatever with the oppression and terror of a nation-wide secret-police system that checks and preys upon every individual citizen. And here in the United States we have had but a single major depression in the memory of most citizens. Even this had slight educational effect on those Americans now aged thirty or less. The production boom of the second World War rescued our country, temporarily, from facing the unsolved problems of the 1929 crash. War-born prosperity served as a sedative against future economic uncertainties.

Americans of our generation have also had much less personal exposure than Europeans to the menace of powerful industrial monopolies and trusts. Outside of labor-union membership we have no widespread public awareness of the steadily growing size and power of our greatest industrial corporations. Will Big Industry eventually control the government and the state? Or will the state be compelled to place much sharper curbs and controls on great corporations? The United States is open to evolution in several directions: toward the corporate state of Fascism; toward a Communist economy; or toward some degree of socialistic state ownership.

This is part of the broader economic quandary that confronts the American people. Can our greatly expanded laissez-faire capitalism maintain itself safely much longer without being streamlined and modernized by certain fundamental reforms? A great many Americans fear another depression. When they do so they are really asking this very question. Yet our public concentrates upon possible consequences of a recession or a slump. It remains little concerned with attempting to discover and remove the *causes* of depressions. We have not been trained by experience to ask those questions which might show us how to make our free-enterprise system more stable, more just, and much safer for all.

A human target is like a boxer—wide open to being knocked down or knocked out *unless* his defenses are up. But in our kind of world America's defenses are military in part only, and those which are non-military may indeed prove to be the most decisive. Through the "Voice of America" program and in other ways we have been learning slowly that ideological defenses are also very important. In a democracy the state of public morale is likewise an essential of defense. And in a powerfully industrialized nation the strength or weakness of the national economy—of capitalism itself—are clearly matters of defense.

The winning boxer anticipates, swiftly and accurately, what type of blows will be most dangerous to him. In the same fashion the citizens of a modern democracy must be capable of advance comprehension. They must understand what forces threaten their form of society most seriously.

They must also differentiate between anti-democratic forces of change and other instruments of change that are inherently democratic. Such a distinction is the very emphatic one between Soviet Communism and European liberal Socialism. It is one thing for Americans to have their guard up against Red totalitarianism, or against the Fascist variety. But it would be a costly error if we were to confound western Europe's democratic Socialism with Moscow's brand of Marxism. The truth is that western Europe now presents an experimentation of great historical significance and of potentially vital meaning for the United States. This is the experiment of mixed capitalist-Socialist economies, as in Britain, France, Scandinavia, and elsewhere. We in America cannot escape being deeply influenced by this experiment. But how well are we prepared by recent political experience to judge it fairly and wisely?

As an observer and a confirmed independent voter it seems to me that—

The bitter divisions and controversies of Americans over the Roosevelt New Deal have seriously increased our postwar problems.

Let us try to investigate this possibility in a non-partisan manner, as outsiders striving to review events impartially. Since I worked in Europe during the first four years of the New Deal, I had an opportunity to obtain the views of a great many Englishmen, Frenchmen, and others. The general reaction of Europeans was quite different from opinions I encountered at home during F.D.R.'s second administration. Even European businessmen and bankers could not see nearly so much "radicalism" in the New Deal as its chief American opponents attributed to it. Because they understood intimately the program and policies of their Old World Socialists, Europeans saw very little in the New Deal that was socialistic. They could understand sharp criticisms of WPA for being wasteful, or of NRA for various reasons. But they could not regard U.S. democracy as being menaced or U.S. capitalism as being undermined.

After working in Washington as a correspondent and traveling much across our country what alarmed me most in the United States of the late thirties was this: leading elements of the Roosevelt opposition voiced the same extremism that I had heard the most reactionary Europeans express, on other issues, in a dozen Old World countries. I had never imagined that so much animosity or outright hatred could dominate so many Americans of property, influence, and unquestioned privilege. Even the feudal barons of Spain or Hungary could not have been more violent. You wondered whether there could be such a creature as the "feudal capitalist."

During the Landon-Roosevelt electoral campaign of 1936 I heard and read more alarmist talk than I had encountered anywhere, except in Hitler's Germany, during nine years as a foreign correspondent. Common charges against the New Deal were Socialism, the end of free enterprise and free government, and dictatorship. Obviously, the New Deal had many shortcomings, including bureaucratic abuses and administrative inefficiencies. But the conservatives and ultra-conservatives indulged in almost incredible exaggerations and distortions. Even after twelve long years of Franklin D. Roosevelt as President, there has not been and is not today anything remotely resembling dictatorship in the United States. Free enterprise pushes on with the largest corporation profits and greatest employment in our nation's history. There is not a single law imposing Socialist state ownership in any branch of our economy. Year after year the opposition cried: "Wolf! Wolf!" and for four successive times F.D.R. was elected by remarkable majorities. The American people refused to be frightened out of their wits—or out of their freely reached opinion.

It seems probable that political exaggerations were never so profuse and abusive in the United States since Lincoln's day as during the New Deal years. Here I am not in the least concerned with defending the New Deal, or with its merits or faults. I am concerned only with the poisoning of American political atmosphere through acrimonious charges and counter-charges, a large proportion of which were highly distorted. What has this habit of exaggeration done to the American people? Today we must discriminate clearly between what is or is not dictatorial; what is or is not Communist or Fascist; what is or is not socialistic. But we have had no recent training in precise political and ideological distinctions. On the contrary, our people have been encouraged to confuse anything liberal with "communistic" and anything conservative with "fascistic." This is an exceedingly dangerous preparation for the acute and complex problems we face in the years immediately ahead.

Again, it seems to me as an independent observer, that American reactionaries—the ultra-conservatives—were more responsible for the extreme distortion in political catchwords and slogans than any others. They had such means for propaganda, and they were aroused to such antagonism, that their alarmist denunciations reached everywhere. In the coming decade neither Communists nor disguised Fascists can hope to do much more than equal their exaggerations. But this habit of reckless approach to our gravest problems can only make safe and prudent decisions by U.S. voters inexcusably difficult. When we most urgently need clear sight, we have been encouraged to throw sand in each other's eyes. In the end it may cost the ultra-conservatives much more proportionately than anyone else.

Will U.S. citizens seek internal security through moderate solutions and a middle course? Or shall we return to the destructive Right-Left extremism of the New Deal era?

How we answer these questions within the next ten years is almost certain to determine whether the United States can maintain relative prosperity and avoid another great depression. How we answer them will decide whether American democracy can remain strong enough and united enough to resist Communist and Fascist ideologies. How we answer them is also extremely likely to make the supreme calamity of another war much more remote or to leave our nation and people most dangerously exposed to involvement in war.

Perhaps the most disastrous thing that could happen to the American people at an early date would be a relapse into the same bitter and vicious controversies which raged between our reactionaries and ardent New Dealers in the 1930's. Neither an extremely conservative Republicanism nor an extreme Left-wing Democratic program can provide sound and tolerable solutions for our country as a whole. And neither one nor the other can offer us an adequate amount of internal unity, or anything resembling internal security.

In the 1948 Presidential campaign it was the great merit of Governor Thomas E. Dewey that he refused to stoop to those demagogic exaggerations which had so sharpened our political divisions and poisoned our spirits in previous elections. By his moderation and his emphasis on the need for national unity Governor Dewey, even in defeat, made a positive contribution. President Truman's remarkable November victory at the polls was also a vindication of basic New Deal liberalism. A majority of those who cared sufficiently to cast their votes vigorously repudiated the record and reckless indifference of the "do-nothing" Eightieth Congress. It appeared that the American people were considerably less conservative than had been supposed. In any case it seemed unquestionable that the American majority (as of then and the immediate future) was in no sense ultra-conservative.

But those reactionaries who hated with a glandular fanaticism everything connected with the New Deal and F.D.R. remain unrepentant and unchanged. Because they have been frustrated for so many years they chafe to settle old scores. If they could have their way they would make the postwar Republican Party an instrument of Rightwing reaction, dedicated to uncompromising combat with the ghost of Roosevelt's New Deal. It is the temptation toward such extremism and reaction that makes a middle and moderate course infinitely more difficult today than the realities of our domestic situation require them to be.

Along with its failings, the New Deal produced certain notable benefits for conservative businessmen. The nation's banks were restored to a position of health and strength. Through the Reconstruction Finance Corporation a great many corporate and smaller private enterprises were rescued from distress. These were not exactly "socialistic" measures. Nor was there anything "Red" or anti-capitalistic about reforms that eliminated excesses in stock-market transactions. On the contrary the stability of our entire structure of capitalism was greatly increased by them. But the rabid partisanship engendered by intemperate opposition to almost all aspects of the New Deal lingers on in powerful places. Our moderation and habits of restraint have been perverted in many respects. Whatever our personal views may be, we have not been prepared for objective judgment and responsible discussion of the issues.

Today we have a peculiar need to re-examine the record of the Tennessee Valley Authority alongside the original denunciations which ultra-conservatives made against that uniquely successful project. They charged that TVA was "socialistic" and "dictatorial"; that it would undermine and destroy government by the states in that region; that it would seriously reduce free enterprise in the seven states "dominated" by its public power.

In its first ten years TVA raised the purchasing power and standard of living of nearly 5,000,000 occupants of its vast region to an extraordinary degree. It brought electric power to 85,000 farms for the first time; a previously unknown prosperity to 1,350,000 people living on farms. TVA made possible the creation of hundreds of new factories and local enterprises—a remarkable extension of capitalistic production. It became the second largest producer of power in the United States. When World War II came, TVA proved to be our most decisive arsenal of democracy. Without its tremendous quantities of electric power—including the great aluminum plants and the Oak Ridge atomic plants fed by its power—America's production of weapons and materials would have been tragically reduced. The war would have been prolonged by many months, probably by more than one year—at a cost in money alone of tens of billions of dollars.

As Representative Gore of Tennessee reminded Congress, TVA earned a net profit—after depreciation—of $40,000,000 in 1947. These were public earnings, to the benefit of all U.S. taxpayers. But the profits of private business had increased just as impressively as a result of new private enterprises and new customers created by TVA power. In 1934 the Tennessee Valley had been this country's "zero" market for electrical appliances. A few years later it was the nation's leading market, providing spectacular increases in purchases of electric ranges, refrigerators, and numerous other products of General Electric, Westinghouse, and similar corporations. Through its federal agency of TVA the government kept its "interference" down to a minimum. State and municipal authorities were encouraged to assume all possible responsibilities. Instead of centralized governmental controls, decentralization was promoted. *

Thus TVA has failed completely to become the bureaucratic, socialistic, anti-free-enterprise monster that the spokesmen for private utilities and ultra-conservatives so violently described. Rugged individualism and democratic co-operation have expanded amazingly throughout the entire region. Simultaneouly TVA has become a worldwide model for planned development of national resources through electric power. Even some of our most conservative capitalists favor TVA-style systems for bringing flood-control and modern industries to China's great river valleys. The disastrous floods of 1948 in our Columbia River valley caused huge losses. An equivalent amount of millions of dollars would have gone far toward building a CVA system. It has been clearly demonstrated that the ultra-conservative opponents of TVA merely resisted an enormous extension of self-government and free enterprise.

We are concerned here with the needless, and often unpardonable, confusion of ideas and issues in our contemporary United States. We are unnecessarily confused because we are the victims of many years of fantastically loose talk. *Too many of us, for too long, have made little or no effort to base our political or economic arguments on definable realities.* It is easier to call David E. Lilienthal "communistic" than to examine closely what TVA accomplished under his management. It is easier for Communist agitators to denounce any big industrialist or banker as a "Fascist." But the time has come when, for our very survival as a democracy, it is necessary to determine precisely what Communism and Fascism are, and in what

* For a documented statement of its record see David E. Lilienthal: *TVA: Democracy on the March* (New York: Harper & Brothers; 1944).

manner Socialism differs from totalitarianism by adhering strictly to democratic practices. Alarming numbers of our recent and present Congressmen are incapable of making these absolutely essential distinctions. So long as this remains true, in Congress and in our electorate, democracy in the United States will be exposed to destruction by demagogues. *Much more than by outside forces we are menaced by our own superficial and highly emotional habits of mind.*

What are some of the more serious handicaps of Americans in a world of revolutionary social change?

First of all, there is the obstacle of U.S. conservatism, the extreme resistance of many of our most powerful interests to even a moderate degree of social change. Much as our safety is linked to western Europe, the United States is a stronghold of conservatism compared to the more experimental democracies of our closest allies. In a world where everything is in profound transition the United States stands virtually alone as a champion and symbol of the status quo. In a world-wide revolution we are the great anti-revolutionaries. Those who have most always are. And the role of an anchor in a storm can be extremely useful at certain junctures. But shall we prove capable of recognizing in time when an anchor must be shifted? Sometimes even the largest and most modern ship is compelled to shift its direction somewhat, to adjust itself to winds and waves, in order to avoid capsizing in a gale. You cannot plunge head-on into a hurricane with a lashed wheel and expect safety.

This is where angry, emotional, and flatly uncompromising conservatives are as much a menace as Red agitators at the opposite extreme. Our problems of economic and political security are much too complex. There can be no security for anyone in no-compromise. The intelligent conservative understands this because he is capable of hard thought and of learning from the mistakes of others. He recognizes when at least a minimum of compromises can no longer be safely postponed. British conservatives and Scandinavian conservatives have done this with extraordinary insight at crucial moments. Czarist Russia's ruling class failed to do so. So did the feudal landlords of Poland, East Prussia, and Hungary. In every revolution the privileged classes pay an exorbitant and entirely unnecessary price for their failure to be intelligently conservative.

We are also handicapped in the United States by the time-lag between our own situation and the outer world's developing crisis. Those disruptive forces and radical ideas which have struck Europeans with their full impact are only beginning to be felt here. This is our temporary good fortune. But it is likely to make it much more difficult for Americans to trim their sails when the necessity arises for urgent economic reforms and political readjustments. Another depression would certainly create such a necessity for urgent reforms. The popular demand for them would be more emphatic than in 1932. The point is that *even the powerful United States cannot resist all currents of change in a profoundly changing world. We can temper change, but we cannot prevent it.* We can choose many or most of the changes we have to make, providing we are in a frame of mind to face and deal with realities.

A time-lag, however, serves to create a mind-lag. When we think we have plenty of time we yield to complacency or wishful thinking. This has been the general tendency of average Americans in these postwar years. Our middle men have not done much perceptive observing and thinking about where they are, what is happening to them, or what they can and should do. Yet our own middle class is seriously exposed. It has a greater need of a precise understanding of its position than any other middle class in the world. A mind-lag is an exceptionally menacing thing for those who are the major target of the totalitarians.

We are handicapped further by a misleading and false assumption: the assumption that our current situation differs fundamentally from that of western Europeans. But the Europeans, in reality, are merely in the front sectors of a common struggle to keep democratic institutions from being undermined and overthrown. Where economic insecurity and Communist-Fascist ideologies threaten their freedoms today, the same forces will seriously threaten our American freedoms if a great depression should come tomorrow. The growing insistence of the underprivileged upon social reforms and improved standards of living is limited by no national boundaries. To avoid being much more radical, Americans, like the Europeans, will be compelled to be progressive. The experience of all Europe and Asia indicates that this is the only direction in which the people of the United States can hope to find reasonably safe solutions.

It may well be that no heavily industrialized nation can escape some degree of merging of capitalist and Socialist practices in this century. We have no surety that the United States can remain indefinitely a unique example of uncurbed capitalistic enterprise. Perhaps we too shall be compelled to find, in the phrase of Professor Arnold J. Toynbee, "a working compromise between free enterprise and Socialism. . . . Get the issue off its ideological pedestal and treat it, not as a matter of semi-religious faith and fanaticism, but as a common-sense practical question of trial and error." In other words, what will work best and provide the most economic stability? Whatever changes may come, the vital matter would not be a mixing of capitalist and Socialist techniques. The truly important question will always be whether our democratic freedoms are strengthened and preserved.

Rather than yield ourselves to ideological nightmares, we in the United States can first turn our attention to a more immediate and practical problem. Lack of solidity in the center is what menaces representative government in western Europe. If these nations possessed a middle class so proportionately numerous, so entrenched and prosperous as our own they would not be forced into sweeping economic reforms; they would not be in danger of dictatorship from the Right or the Left. Our best defense lies in understanding—

Why the United States needs a strong political Center.

Because of our two-party system it has been impossible to create an effective center party in the United States. Our exceptionally large independent vote turns the balance of power from Republicans to Democrats and back again. Yet the actual political middle also belongs to a large membership in both these parties as well as to independent voters. Our political center ranges all the way from those Republicans who are intelligently conservative to the small Socialist minority on the opposite side. All of these people, chiefly of the middle class, are the main target of Communist or Fascist totalitarians.

Professor Arthur M. Schlesinger, Jr., is completely realistic in emphasizing the need of consolidating the political center in the United States.* As he has pointed out, much of our confusion rises from confounding liberals or Socialists with Communists; and equally from lumping all sorts of conservatives with Fascists. We should have much greater clarity on both domestic and foreign issues if we recognized the existence of two modern political actualities; the non-Communist Left and the non-Fascist Right. New Dealers

* Cf. *New York Times Magazine,* April 4, 1948.

like Chester Bowles and Leon Henderson are in no sense
"communistic." They are liberals and progressives. Conservative Republicans like Senators Byrd or Russell are
certainly not "fascistic." Rather they are deeply conservative. As chief of the C.I.O. Philip Murray has demonstrated
his anti-Communism as well as his hard-hitting liberalism.
In a democracy these wide differences of political opinion
are natural and indispensable. They have the great common quality of acting within the framework of democratic
practices and principles.

It is the true function of the American middle class,
then, to keep the liberal political elements from being too
radical and to keep the more conservative elements from
being too much of a brake and outrightly reactionary.
Just as a not too radical liberalism is necessary to the
Democrats, a moderate conservatism offers the Republicans their only hope of sustained electoral support in our
times. We already possess a strong non-Communist Left
and a strong non-Fascist Right. Our urgent need is to
discontinue the dangerous habit of calling each other by
the wrong names, thereby tearing down the defenses of
our democracy.

As Professor Schlesinger insists, "the problem of United
States policy is to make sure that the Center does hold."
The Center means the American middle class, which is
the electoral majority, representing public opinion in the
United States. Since we are the target of the extremists we
can only hold by defending both moderate conservatism
and enlightened liberalism against the totalitarian extremes. We cannot succeed in doing this by confusing
Thomas E. Dewey with Huey Long, or William O. Douglas with William Z. Foster. But the Left-wing, Right-wing
dual assault upon the legion of Americans in between must
be clearly understood before it can be effectively repulsed.

Here we come to the essential quandary and the vital

role of the American middle class today. Where are we being attacked? In what ways are we divided and pulled apart? Do we yet begin to make adequate use of the remarkable amount of common ground we still possess? If we look more closely, we shall be better equipped to preserve the unexpendable center of our American society.

Chapter VII

THE CROSSFIRES OF TOTALITARIANISM

While Communists and Fascists struggled for domination of Italy after World War I the outcome seemed of no personal significance to most Americans. While the same ideological adversaries fought bitterly for control of Germany throughout the 1920's a majority of our citizens saw no direct connection with their own future and that of their country. The illusion of United States immunity to totalitarian concepts persisted stubbornly. A second global conflict was necessary before the American people began to conceive the universality of the isms. Even today most of us are seriously concerned only about Communism, rather than with every manifestation of police-state doctrines.

Yet America's middle men are not under constant challenge and assault from a single dictatorial ideology alone. Although the Communists' offensive is at present better organized and more aggressive, and therefore more obvious, the lure of Fascism as a counter-measure to Leninism has by no means been stifled or discredited. In reality Europe's ideological struggle between the wars has merely spread to many other parts of the globe. All the elements of Europe's struggle are discernible in the United States. At present they are simply in a less developed and less acute stage.

Today Mr. American Middle Man lives in the crossfires of totalitarian advocates and tendencies. Because he is keenly aware of Communistic methods and tactics he is partially armed. Because he tends to ignore the fact that

military defeat could not destroy the ideological appeal of
Fascism he is in other respects dangerously disarmed.
Universally the anti-democratic pressures come from various directions and in many different guises. They cannot
be of but one political coloring, nor fed by a single doctrinal source. Like Europe's middle class the majority of
Americans are caught between the pull of Communism on
the extreme Left and the counter-pull of Fascist-style reaction on the extreme Right. This is the chief reason for
John Between's ideological perplexities and confusion. If
his choice were only between Moscow's Marxism and
democracy, he would be much less confused and in far
less danger of being taken in. The Fascist possesses a terribly seductive weapon: the reassuring promise that his
only objective is to defeat or eliminate Communism,
without regard for his own totalitarian methods and aims.

What is the nature of the totalitarian crossfires in postwar America? First of all they are based upon an abusive
use of propaganda. Where the Communists are a small
minority and Fascist-minded groups cannot hope to win by
admitting their real motives and objectives, they must resort to highly doctored molasses in order to catch flies.
Prejudices and emotions must be enflamed by propaganda.
Truth must be distorted. In this deliberate process Communists and Fascists are everywhere equally shameless and
skillful. Red agitators and supernationalists employ the
same tactics. The great barrages to win a mass following
are always propagandistic. They are more effective because
they seldom carry their totalitarian labels, because they
are without scruple for fact. Their object is to sow dissension, to poison decent minds, to tear John Between
away from the moorings of his democratic principles.

This is where the crossfires of the totalitarians can be
clearly detected in our contemporary American society.
Propaganda against U.S. democracy and the American way
usually employs the sneak attack rather than the frontal

attack. It consists of a subtle but perilous mixture of misrepresentation, distortion, and deliberate falsehoods. It may be relayed unconsciously quite as much as consciously, and by many others than those who are outright Communists or Fascists. The pressures of anti-democratic propaganda never cease. Because we are caught interminably between them we might begin by examining a few samples of—

The lies that we are persistently told.

The Soviet press and Communist spokesmen everywhere specialize, as the Fascist-Nazis did, in perverting truth through gigantic distortions and falsehoods. Fortunately the devotees of Lenin and Stalin employ this technique with such flagrant exaggeration that the average American is seldom fooled by their major propaganda efforts. But these seemingly obvious perversions of truth are not intended for rationally minded or reasonably well-informed persons. They are addressed primarily to potential converts in less-favored lands; to those who distrust America's power, or to the legion of the world's under-educated, underprivileged, and most exploited. As an example:

David Zaslavsky, political commentator for Moscow's official Communist party organ, *Pravda,* on September 25, 1947 compared President Truman to Adolf Hitler, and Secretary Marshall to a Japanese war lord. "Truman wants to be a universal ruler," Zaslavsky wrote. A new source of "criminal aggression . . . is in the United States. Its headquarters are on Wall Street. Its heads are Truman and Marshall. Its agents all over the world are American generals and diplomats."

Here Communist distortion concentrates upon portraying all American capitalists as "plotters of war." A cartoon in *Izvestia* portrays a fat Uncle Sam reaching a clawed arm around the world, with the caption: "War Incendiary, clutching an atomic bomb." This is typical Red propaganda because it is based on widespread foreign fears of the United States' formidable industrial power, and on mass fear of an atomic war. In the same way the Communists bitterly condemned the Marshall Plan as an "instrument of American economic imperialism." This charge could only be true if our European Recovery Program were so misused and abused as to give U.S. capitalists control of major industries in western Europe. ERP was not adopted by Congress with any such intention. The proof of the pudding also exists in the eating. But the Red propagandists did not even wait for ERP to organize and begin to function. Moscow's political purposes could best be served by an immediate lie.

The Communists' world-wide "party line" is based upon the fantastic claim that Moscow and the Politburo can never be wrong. In a hopeless effort to keep in step with this remarkable doctrine U.S. Communists have been performing a frantic series of backward somersaults over a period of years. So long as the Nazi-Soviet "nonaggression" pact was intact, and until the very day when Hitler invaded the Soviet Union, U.S. Communists shrilly denounced World War II as "the imperialists' war." The moment that Soviet Russia was attacked this same conflict became "the war of the peace-loving democracies against Fascism." In New York the Communists' *Daily Worker* performed such an abrupt about-face that its editors tripped over their pet falsifications of many months previous. When Moscow excommunicated Marshal Tito and the Yugoslav Communists in 1948, U.S. Reds again reversed themselves. They forgot their fulsome praise of Tito's orthodox Marxism and abjectly adopted the Moscow line. Communists, at least, are sufficiently obliging as to tell the world, publicly and officially, what tremendous liars they have been upon occasion.

But the half-truths and distortions that Communists consistently employ retain a considerable influence among the underprivileged and the victims of racial discrimination. Where Communists control certain labor unions they fight aggressively for better wages and working conditions for the members. They defend many legitimate rights of the workers, including their legal right to strike under certain conditions. Simultaneously the same Communists drastically distort truth by ignoring the fact that workers under the Soviet dictatorship and in satellite Communist countries do not possess the right to strike. Capitalists are the only "exploiters" of labor, the Red propagandist maintains. The only real democracy is Soviet "democracy." The only true "progressive" is a party member or a fellow traveler.

By great good fortune the Communists themselves have torn away a large assortment of their masks. Their distortions and falsifications still pay off among the underprivileged, rebellious, and uninformed. But the great majority of Americans see through the tawdry gauze of their twisted protestations. Even so, Communists gain much influence and support outside their party ranks by their own favorite exploitation: the propagandistic exploitation of the half-truth or the part-truth. These are the very devices that the Reds employ most effectively to win the support of liberals and idealists as well as of Negroes, Jews, and other minority groups.

In the crossfires of the totalitarians many other forces besides the Communists are represented. The confusion of America's middle men may be said to arise chiefly, in fact, from sources that are neither Communist nor outright Fascist. Our mental and moral defenses are more consistently undermined by—

*Half-truths, distortions, or lies that are the
products of prejudice or ignorance.*

In this respect the supernationalists and rabid isolationists in the United States continue to be grave offenders.
Editorials and featured columns in the Hearst press consistently preach an extreme American nationalism, based
upon jingoistic appeals. The Communist and the Fascist
technique is to omit all pertinent or qualifying facts that
would weaken the all-out, black-and-white case they are
intent upon building up. The supernationalist uses exactly
the same technique by appealing to chauvinistic, racial, or
other susceptible prejudices.

During the debate on the postwar $4,000,000,000 loan
to Great Britain the *New York Daily News* (February 1,
1946) had this to say: "It seems to us that the sensible
thing to do would be to teach England that war is a horrible and costly jag, by letting England sweat out its World
War II hangover unassisted."

We do not question the *Daily News* editorialist's right
to this opinion, but any thoughtful reader is compelled to
ask how much demonstrable truth lies behind the statement. As it is expressed, this statement has certain definite
intimations and insinuations. It insinuates that the British
government and people actually sought or welcomed the
"horrible and costly jag" of World War II. Nothing could
be farther from the truth. On the contrary, both the Baldwin and the Chamberlain government, backed by British
public opinion, made the most pronounced efforts to avoid
involvement in war.

The same statement also intimates, with a nauseous
holier-than-thou overtone, that the British people have
not yet learned what a terrible and vicious thing modern
war really is. By its implication that is an inexcusable libel
of the courageous British people, who withstood the

deluge of Hitler's bombers, completely alone, for a full year. The British learned the full cost of war as we Americans have never known it. To deny this, even by intimation, is an unpardonable falsification.

In this same single sentence there is a third serious distortion. The reader is urged to believe that whatever misery and physical weakness afflicts democratic Britain is of no consequence to the interests and safety of the American people. Yet Great Britain is still the strongest and most important ally of the United States anywhere in the postwar world. The entire isolationist argument of the *New York Daily News* in this editorial is founded upon shocking distortions of demonstrable facts.

In our pre-Pearl Harbor period Brigadier General Robert E. Wood of Chicago was a leading member of the isolationist America First Committee. In September 1939 General Wood predicted that "if we get into the war we will get Fascism, Communism or some other ism as the inevitable result." Undoubtedly he believed this when he said it. That, however, does not excuse a colossal error in judgment. The United States could not escape involvement in World War II. After having been sneak-bombed into the global conflict, what have we now got? We have President Truman serving a full term in his own right. We have had a postwar Presidential election that astonished the world, as well as a great many U.S. citizens, as a demonstration of freely expressed opinion by democratic processes. After nearly ten years General Wood's prediction stands only as a gross exaggeration. Neither a Communist nor a Fascist could have distorted basic realities more irresponsibly.

In July 1947 General Wood remained entirely unabashed by the extraordinary inaccuracies of his prewar prophecies. At a hearing before the Joint Congressional Committee on the Economic Report he expressed his belief (as reported in the *New York Times*) "that to a con-

siderable extent Europe was 'finished' and that the only
thing left for Britain, Holland and Belgium was to export
some 20,000,000 to 30,000,000 of their population." Con-
currently, he favored curtailing most of our aid to Europe,
"except perhaps some 'charity.' " *

This was typical of U.S. isolationists who opposed the
Marshall Plan and any effort to restore the economic
strength of our democratic allies in western Europe. What
did General Wood mean by saying that Europe was "finished" to a considerable extent? He was implying something that has been denied by history for many hundreds
of years. The European peoples' record of recovery from
countless wars and catastrophes is simply astonishing. They
have never been "finished," not even "to a considerable
extent." Even as the general spoke, Belgium already offered a remarkable example of recovery. Despite their
severe impoverishment, Italian workers had amazed foreigners by rebuilding thousands of bridges and trestles,
by reopening their entire railroad system and most of
their disrupted highways. The British were laboring heroically under "austerity" rations lower than in wartime.
General Wood was indulging a defeatism about Europe
such as even European Communists did not dare to dis-
seminate. Since he voiced his gloomy opinion, the recovery of western European nations has been steady and
increasingly impressive. Once again Chicago's leading
isolationist merchant has shown himself a most unreliable
interpreter of international developments.

Colonel Robert R. McCormick's *Chicago Tribune* is
an uncompromising and blatant champion of supernation-
alism and isolationism. It scorns and belittles the United
Nations. It denounces almost every field of international
co-operation participated in by the United States. Its tone
and journalistic methods are as rabid and distortive on the
extreme Right as those of the Communists on the extreme

* Cf. *New York Post*, July 17, 1947.

Left. The frightening meaning of the atomic bomb may be fairly clear to millions of ordinary citizens as well as to great scientists like Doctors Einstein and Urey. It has not penetrated to the autocratic occupant of the Tribune Tower. Colonel McCormick and his newspaper have declared war on all Americans who are convinced that our very survival, in an atomic age, depends upon the establishment of a world law through world government.

In a three-column special article on the first anniversary of Hiroshima the *Chicago Tribune* (August 6, 1946) charged that "a combination of radicals and men of wealth," ostensibly working for world government, was endeavoring "to defeat candidates for public office opposed to the surrender of the nation's sovereignty." An accompanying cartoon described a "campaign to surrender America and our atomic bomb to a world supergovernment." Leaders of Americans United for World Government (now merged into United World Federalists) were accused of being "radicals" and associated with members of "Communist front groups." Among prominent Americans thus branded by the *Chicago Tribune* were Professor Harold C. Urey, Henry Seidel Canby, Clifton Fadiman, Marshall Field, Jr., Thomas K. Finletter, Jonathan Daniels, Raymond Swing, Russell Davenport, Norman Cousins, Mrs. J. Borden Harriman, James P. Warburg, Mrs. Gifford Pinchot, Douglas Fairbanks, Jr., Edward R. Stettinius, Robert Sherwood, and many others. When such a representative group of distinguished American citizens can be maligned for their efforts to promote understanding of the imperative necessity for One World, the menace of distortion in our national society must be evident.

We must understand that distortions, half-truths, and lies are the stock in trade of extreme Rightists and extreme Leftists alike. Whether these tactics are employed consciously or unconsciously does not alter their consequences.

Their effect is to confuse, antagonize, and divide otherwise well-intentioned members of the middle class. With this in mind we can consider the specific crossfires of totalitarianism in the United States. As a natural starting-point we may examine:

How the Communists conspire for political power.

By now the major methods of U.S. Stalinists should be self-evident. They can be summed up in a few sentences:

1. Infiltration of Communists into liberal and progressive organizations, political or civic.

2. Establishment of Communists in key positions of control in labor unions wherever possible.

3. Promotion and mobilization of class warfare.

4. Exploitation of true grievances of all racial groups that suffer from discrimination.

5. Creation of political groups or a party that can be used as a "front" and managed by Communists, directly or indirectly.

6. Defense of Soviet actions and policies on all issues and by any practical means.

7. Exploitation of the American people's desire for peace by demanding concessions to Moscow, regardless of how much is at stake; also by opposing U.S. preparedness, no matter of what degree.

8. The use of double-talk, by distorting and abusing terms like "democracy," "freedom," "Fascist," and "the will of the people."

Wherever the New Deal endeavored to improve the lot of the lesser-privileged, the underprivileged or the workers, U.S. Communists—for their own strategic reasons—were compelled to approve. Reforms like the Social Security Act and the Wagner Labor Relations law were not in the slightest sense "Communistic." On the whole they were what Americans, by their votes, demanded at the time. But the Communists could not pose as champions of the masses if they did not support these fundamental reforms. In the process, with national unemployment averaging ten million persons or more over a period of many years, Communists made their first notable infiltration into various liberal and progressive organizations, and also into a number of U.S. labor unions.

The Communists shrewdly concentrate their proselyting upon the most exposed and susceptible elements in our population. They recognize the justified complaints of thirteen million Negroes; of the Southern sharecroppers; of Jewish, Puerto Rican, Mexican, and other minority Americans who are subjected to many discriminations. All these constitute fertile fields both for class warfare and for Soviet-Marxist doctrines. Where U.S. democracy has been most negligent or indifferent is precisely where Communism can effectively profess to offer real improvement. For this reason we are certain to have a Communist problem of varying dimensions as long as American democracy fails to extend more rights and create better conditions for those who exist in the lower twenty-five- or thirty-five-per-cent bracket in our economy.

The only practical answer to the Communists is to beat them where they thrive and grow. The phrase of Sir Samuel Hoare (Lord Templewood) bears repeating: "So set your house in order that your social and political conditions will silence any demand for Communism's introduction." To do that, any great depression in the United States obviously must be prevented. To do that, fair employment practices must be established nationally. To do that, a civil rights program, such as President Truman courageously championed, must be enacted and consistently expanded. In other words, the Communists can be reduced to relative impotency—to being a noisy nuisance and nothing more—only by a liberal and progressive domestic program; by the consistent extension of our democratic rights, privileges, and opportunities.

But the long-term menace to American traditional freedoms comes from our extreme Rightists quite as much today as from the Reds. The American middle class is like a rabbit hypnotized by a cobra. It is dominated by fear of Communism and fear of Soviet Russia. For this reason most of our citizens refuse to see that other totalitarian elements seriously threaten from the opposite direction. We are already between the crossfires because of—

Dangerous Right-wing activities of U.S. reactionaries and supernationalists.

The House Committee on Un-American Activities has been curiously single-focused in its investigations. It has spent virtually its entire time and cash in probing "Communistic" influences, some very real and others exaggerated. But it has repeatedly ignored even the most obvious pro-Fascist organizations. Up to this writing, for instance, it has never taken steps to present the ugly facts about the Ku Klux Klan and Columbians, Incorporated, in Georgia; nor has it taken steps to curb the hate-mongering of the notorious Gerald L. K. Smith and similar American-born "little Hitlers." According to its record under Representative Thomas, nothing un-American is being practiced in the United States except by the Reds or by persons who are Left of center politically. The Congressmen did appoint a subcommittee on Fascism—which held a single ten-minute session during its first several months of existence. Representative John McDowell of Pennsylvania had the following to offer as an excuse: *

> We're not finding much in the way of things that could grow into Fascism. Fascism is down all over the world. There are groups here that hate Catholics and Jews, and hate one

* See *New York Herald Tribune*, May 26, 1948.

thing and another. But as far as I can find there is no evidence that they're dangerous. The only danger is *if they join together* [italics mine], and you need money for that. The hate groups have done no harm so far.

The only charitable thing to be said about this statement is that Congressman McDowell is as qualified to look for Fascism as a ten-year-old child—and no more so. Fascism *is* hatred and racial discrimination linked to jingoistic nationalism. These three elements are dominant in every Fascist. Speaking conservatively, they are also dominant in the prejudiced convictions of several millions of U.S. citizens today. In the depths of a depression—as in Italy and Germany—they could easily be made to appeal to many millions more. To assume that Fascists do not exist in the United States simply because they are too clever to call themselves by their correct name amounts to fantastic naïveté. When those chosen to defend our freedoms adopt this reasoning they are guilty of an attitude, whose consequences may open the door to treason.

For many months Dr. Douglas M. Kelley, as an official U.S. psychiatrist, conversed intimately with Göring, Ribbentrop, Streicher, Ley, Frank, Schacht and the remaining twenty-two top Nazis in their cells at Nuremberg. After this unique experience he ranks unquestionably as an authority on what makes a Fascist. Upon his return Dr. Kelley wrote: *

> I am convinced that there is little in America today which could prevent the establishment of a Nazi-like state. . . . We are similarly inclined to base our thinking on emotional rather than on intellectual evaluations. And no one can deny that the basic appeals that Hitler used—demanding minority persecution, demanding development of a stronger nation . . . demanding government control of private business—all are present in the United States today. It is a deeply disturb-

---

* Cf. Douglas M. Kelley: *22 Cells in Nuremberg* (New York: Greenberg, Publisher; 1947), pp. 258–9.

ing experience to return from Nuremberg to America and find the same racial prejudices that the Nazis preached being roused here in the same words that rang through the corridors of Nuremberg jail.

Congressman McDowell offers the soothing syrup that "Fascism is down all over the world." Yet scores of crackpot organizations are active today throughout the United States, preaching anti-Semitism, nationalistic supremacy, and a so-called hundred-per-cent "Americanism." Unlike the Reds, *they infiltrate openly,* without any marked public opposition or concern. They receive virtually no attention from the House Un-American Activities Committee, although they are as un-American as any Communist fanatic in every demagogical idea they put forth to poison and undermine our democratic system. We do not even have any assurance that the FBI pays close attention to these dangerous hatemongers.

Over a period of twenty years I have observed both Communists and Fascists in Europe, Asia, Latin America —and in the United States. Today we Americans are caught in between. While our attention and fears are concentrated overwhelmingly upon the Communists in our country, we are ignoring almost completely an equally serious Fascist fermentation. One of the most sobering aspects of our present situation is the unquestionable fact that—

Fascist-thinking and Fascist-inspired organizations are extremely active in the U.S.A. today.

The Christian Fronters of prewar days were strictly Fascist in their outlook; and they now operate under other names, with the same slogans and objectives. An alarming number of bitterly anti-Semitic organizations exist currently in the United States, spreading hate propaganda that might have been written by Goebbels and Streicher. The Silver Shirts, headed by Homer Maertz of Chicago, is but one among dozens. The Thomas committee obtained secret testimony that the Silver Shirts and a wealthy member of the German-American Bund were supplying anti-Semitic literature to other "movements" suggested by Maertz. Curiously enough, the transcript of this testimony was never released by the Thomas committee. It was reportedly testified that the groups were "patriotic movements."

There are scores of patriotic movements in the United States. Sincere as their members are, many of these organizations are extremely conservative; most of them are strongly nationalistic; a good many of them are receptive to anti-Semitic propaganda, or are anti-Negro. As such they offer a fertile field for Fascist ideas. Spokesmen for the race-prejudice groups have frankly admitted they were looking for a "strong leader." They and other super-nationalist organizations have maintained close relations and worked together for at least fifteen years, as I learned while making a journalistic investigation in Washington in 1937. If Senator Huey Long had lived, he might well have proved to be an ideal leader for an American Fascism. Within the next ten years the chances are great that another ambitious, spellbinding demagogue of the Huey Long type will emerge on the extreme Right.

Gerald L. K. Smith has renamed his America First Party the Christian Nationalists—and the word Christian attached to any U.S. *political* group is a foreign importation.

In the Hearst press of March 24, 1946 Washington columnist Paul Mallon made some astonishingly frank statements. Rabbi Benjamin Schultz of Yonkers, New York, had inquired (he wrote) about "some recent slight report in this spot on the possibility of *Christian dictatorship* in America in the event of depression—a report gleaned from travel and talk *among many American leaders*" (italics mine). Mr. Mallon added that only two important "politico-religious" forces are struggling to lead and control world thought today—"the God-fearing people on one side and the atheists of Communism on the other." The preponderant majority of Americans, he wrote, are Christian in their principles and essential ideology. Then came the propagandistic pay-off:

> If some future depression hinders the operation of their political democracy, and [these Americans] are *forced to seek refuge in strong-arm government,* it is wholly unlikely that they would renounce their basic principles and accept Communism. As the large majority of the people are Christian, they are unquestionably likely to work out some *Christian method* to meet their needs for government. *In all reasonable expectations, then, any future totalitarianism in this nation is apt to be Christian in essence.* I found this feeling among many men, although I must confess not among all our leaders. [Italics mine.]

Mallon did not explain how there can conceivably be such a self-contradictory phenomenon as a "Christian dictatorship"; nor how any totalitarian government, based upon terrorism and oppression by the police state, can possibly include "Christian methods." But the profoundly significant thing about his article is this: in a powerful chain of newspapers the idea has been placed boldly in print that another depression may well justify—presumably for lack of any alternative—the establishment of a so-called "Christian totalitarian dictatorship" in the United States. In essence that is a Fascist idea: an invitation to a clerical Right-wing totalitarianism. In every respect it is an un-American idea, violating the basic stipulations of the United States Constitution and the Bill of Rights. When fear of Communism prompts anonymous "American leaders," some or many, to envisage the employment of the word Christian to offer an advance excuse for dictatorship in the United States, Fascism is already a direct menace to our country.

We have no reason to doubt that our Communists will encourage violence and armed strife in the United States if they believe they stand to gain sufficiently by such actions. That is part of the Red record everywhere. But it is equally part of the Fascist record everywhere. For this reason we need to understand clearly that—

A potential threat of ultimate resort to armed force also exists among U.S. pro-Fascists and reactionaries.

When leaders of supernationalist organizations openly repudiate many of our basic democratic practices and preach bitter hatred of certain groups of citizens, they are planting violence in the hearts of their followers. In times of desperate economic want these burning resentments erupt into gangster beatings, riots, street murders, and mob rule. They can lead, as they have in Europe, to civil war and dictatorship. More than ninety per cent of the dictatorships of this century have been Right-wing or Fascist. Because they are anti-Communist—although employing all of the Reds' methods of totalitarian oppression —the counter-revolutionaries always get the support of influential men of wealth and power.

Under Merwin K. Hart, president, the National Economic Council, Inc., has an impressive list of outstanding American industrialists, businessmen, and lawyers on its board of directors. The NEC was first organized as the New York State Economic Council in 1931. One of its announced objectives was "to prevent legislation harmful to those who live by private enterprise." This legitimate objective could be of personal interest to most capitalists. But whatever the sentiments of its membership may be, Merwin K. Hart, a frank scorner of democracy and an ardent champion of Franco's dictatorship in Spain, has made the National Economic Council an instrument of extreme Right-wing reaction.

The weekly NEC *News Letter* of January 15, 1948 published some revealing and astonishing statements over the signature of Merwin K. Hart. The most significant ones are as follows: *

> Our Republican government has been weakened and something called democracy has tended to take its place. . . .
>
> This "non-partisan foreign policy" (the Marshall-Vandenberg policy) was conceived in appeasement of Soviet Russia and Collectivism generally. . . .
>
> Under false and misleading influence we were swept into a war that cost 300,000 American lives . . . we were led to acquiesce in the vindictive policy of unconditional surrender . . . were lured into a thing called the United Nations. . . .
>
> It has been the habit for some years in this country, under systematic intimidation by a small minority of aggressive Zionists, to skirt around any problem in which Jewish influence figured. We believe the time has come for all Americans to speak out, unafraid. . . .
>
> The danger from American Communists—even if there are only 75,000 of them in the United States—is so great that before the ordinary American citizen woke up, war with Russia might be well-nigh lost right here on the domestic front.

After more paragraphs in this vein Mr. Hart got down to recommending a course of action for all Americans who might share his viewpoint.

> We have one concrete suggestion to make to every citizen who is impressed by the potential danger. Let him possess himself of one or more guns, making sure that they are in good condition, that he and other members of his family know how to use them, and that he has a reasonable supply of ammunition. To buy and possess such guns will, in most states, require a license. . . . No license is required to own a rifle or a shot-

---

* *Weekly News Letter of National Economic Council,* January 15, 1948; also *PM,* January 16, 1948.

gun. *Every citizen should make sure that he has lawfully in his possession either a pistol or a rifle, and if he has more than one it will do no harm.* . . .

In certain jurisdictions it will be found relatively easy to obtain gun licenses; in others more difficult. Where it seems too difficult suspicion would be warranted as to why. *Interested citizens might well counsel together to see what could be done about it.* [Italics mine.] . . .

In any event we advise all our readers to proceed lawfully to equip themselves so they and their households may not be defenseless if what happened in Spain and France happens here. It will be better to have guns, and have them ready, and not have to use them, than to have the need for them arise and not have them. [Italics in this paragraph are Hart's.]

Speaking before the Union League Club in New York City on September 19, 1940, the president of the National Economic Council is quoted as saying: * "It is time to brush aside the word 'democracy' with all its connotations . . . we have been overdrilled into believing we are a democracy."

One must assume that the majority of Americans would be shocked and revolted by the "get your gun and have it ready" appeal. What does this document reveal? It is not merely anti-Communist. It is anti-democratic, anti-Semitic, anti-bipartisan U.S. foreign policy, anti-American participation in the war, anti-United Nations—pro-Fascist and pro-Tojo in calling the demand for unconditional surrender by those who attacked us vindictive. In a word, it is rabidly isolationist, supernationalist and Fascist in its major contentions. How many of the wealthy and prominent industrialists who are members of the National Economic Council are in agreement with the opinions expressed by Merwin K. Hart? It may be that most of them are not, but it is probable that some of them are. The NEC and its *News Letter* remain active and influential in high places.

By this time it should be amply clear that U.S. reaction-

* Ibid.

aries and pro-Fascists also constitute a menace to the preservation of our representative government and our democratic freedoms. It should be equally evident that they
masquerade under extremely misleading or seemingly
innocuous names. They appeal to bigotry, prejudice, and
hatred. They denounce the United Nations and international co-operation. They lump liberals and progressives
of whatever degree with Communists and "subversives."
Openly or clandestinely they preach and encourage violence. They are eager to exploit the Communist danger
as a means of imposing a Right-wing, nationalistic totalitarianism upon the United States. *Where has all this
happened before?*

In these pages I have endeavored to point out, fully and
realistically, how U.S. Communists conspire for power and
the true dimensions of their threat to our institutions. On
the basis of all my observation and experience, however,
I cannot escape one conviction: there are important
reasons—

*Why an American Fascism is more likely
than Communism to become a serious threat
to U.S. democracy.*

I am willing to go on record, in this fairly permanent
fashion, by saying that I do not believe Communists *can*
seize governmental, nation-wide power in the United
States at any time in the next twenty-five years—unless our
country should be thrown into chaos by atomic war and
destruction. On the other hand, I firmly believe it is possible that a Fascist-style dictatorship *may* find means of
dominating the United States during the next quarter-
century—and conceivably within ten or twelve years. I
hold this very unpleasant conviction for reasons that are
practical and realistic:

1. Fascists could destroy U.S. democracy much more

easily than Communists could because the overwhelming majority of Americans are aroused to the Red peril, while seriously underestimating the dangers of Black reaction.

2. The broad American middle class is infinitely more susceptible to jingoistic, extreme nationalism than to Marxism of any kind.

3. Anti-Semitism and other racial prejudices and hatreds are being recklessly and ruthlessly spread in our country.

4. Middle-class resentment against U.S. labor unions is widespread. At any time a demagogue who promises to put "the Reds, the Jews, and the unions in their place" may whip up a powerful mass following in the United States.

5. Many American conservatives and reactionaries in industry, business, and banking—as their taxes go up and their profits are acutely reduced through our huge military expenditures—will inevitably be open to the kind of "special benefits" propaganda that Fascists exploit insidiously.

6. A certain percentage of wealthy industrialists and capitalists, in any country, can always be persuaded to contribute vast sums to a Right-wing, anti-Red, and supernationalist movement. U.S. Communists can never get tens of millions of dollars in donations and subsidies in our country. Under skillful patriotic camouflage, and especially in times of strikes and civilian disorders, Fascists can be expected to obtain very powerful financial support. All they would need to do would be to talk "law and order" and maintain a front of relative respectability.

7. The rapidly increasing military influence in the United States will inevitably tempt some of our generals and admirals to combine with and support reactionary movements.

8. Any future depression or future war will greatly increase the strength of the Right-wing forces.

9. The Catholic Church in the United States, although

strongly mobilized to combat Communism, is in no notice-
able degree organized to expend similar efforts to prevent
Fascism.

10. The American people as a whole show an alarmingly slight inclination to prepare to defend their liberties
by learning exactly what Fascism is and how it operates.

This is not to say, even for a moment, that we cannot
escape Fascism. Rather it is to insist that the odds are
against our doing so in America *unless* we become aroused
to the fact that Fascism is already a menace—that it can
never be exterminated as an idea—and that it will remain
a potential menace as long as we live.

When the time and circumstances are propitious we
shall have a new Right-wing, Fascist-inspired party in the
United States. Its members may call themselves "American
Constitutionalists." Or the movement might be called the
"United American Party." Whatever the name, it would
be super-patriotic in sound; but what it preached and how
it acted would be utterly different. The "Christian Nationalists" are typical of what to expect. Because our citizens are predominantly conservative they cannot go radically Left in great numbers. As in Italy and Germany our
middle class, under stress and provocation, would be much
more certain to go radically Right—to the Right-wing
Fascist extreme. In such a situation they would be assisted
by all those reactionaries who are consciously or "unconsciously" Fascist.

In these Communist-Fascist crossfires it is nevertheless
possible for Americans, if we are alert and understanding—

To keep conservatism free from disguised
Fascists, and to keep liberalism free from
Communists.

When the majority of New Dealers and the A.F.L. and
C.I.O. leadership refused to climb on the Third party

bandwagon of Henry Wallace they rendered a notable service to democracy in the United States. Although they were liberals and progressives, they were prompt in rejecting any political alliance with the Communists who so aggressively supported the Wallace candidacy for President. At Philadelphia the Wallace-Taylor enthusiasts deceived extremely few Americans, liberals or otherwise, by choosing the name of the Progressive Party. The Communists' domination of the Wallace political organization was abundantly clear at Philadelphia, and long before that for those who were at all informed.

Long previous to the Wallace convention Philip Murray and his closest associates had cleansed the national C.I.O. leadership of Communists. The most liberal and democratic of the Roosevelt New Dealers had formed Americans for Democratic Action, specifically excluding any Communist ties or participation. The young and able American Veterans Committee repudiated the efforts of Communists to control their organization. On this issue they won an outstanding victory in their national elections. The alert membership of the American Newspaper Guild also fought the "Communist control" issue and won.

These were all heartening examples of the non-Communist Left sticking to its democratic principles. By free choice and intelligent leadership infiltration by Communists was blocked and prevented. Perhaps the most significant of these liberal victories was scored by courageous and realistic Walter Reuther when he rallied a majority in the powerful United Automobile Workers union to defeat smashingly the Stalinists who sought to control it. Reuther won a very tough fight by strictly democratic means. By so doing he not only took one of the greatest of our unions into the non-Communist front; Reuther also placed the entire nation, beginning with conservative businessmen, in debt to his vision and fearlessness. Was it an accident that Walter Reuther became the victim of a dastardly attempt at assassination? Only this much is certain. At the time he was shot, in a sneak assault through the window of his Detroit home, there was only one group of people in the United States who had an obvious motive for the crime.

American liberals, then, have given recent and convincing evidence that they understand how to keep free from Communist infiltration and controls. They were not fooled by the Wallace-backing Reds when they sought to camouflage themselves behind the designation of "Progressive Party." They remained the true progressives, demonstrating that the term is essentially anti-Communist and anti-totalitarian today, as it always has been in the United States. The greatest service of our liberals of the non-Communist Left is this: by their actions they have proved that whoever describes these genuine liberals as "communistic" is indulging in Fascist-style distortion and falsification.

Unfortunately, it is considerably more difficult for American conservatives to keep free from cleverly disguised Fascist elements and influences. When Thomas E. Dewey supported the main features of our bipartisan foreign policy during the 1948 Presidential campaign, he offered one encouraging example. He repudiated the pro-Fascist, supernationalist viewpoint of men like Merwin K. Hart, whose appeal (as quoted in this chapter) was addressed particularly to Republican leaders. All conservatives who refuse to accept the isolationist-nationalistic attitude of the Hearst-McCormick-*Daily News* press and their kind are in reality resisting a major pro-Fascist influence.

But there are pitifully few organized groups in the United States, with large membership and ample funds, devoted to combating organizations that promote anti-Semitism and other forms of racial hatred. It is dangerously easy to forget that Fascism gets its start from Silver

Shirts, the Ku Klux Klan, and a host of similar activities. It is also difficult to build an effective defense against the super-patriotic appeal of extreme reactionaries. Jingoistic nationalism thrives on emotionalism. It is a slow, hard task to fight emotionalism with logic and reason. Fascism can be combated successfully only by a broad, popular understanding of what leads toward Fascism and therefore is essentially Fascistic. We also have many reactionaries who are not at all interested in making these vital distinctions, and in making them stick. It may better suit the personal interests of a good many people to be "unconsciously Fascist," without ever facing what their prejudices and attitudes actually add up to.

Since we live, and must long live, in the crossfires of Red and Black totalitarianism, we would be prudent and foresighted if we were to examine—

The handicap, and perhaps the menace, in American character and habits.

Like all other peoples we Americans have the faults of our virtues. When you have spent many years observing and comparing different national groups, you are particularly impressed with the dominant characteristics of United States citizens each time you settle down again in your native land. The outside view throws many things into sharp perspective.

It would be easy, therefore, to make a long list of qualities typical in Americans: extraordinary hospitality and friendliness—remarkable energy—a youthful effervescence and boisterousness—a fondness for bigness—love of companionship—marked enjoyment of team-play and team-work—a pronounced inventiveness. Many other items could be added to these which come first to mind. Perhaps none is more universal or significant than our average citizen's deep conviction that almost anything American obviously is best. By nature and education we are an extremely Nationalistic people—spelled with a capital *N*.

On the opposite and negative side of the ledger are those human shortcomings which are the inevitable counterpart of our major American qualities. Do they combine to expose United States citizens to the calculated appeals of certain types of totalitarianism, and especially to the Fascist appeal? Let us jot down some of the most notable weak spots in the make-up of average Americans:

1. *Strong emotionalism and proneness to extremism* Americans are quickly aroused. Their feelings are close to the surface. They can be consumed by resentment and anger as swiftly as by a sense of injustice. In the majority their glands or their hearts rule their heads. On any burning issue they tend to ignore or reject logic and reasoning. They are quick to hate as well as to love.

2. *Impatience and lack of self-discipline* The American wants action—to get things done. "Try something, try anything, but don't wait!" This is his general attitude when up against a tough problem. He would rather be doing something than plan it through carefully beforehand. Therefore any simple formula or explanation tends to catch his fancy. Being used to a land of vast resources and opportunities, he resents having to make any prolonged sacrifice to attain what he desires. He is wide open to the fellow who promises an end of his present troubles —very soon, with the least possible personal sacrifice.

3. *Intolerance* The American is much inclined to feel superior to foreigners of any nationality and to peoples of other races. If they get into wars and have much lower standards of living, it's probably "their fault." Why don't "they" have bathtubs everywhere? Why don't "they" educate their people? If they weren't so backward, or so lazy, "they" wouldn't be where they are. . . . No mention of the systems under which Europeans, Asiatics, or Latin Americans have been forced to live. No consideration of

the severe limitations of geography or resources. During the war millions of our men overseas exhibited this attitude of intolerance—an aggressive or unconscious expression that they belonged to a super-race.

4. *Extreme nationalism* Having been brought up on the doctrine that the United States is, *in all respects,* "the greatest country on earth," what could we expect? By the grace of a generous Providence this is true in many respects. But an exorbitant national pride must eventually be followed by a fall. The powerful must also know how to walk humbly—if they would retain their power. The intensity of American patriotism and nationalistic fervor also contains elements of great danger. The Germans had the same thing, and Hitler exploited it diabolically.

5. *From teamwork to mass movement and mass organization* This can be a quality or a fault, depending entirely on whether it is used constructively or abused. Americans love to organize, and are extremely capable at it. They also love "to belong," to share in group endeavors, to adopt common slogans and common programs, to march in veterans' parades or wear the cap and regalia of a fraternal order—or perhaps the sheet of a Klansman. They love to wear insignia and medals.

Perhaps these five points are sufficiently pertinent and revealing. Suppose, in a period of nation-wide hardship and inflamed popular resentment, an adroitly veiled nationalist-Fascist movement should seek to wrest power from our two major political parties. Suppose it should shape its program and appeal to the five predominant American characteristics enumerated above. Suppose it kept its ultimate goal of dictatorship prudently and cleverly under wraps. Or suppose that most people were so fearful of Communism and so incensed against it that in a time of widespread impoverishment they didn't much care.

Suppose.

Perhaps the preservation of American democracy will depend largely upon how clearly and persistently American citizens—particularly those of the great middle class—keep in mind that the crossfires of totalitarianism come from *both* the extreme Right and the extreme Left; that they will continue, in one guise or another, throughout our lifetime; that free men must comprehend and combat *every* assault upon their freedoms from every direction.

If we are to do these things adequately, America's democratic capitalistic system cannot afford to plunge again into a general blockage of production and widespread unemployment. It is likely that our long-term political and ideological security will be determined chiefly by the degree of economic stability that the world's most highly industrialized nation is capable of maintaining.

Chapter VIII

BETWEEN BOOM AND BUST

"The Communists, both here and abroad, are counting on our present prosperity turning into a depression. They do not believe that we can, or will, put the brake on high prices. They are counting on economic collapse in this country."

President Truman opened his message to the special session of Congress with these words on July 28, 1948. He was not exaggerating in the slightest. For at least three years Politburo strategists and Communist leaders everywhere had based their plans on an "inevitable" great depression in the United States. Some of them frankly told western journalists that our impending economic crash would exceed anything Americans have previously experienced, and that it was certain to happen before or by 1953. This conviction had much to do with the boldness, intensity, and inflexibility of Moscow's European policies in the early postwar period.

Curiously enough, a great many western economists and U.S. capitalists found themselves unfamiliarly close to agreement with this one section of the Soviets' party line. Aside from the date of its possible advent, many of them regarded a postwar depression as almost as certain as death and taxes. Some dared to insist that courageous anti-inflationary measures could prevent another American "big bust." More frequently economists speculated when it would come, or how it might be postponed, or whether it could be restricted to something milder called a "recession." There seemed to be an alarmingly widespread notion that American capitalism was a fine, handsome, lusty fellow who simply had to go on a terrific bender every third or fourth Saturday night. Very few businessmen or politicians wanted to form an Alcoholics Anonymous to help keep the prosperous chap away from the bottle which might ruin him.

The orthodox Marxists and Politburo brain-trusters counted on a fairly early economic collapse in the United States for various reasons. According to Communist doctrine, the "basic contradictions" in the capitalist system make recurring major depressions inevitable. Communists believe that uncurbed appetites, monopolies, and other abuses operate at disastrous cross-purposes under free enterprise. Without mutual sacrifices by different segments of the population, stability is impossible in a capitalist economy. Americans have also been strongly opposed to a planned economy or controls by the state. The enormous expansion of U.S. industry in wartime contributed another element of unbalance and uncertainty. So the Soviet hierarchy confidently expected a repetition of 1929, on a bigger scale.

Actually, the Stalinist leaders and political strategists had a deep need to center their expectations upon another serious crash in the United States. The very solidity of the ground on which they stand—their basic philosophy—depends upon capitalism demonstrating a great and incurable lack of stability. The success of Communism's appeal around the world depends very largely upon U.S. capitalism presenting a spectacle of economic chaos and rampant breakdown. If our free-enterprise system turns out to be capable of maintaining prosperity and an unrivaled standard of well-being for all, then any considerable expansion of Soviet-Marxist ideology and power is doomed. The greatest and gravest blow to the Communists' faith and dreams cannot be dealt by super-bombs and guns. It can only be dealt in this generation by an American capitalism that becomes more balanced and more effective in producing general welfare—if it does.

But Moscow's confident expectation of an early U.S. depression received a rude blow from a totally unexpected quarter in 1946. The Soviet Union's most authoritative economist, Eugene S. Varga, published a book that upset the Kremlin's occupants almost as much as a blockbuster bursting in adjacent Red Square would have done. It is quite important for Americans to understand the implications of—

The heresy of Comrade Varga.

Economist Varga was immediately demoted for his unorthodox conclusions in defiance of the prevailing Communist party line. At the time he wrote, however, he was director of Moscow's Institute of World Economics and World Politics as well as a Soviet Academician. In substance he wrote that there is no necessary conflict between the economic interests of Soviet Communism and western capitalism, at least in the first postwar decade. Beyond that, he boldly and completely rejected the Politburo's central economic theory about western and especially U.S. capitalism. Varga stated that there was no likelihood of a severe economic crisis in western capitalism during the first ten postwar years. He believed that our capitalism's "basic contradictions" would not reappear until the decade beginning in 1955.

The institute that Varga directed was suppressed. The Soviets' long-favorite economist was shunted into a lesser job. He was also subjected to something approximating a heresy trial by twenty other Soviet economists. Like Galileo, he had affirmed something that the ruling powers could not accept without feeling their whole ideological position shaken at its foundations.*

* Cf. *New York Times*, January 23, 1948.

The Varga blockbuster reverberated in high Soviet circles throughout 1947, although confirmation of what he had written did not reach the outer world until early in 1948. But by the following midsummer there were important indications that the Kremlin brain-trusters had begun to accept Varga's main contention, however reluctantly. In *Pravda* a prominent Soviet writer admitted that two factors might "postpone the onset of the inevitable [U.S.] economic crisis": the Marshall Plan and our huge armaments production program. In July 1948 Alexander Werth, the most experienced and best-informed foreign correspondent then remaining in Moscow, reported: "So the party leaders are evidently not quite so sure that Varga was wrong. Their doubts about the imminence of a capitalist collapse are already reflected, and may be increasingly reflected, in an attempt to find a *modus vivendi* with the outside world. In other words, they may modify the foreign policy of the Soviet Union for some years to come." *

It should be of considerable cheer to Americans that Soviet leaders are no longer so certain about an early depression in the United States. Nevertheless, the specter of a possible economic crisis continues to haunt most U.S. citizens. High prices and the upward sweep of inflation have aroused deep anxieties and fears. These have been in no sense diminished by—

The expectation of many U.S. capitalists of a major depression.

It is a matter of plain fact that the postwar policies of a large number of American industrialists and businessmen have been based upon an assumption of hard times to come. Financial reporters and economists have long known

* Cf. Alexander Werth: "Russia: The Economists' War"; in the *Nation*, July 31, 1948.

this to be true. Those who talk privately with executives of large and important enterprises are often sobered and depressed by their expectation of a severe economic crisis; perhaps within five years, perhaps a little later. Many of the big corporation and business leaders, who collectively have a far more powerful influence on U.S. economy than any other single group, are resigned to the fact of cyclical breakdowns in our capitalist system. It is not surprising that public confidence is no greater than their own.

Our punishing and dangerous rise in prices was still in its relative infancy in May 1947. Even then the "boom and bust" philosophy was disturbingly prevalent. Down in Wall Street the *New York Post*'s extremely able financial writer, Sylvia F. Porter, was shown a secret chart drawn up for an internationally prominent concern. The chart illustrated the diagnosis of our economic future by some group of experts: lines for prospective production, employment, sales, profits, and the like. The black lines curved sharply downward between the early and middle 1950's. In the light of ERP and the armaments boom perhaps the lines have been revised for a few years; but the prediction of a crash was there, and probably still is.

A corporation executive told Miss Porter (as of May 1947): "It's not the next few years that we're thinking of. Demands for our goods here and abroad are too high to permit any lasting decline."

"After these next few years?"

"Well, look at history. Every major war has been followed by a major depression. . . . Do you see any reason why history shouldn't repeat itself? *What are we doing to prevent it?* As far as our company is concerned we are trying to be prepared financially and in every other way to fit into the times and pull through, whatever comes." * (Italics mine.)

We cannot blame businessmen for being realistic about

* *New York Post*, May 23, 1947.

future prospects and a rainy day, or even a deluge. But Miss Porter's accompanying comment seems to me unanswerable: "The time to prevent a calamity of this nature is now—before calamity threatens. The time to plan for a stable economy in the '50s is during these next few years of postwar activity. This is our chance."

The owners and managers of U.S. industry exercise the greatest power and influence in our capitalist system. Yet they have little or no faith that the system can be kept from intermittently smashing on the rocks. They fear radicalism and Communism, yet they produce no coordinated program to prevent a depression that would spread radicalism, both Communist and Fascist, to an unpredictable extent. Could this also be one of the "basic contradictions" of capitalism, that its greatest champions refuse to impose the self-discipline that alone may save it?

Even as inflation gathered speed and zoomed upward, our major corporations were in an exceptionally favorable position. They had available abnormally large earnings, out of which anti-inflationary "war chests" might have been created. Corporation profits, after taxes, registered constant and consecutive record-breaking highs through 1947 and 1948. These followed five full years of excellent wartime business. With billions and billions of war contracts at "cost plus ten per cent," U.S. enterprises had been exposed to extremely few cash sacrifices for the common cause. Would they use a reasonable proportion of their impressive surpluses to keep prices curbed, and thus prevent Uncle Sam's vast industrialized machine from rushing into boom and bust? Could they absorb a round of wage increases without raising their prices?

The cost of steel dictates production costs for thousands of American manufacturers. Big Steel was doing tremendous business, sure of capacity production for years to come. For the second quarter of 1947 the net profits of the U.S. Steel Corporation alone totaled $29,336,000. They continued at a similar pace, sometimes higher. Bethlehem and other steel giants prospered equally. But with each wage increase, up went the price of steel.

During the first half of 1948, General Electric netted a record of $54,602,339—the highest earnings in its history. In this same period G.E. reduced some of its prices for a while, then abolished the cuts. The expense of another wage increase was again passed on to the consumers.*

For the first six months of 1948 the General Motors Corporation reported profits of $206,763,000. This was an increase in earnings of more than $69,000,000 over the same period in 1947, which was already a tremendously profitable year. Similar prosperity was enjoyed by Ford, Chrysler, and all of Big Motors. Except for a few scattered efforts to reduce prices, Big Motors passed on virtually the entire cost of successive wage increases to the general public. Owners of a common share in G.M. had earned $2.97 in the first half of 1947; then $4.55 per share for the same period in 1948.† But the managers and directors of heavy industry evidently could not tolerate the idea that their stockholders might well afford to contribute—out of record-breaking profits—perhaps one dollar per share toward the safety of U.S. capitalism. If someone was to set an example of "doing with a little less" for the sake of preventing a national economic catastrophe, apparently it would not be the masters and key managers of our free-enterprise system.

So America's perilous inflation went on and on. By mid-summer of this second year of huge corporative profit-making Marriner S. Eccles, former chairman of the Federal Reserve Board, told the Senate Banking Committee he regarded an economic slump as "inevitable." Mr. Eccles had fought the inflationary follies most courageously until he was shelved by President Truman—not exactly a con-

* Cf. *Time,* July 26, 1948.
† Cf. *New York Times,* July 29, 1948.

sistent enemy of high prices. Now Eccles insisted that dis-
equilibrium between farmers, businessmen and others
earning exorbitant profits and white collar workers, pensioners and others most seriously pinched by high prices
would finally precipitate "some unpleasant adjustments."
As in Europe, now in the United States the middle class
was being tormented and leveled down by inflation. It is
necessary to keep in mind that inflation is a direct ally of
social unrest and totalitarian agitation. Permit it to run
with the bit in its mouth and these consequences cannot
be avoided.

Citizens of the United States live today in a state of nonsensical but fearful paradox. Ours is the richest, most
powerful, most technically advanced nation on earth, yet
the people of this privileged land exist in an unrelaxed
nightmare of boom and bust. Even the world's highest
standard of living provides us with no reliable security
for tomorrow. To most of us every meal is a reminder that
we must buy fewer clothes or do without this or that.
Every meal is a reminder of our collective fears, our collective folly, and our collective failure to unite to defeat
inflation.

Was the punishment of high prices necessary?

The Office of Price Administration was abolished by
large Congressional majorities in June 1946. Republicans
and Democrats both had a full share of responsibility. So
did the public. Most Americans were fed up with wartime
rationing. Most organized groups, business or agricultural,
were incensed over what they regarded as "bureaucratic
interference and inefficiency" by OPA. There was a heed-
less and adolescent urge to get rid of all wartime regula-
tions and inconveniences. Back to normal—and to hell
with the risks involved. Those who accurately warned Con-

gress and the public of what would happen were ignored, scorned, or vilified. In the most popular and repetitive of American traditions the American people were going to have their cake and eat it too. Within twelve months cake and everything else was costing a great deal more.

Those down-to-earth governmental leaders who fought courageously to preserve price ceilings for another two or three years were repudiated by Congress. Conservatives of both parties were especially jubilant. Paul A. Porter, Price Administrator, warned that the "scuttling of price control" would bring skyrocketing prices, with an "inevitable aftermath of depression." The OPA issued estimates of additional costs for food, clothing, and other consumer goods running into hundreds of millions of dollars. In a matter of months they were exceeded. Eventually they ran into many billions of dollars.

In the all-out 1946 offensive to kill the OPA the National Association of Manufacturers spent huge sums in display advertisements. As the voice of the nation's most influential businessmen N.A.M. assured Americans: "If price controls are discontinued, production will step up fast. Prices, after a brief rise, will quickly seek reasonable levels." This would happen, N.A.M. insisted, "through free competition." Two years later the "brief rise" in prices was still soaring toward the inflationary stratosphere, completely unchecked. The ordinary citizen—as he paid ten extra dollars for a small radio or a dollar ten or more for a pound of ground beef—was entitled to ask: Do the nation's industrialists really know what they are talking about? Or only now and then?

The cost-of-living index issued by the Bureau of Labor Statistics stood at 131.1 in April 1946—with OPA in effect. That was less than two points higher than when World War II ended. By June 1948 it had risen to 171.7—the highest on record in the United States. Not a living soul in America, not even the officials of N.A.M., could regard

these devastating price increases as remotely connected
with "reasonable levels." In two years' time abolition of
price-controls had taken many billions of dollars out of
the earnings and the savings of U.S. citizens. No democratic people in modern times had ever paid such a huge,
cruel, and unnecessary price for throwing their economic
safety brake down the well.

But the word "controls" had been anathema to many
Americans, and especially businessmen. In their view—
then and now—controls of any kind are bad, or maybe intolerable. It is like saying that all kinds of medicine should
be abolished because they often harm you when you take
an overdose. It is like a man's saying that he has to get
drunk on Saturday night, no matter how hungry his family will be as a consequence. The "control" of a couple
of beers or a highball per evening would be "dictatorial."

More than either political party, American industrialists and businessmen were predominantly responsible for
the elimination of price-controls and the great inflation
that followed. They are gravely responsible because groups
like N.A.M. and the U.S. Chamber of Commerce enjoyed a tremendous influence in Congress and on public
opinion. If thousands of businessmen throughout the land
had supported a *delayed and gradual removal of price
ceilings,* a majority of politicians undoubtedly would have
fallen in line. But U.S. capitalists—save for occasional and
notable exceptions—refused to champion a course of restraint and moderation. They wanted "freedom from all
controls." Yet even a high-school student could have fig-
ured out the inevitable consequences. When you have
only ten apples, and sixty people, with five-dollar bills, are
clamoring for an apple, do you sell them for five cents?
Or do you ask for a dime? Is there really much "free competition" in such a situation? The supposed authorities
on free enterprise evidently hadn't the slightest idea. Being in the highest brackets of U.S. income, they have pre-

sumably learned the least, even today, because they are least hurt.

By the autumn of the 1948 Presidential election, high prices and inflation had become a political football, but also our Public Enemy Number One. Even Stalin and the Communists were secondary by comparison. The special session of Congress arrogantly disregarded President Truman's demand for drastic action to curb inflation. Month by month hundreds of millions in savings were being devoured by high prices. Week by week millions of citizens were being "priced out" of one consumers' market after another. Who was to blame for this disastrous upward ride toward boom, then bust?

An outside observer would have to include all of the main divisions of our free-enterprise system, in one degree or another. Our big corporations, whose profits after taxes remained amazingly high, showed themselves unwilling to sacrifice a part of their exceptional earnings. Farmers, even after enjoying eight or ten years of extraordinary prosperity, were still seeking subsidies and governmental guarantees to keep their abnormal earnings at their recent peak. The labor unions were fighting to keep wage adjustments scaled to each important increase in the cost of living. No single group in a position to make some sacrifice for the common good seemed willing to do so for the sake of saving our free-enterprise system from another smash-up. As always, the teachers and white-collar workers and civil servants and pensioners were being ground into steadily reduced circumstances. America's middle men were beginning to learn one of the things that cause the unrest and rebelliousness of "those Europeans." Our most vociferous defenders of free enterprise and capitalism had failed to defend the system's central bastion—the American middle class.

After two years of a rip-roaring price jag some former anti-control businessmen showed signs of sobering up. The

huge arms production program, topping ERP, promised
to add enormously to inflationary forces. At this prospect
one banker remarked: "We'll have to have controls as we
never had them before. If we don't have them, God help
us." But this banker was a minority voice piping in the
wilderness. Most of the august executives in the membership of the National Association of Manufacturers still
preferred to rely exclusively on God. It was not exactly
evident why He should be expected to do what human
intelligence could, at any time, make an intensive effort
to accomplish.

As a matter of fact, industrialists, labor leaders, politicians, and the rest of us had some quite unusual human
intelligence immediately available. On January 19, 1948
Mr. Bernard M. Baruch made urgent recommendations
of most exceptional importance before the Senate Foreign
Relations Committee. He startled the Senators by presenting a detailed program for a war on our domestic inflation
"to stabilize the nation for peace." Among eleven Baruch
recommendations these were outstanding:

Postponement of tax reduction for two years. (Congress
immediately voted a sweeping tax reduction.)

A reduction of "major food and agricultural prices."
(Consistent opposition from farmers and wholesalers.)

Acceptance of a stabilization of wages by labor.
(Promptly opposed by the labor unions.)

Restoration of the excess-profits taxes to fifty per cent
of wartime levels. (Most vigorously opposed by industrialists and business groups.)

Mr. Baruch declared:

> It is my belief that few controls would be needed today
> . . . if inflation were tackled vigorously by putting off less
> essential activity . . . postponing tax reduction, reducing
> farm prices, holding wages stable, taking smaller profits and
> increasing production.
>
> *If we do not show the wisdom and restraint to make these*

rather small present denials for greater future gains, then I can see no other alternative but to impose a ceiling over our entire economy as in wartime, to save America from being wrecked.

Unquestionably Bernard Baruch is one of the most authoritative and able U.S. capitalists of this century. No one questions his unique experience and knowledge, nor his loyalty to the free-enterprise system.

Who was interested in rallying around Mr. Baruch's common-sense program to preserve the stability of American capitalism? What vital groups in our society would contribute something real "to save America from being wrecked"? Bernard Baruch, for all his experience and wisdom, might as well have announced his program to the sands of the Sahara Desert. The same industrialists, bankers, and assorted capitalists who praise Mr. Baruch so extravagantly when he is not voicing unpleasant realities now gave him the silent treatment. "Taking smaller profits"? That was heresy quite as great as Eugene Varga's in Moscow. If the further progress of inflation should require the imposition of "a ceiling over our entire economy as in wartime," economic forces would then take a bitter revenge. Whether the controls were Communistic, socialistic, anti-capitalistic or what, controls we would have—at the direct invitation of whom?

A minority of U.S. industrialists and businessmen had urged their associates much earlier to show "economic statesmanship." Back in May 1947 the National Planning Association issued a statement among whose signers were S. C. Allyn, president of the National Cash Register Company, Charles E. Wilson, president of General Electric, Beardsley Ruml, chairman of the board of R. H. Macy & Company, and others. In part their statement said:

If orderly price reductions do not become more general, business must share the blame for the slump that is then sure to come. . . . We are here concerned, not with placing

blame for the present situation, *but with placing responsibility for leading the country out of it. That responsibility
is squarely up to business men.* [Italics mine.]

Along with soaring prices, the responsibility of businessmen, farmers, politicians, and others has soared proportionately since May 1947. Even by the end of that year
"one fourth of U.S. family units spent more than they
earned. Low-income people were spending past savings
predominantly for current expenses." † Day by day, as
President Truman reminded Congress, inflationary forces
were "imposing additional hardships upon countless families; day by day undermining the foundations" of our
postwar prosperity.

With a new administration in Washington, 1949
brought Congress and the American people face to face
with an inflationary menace of a long-term gravity that
could scarcely be exaggerated. The United States was riding a bobbing boom-balloon. In the midst of extraordinary
production and much prosperity, boom-and-bust was an
inescapable national problem. Fears of another great depression were prevalent among all classes of citizens. The
danger was pretty generally understood, but something
much less considered and appreciated was—

The crisis that the New Deal never solved.

This is a brutal fact that no category of Americans can
much longer ignore. Our present economic troubles were
not caused by World War II. They were merely accentuated by it. Our fundamental difficulties began long before
the 1929 crash. Ever since then the same elements of disorder—contradictions if you will—have remained uncon-

---

* Cf. *New York Times,* May 5, 1947.
† Cf. mid-year 1948 report of President Truman's Council of Economic
Advisers.

quered and almost untouched at the heart of our free-enterprise system.

We would be prudent to remember certain facts about the 1929 crash and its ensuing depression. Production in the United States dropped by 47 per cent, where it had never fallen off more than 10 per cent in any previous economic letdown.* Farm income dropped 80 per cent, and more than 15,000,000 Americans were unemployed. With our immensely increased industrial capacity of today, what would a sudden sharp decline of perhaps 50 or 55 per cent of our production do? What would happen if perhaps 22,000,000 of our people were out of work? How many scores of billions in governmental expenditures would be necessary to keep them alive? For how long?

The New Deal came along in 1933. It improvised WPA, CCC, NRA, and an entire series of expedients to provide some kind of income for the jobless and get production going again. The Reconstruction Finance Corporation provided one kind of "governmental interference" that businessmen found no reason to criticize, because it was bailing them out of their own acute difficulties. Gradually, despite all the counter-charges and curses, our national economy began to function again. Times, if you remember, were not at all bad between 1936 and 1939.

But had the fundamental ills of U.S. Free Enterprise, Unlimited, really been removed? The answer is that they had scarcely been touched. After more than six years of New Deal "pump priming" the pump still leaked very badly. The revealing proof lies in the fact that when World War II began, in September 1939, the United States still had 10,400,000 citizens unemployed. That was almost one out of every five qualified workers.† Thus, for all the bil-

* Cf. Chester Bowles: "Challenge to the Business Man," *New York Times Magazine,* October 5, 1947.

† Cf. Fritz Sternberg: *The Coming Crisis* (New York: John Day Co.; 1947), Chapter ii.

lions that had been spent, our unemployment problem
had not been solved. The U.S. depression spread to Europe. It created very great unemployment in Germany,
hastening Hitler and Nazism to power. There was much
unemployment in France and other Continental countries.
Great Britain's chronic jobless still represented 10.3 per
cent of its labor force in 1938.

Production for European war needs temporarily ended
U.S. unemployment in 1940. But this was purely superficial. No effective solution has yet been found because
we are still producing predominantly for artificial markets
created by war shortages and for armaments.

What kept 10,400,000 Americans out of jobs in 1939?
The chief culprit was, and remains, the machine. The
economists call it technological unemployment. That's a
fancy way of saying that our inventive genius threatens
to strangle the capitalist system. New labor-saving devices
are created by hundreds or thousands every year in the
United States. We invent machines to put people out of
work much faster than we build new factories, or revamp
old ones, to give displaced workers (DW's, if you like)
another chance to earn a living. There are no "controls"
over inventions or technological improvements. In our
heavily industrialized system the machine is a Franken-
stein monster. It threatens to rule men, and to force large
numbers of them into near starvation.

The economists speak of many other difficult aspects of
our 1929 economic crisis. It is sufficient here to remind
ourselves that *U.S. capitalism is now in a crisis that has
lasted for at least twenty years.* Most exceptional understanding and skill will have to be demonstrated even to
prevent it from coming to a more explosive phase. It is an
ostrichism to talk about "the American way of life" as if to
admire and cherish it means automatically to preserve it.
To do this could be as deadly for us as any ism known to
our century. When we have prevented another great depres-

sion and warded off another "big bust," we shall merely
have made a beginning at preserving our capitalist democracy. It remains to be seen whether we Americans are
capable of that much collective intelligence and collective
self-sacrifice.

Meanwhile we are condemned by harsh realities to live
between boom and bust. If you are at all worried about
Communism and totalitarianism of any form, it will be
profitable to ask:

What another great depression would do to the political thinking of Americans.

Since the past thirty years have provided a tragic
amount of evidence, we need not labor the point. Unemployment and chaotic economic conditions plowed the
field for Fascism in both Italy and Germany. The second
World War vastly increased mass adherents of Socialism
and Communism in Europe. It also prepared the ground
for the possible return of Fascist reaction in France, Germany, Italy, and elsewhere. After two World Wars and
persistent depressions European capitalism is already drastically diminished.

In the Roosevelt-Hoover electoral campaign of 1932 we
saw what the 1929 collapse had done to the political thinking of a majority of Americans. They had not gone Communist by a long shot, nor even consciously socialistic.
But they had gone definitely radical for Americans—even
without the middle and lower classes having suffered long
punishment from high prices before the crash came. Today our American middle and lower classes are being
steadily ground down and punished by inflation. If this
continues and then ends in a severe depression, the ensuing economic crisis will be more devastating than after
1929. Mass unemployment would undoubtedly be much
greater. Political radicalism, on both Left and Right,

could not fail to reach proportions that the United States has never experienced.

All these tremendous imponderables are involved in food prices, which are double what they were only a few years ago. Whenever the middle class, in particular, is impoverished by inflation, it is torn away from its anchor in the broad political center. The lower classes of laborers are also pushed toward the extremes. *Boom-and-bust is the road to political totalitarianism.* It might be worth, say, a ten- or even a thirty-per-cent slice of General Motors' recent profits to prevent this situation from arising. It might be worth a proportionate sacrifice by the farmers, our labor unions, and most of the rest of us. The skyscraper of U.S. capitalism is so tremendous that to risk wrecking it is to risk the loss of everything important which we include in the American way.

Is there any escape from boom-and-bust?

A railroad engineer takes many a dangerous curve merely by carefully reducing speed. What does that mean? It means a little more "control." You might even call it "taking smaller profits" on the time-schedule of the run. It is not at all logical to assume that a powerful locomotive can operate without certain controls. Is it any more logical to insist that the most colossal industrialized machine in the entire world can operate safely, especially in a period of crisis, without a considerable amount of "controls"?

I am content to be as radical as Bernard Baruch and the National Planning Association. I do not believe for a moment that the Goliath of U.S. industrial capitalism can function, in our most uncertain times, without many more controls than we have had in the past—nor without much more planning. If planning be treason, it is a form of treason that U.S. Steel and General Motors practice regularly for the benefit of their own enterprises and their stockholders. Is there any reason why planning should be a monopoly of big corporations, or of Soviet or Fascist totalitarians? Planning is also *how* you do it, and *for what* you do it. Controls are what you make them. Those who are most outspoken in their denunciation of governmental planning or controls, you may notice, are perfectly content to use both in their own personal occupations, for their own immediate interests.

Our problem in the United States is to discover new ways and means for national economic stability and safety. We should not be incapable of succeeding if we will set about devising safety brakes large and strong enough to fit the fantastically great industrial machine in which we are riding. If our leaders—industrial, political, and other—are not sane enough to make this effort and to make it succeed, one of two things must happen eventually: either, as Bernard Baruch warned, there will be imposed "a ceiling over our entire economy as in wartime, to save America from being wrecked"; or America *will* be wrecked.

It would be infinitely less dangerous for American citizens to accept an adequate amount of controls, at least for so long as they increase economic stability; infinitely less painful for those with most favorable earnings to content themselves with more modest profits. Inevitably too, if the threat of depression is to be faced and eliminated, most Americans will have to limit themselves to more modest demands. Much as we resent and dislike personal or national self-discipline, it will have to become a much more prominent aspect of our lives. Yet these concessions would be almost insignificant beside the alarming dimensions of the alternative.

Why should we live interminably beneath the suspended guillotine of boom-and-bust? Is there indeed no other way for people to live within our system of capitalistic free enterprise?

We need not accept any such defeatist attitude until Americans, consciously and determinedly, have attempted to solve their still unsolved crisis of 1929. Unless we wait until it is too late.

The totalitarians expect us to wreck our system, thereby inviting them in. The menace of boom-and-bust begins in mounting prices of bread, milk, and meat. Ultimately it destroys the economic foundations of capitalism, thereby jeopardizing personal and political freedoms.

Chapter IX

OUR FIRST DEFENSE IS THE LAW

D r. Albert Einstein is enormously concerned over the supreme menace of atomic weapons. What does he think we must do to escape atomic destruction? Dr. Einstein says: "Our defense is not in armaments, nor in science, nor in going underground. *Our defense is in law and order.*" (Italics mine.)

But the first essential for survival in an atomic age is also a first requisite for survival of free, democratic institutions anywhere. Laws are the central bastions of the American way of life. The law is the guardian of all our cherished freedoms. Long before Communists or Fascists could seize control in the United States, our most basic laws must be violated, perverted, and broken down. Whenever we fail to respect and enforce these basic laws we are blasting holes in the fortress of democracy—for the benefit of totalitarians. Illegal procedures are the initial and required methods of dictatorial movements and ideologists. But preservation and enforcement of the law alone make it possible for free institutions and representative government to exist.

The first defense of U.S. democracy is the inviolability of our laws.

This is true because a free society cannot be kept free unless its laws are obeyed, unless the common rules of individual or group conduct remain applicable to all, unless an important minimum of legal restraints and privileges is maintained without fear or favor. We know

185

that absolute equality under the law is impossible to attain. But we also know that citizens in the western democracies enjoy more liberties and more legal protection than people under any other form of government. Whether in western Europe, South Africa, Australia, most of Latin America, or North America, the sanctity of the Law—its unchallenged sovereignty—accounts for all of the freedoms the people possess.

Since the United States has never experienced a dictatorship, it is perilously easy for Americans to forget or completely ignore the legal source of their exceptional liberties. No honest citizen need fear interference by the police. Our homes cannot be invaded or searched without a warrant. Although habeas corpus may sound vague or confusing to most of us, we know that a citizen cannot lawfully be arrested without a given reason, and that when he is brought into court a reason for his detention must be given. These are fundamental protections that we take for granted. But they have never been tolerated in any Fascist state. They do not exist in Soviet Russia, nor in the Communist-ruled satellite nations; nor in Franco's Spain. They did not exist under Chiang Kai-shek's one-party dictatorship in China. Under the Perón regime in Argentina they are also largely nonexistent.

The law alone makes it possible for us to make our daily rounds of work and pleasure without constant apprehension or interference. Thanks only to its almost invisible presence and authority is it possible for 148,000,000 Americans to live in their various communities in relative peace and security. Freedom of worship, freedom of speech, and freedom of assembly are fundamental liberties that only became realities when they were buttressed by law—and can only persist so long as law prevails. Free enterprise itself was created by law, and that is the only means by which it can be saved from gradual or abrupt elimination.

Any legal expert could provide paragraphs and columns of illustrations of the law as the foundation and framework of our democratic system. But even in remembering its most obvious benefits we immediately comprehend that all our vital freedoms are the product of laws which apply universally within our society. To destroy American democracy its laws must be destroyed. If our most essential legal privileges or protections are distorted or abolished, then our entire way of life will be open to conquest and destruction. Without freedom of thought and freedom of speech what would be left of "government of the people, by the people, for the people"? Yet without law, freedom of speech itself is impossible.

Thus we must recognize clearly that the fate of our democracy will be chiefly determined by whether the fundamental U.S. laws are preserved or destroyed. We need not wait for Communism, Fascism, or some closely associated totalitarianism to become a major organized menace within our borders. Our first defense is to keep the power of established, freely adopted laws supreme in our land. The fundamental rights of any citizen—however much we may disagree with his political ideas or disapprove of his personal habits—must be defended by all citizens, or at least by an impressive majority, upon all occasions. For whenever such basic rights are denied to some while reserved for many others, we open the door for totalitarian exploitation or for infiltration. Communists and Fascists climb to power by violation and perversion of the law. When democratic citizens and societies violate or pervert their own laws they are merely committing the very self-destructive act most desired by the totalitarians—the one act by which anti-democratic forces can profit most.

Because Americans today are the central target of totalitarianism, we are compelled to defend our laws—our essential liberties—with greater understanding and energy than ever before. We have certain high and honorable

claims to the support and allegiance of people everywhere
who love freedom. To contradict our humanitarian principles by our actions would be to forfeit these claims,
while strangling our own liberties. We do not want to do
this. We do not intend consciously to do it. Therefore we
must become, and remain, intensely aware of—

How Fascists and Communists pervert the law to their own ends.

"Law and Order" is what totalitarian movements, Red
or Black, always promise even as they ruthlessly violate all
laws that stand in their way and create disorder through
violence and gangster activities. They respect only such
legal provisions as serve their ends. But one of their in-
variable objectives is to seize and consolidate power by
"capturing the law." There has never been a modern dictatorship that did not take over and completely remake
the existing legal system. This is one thing that Fascists
and Communists do immediately, usually by decrees which
are called laws.

Hitler and the Nazis provided an illuminating example
of what Fascists do to law. As they broke down the resistance of democratic German parties the Brownshirt
stormtroopers and hoodlums committed murder, arson,
and a long series of violent crimes. They cowed the police,
or often bribed them. They infiltrated ardent Nazis into
state and municipal police forces wherever possible. Thus
the German police often failed to interfere when Nazis
were beating up Socialists, Communists, or anyone else.
It is part of totalitarian technique to persuade the police
to refuse to enforce the law.

This is how German Fascists distorted, violated, and
finally abolished all the most important legal protections
in their country:

At the outset the police forces were purged of all anti-

Nazi elements. With that the press and radio were taken over one hundred per cent by Nazi party members. "Freedom of assembly" for other political parties was abolished. Printing of anti-Nazi literature was also forbidden. All the laws that had given ordinary civil rights to Germans for generations were eliminated.

As soon as Hitler obtained power, existing criminal law was violated by a series of decrees. Death sentences were extended to an unprecedented and brutal extent. Life imprisonment was also imposed for a large variety of offenses that had previously received mild or little punishment. The Reich Penal Code was rewritten so drastically that any citizen resident in a foreign country could be convicted of "a treasonable act against the German Reich, or uttering slanderous remarks" abroad against Hitler.*

The Nazis, in the first days of governmental control in March 1933, established special "courts" to prosecute citizens for "political crimes." These special tribunals pronounced death sentences, and their verdicts were final. In another year Hitler's Fascists set up a special People's Court, with Nazi judges in a majority, to try cases of alleged treason. The new laws had such sweepingly broad interpretations of treason that every foreign correspondent working in Germany had a potential death sentence hanging over his head. German citizens were without any genuine legal protection whatsoever.

Whatever his alleged offense, a German could not know the charges of which he was accused or the witnesses or supposed evidence to be used against him. Besides being unable to prepare his own defense, he could not select a defense attorney of his own choice. By March 1936 a Prussian court had ruled that "measures taken by the state secret police, arbitrary arrest, protective custody, confinement in concentration camps, etc., are not subject to

* Cf. Albert C. Grzesinski: *Inside Germany*, Chapter xvi.

complaints or judicial investigation." No citizen had any defense whatever against Gestapo torture squads and police terror. Another Nazi decree deprived any member of an opposition party of his rights to compensation for physical injuries suffered at the hands of Nazi gangsters.*

Meanwhile, of course, every court and tribunal—from Germany's Supreme Court on down—had been purged of all anti-Nazis and stuffed with rabid party supporters. Knowledge of law and personal integrity were the last qualities to serve as requirements. Nazi "justice" was a depraved and brutal mockery of the very word. The only law that remained in Germany was the law of terrorism, execution, and enslavement.

The Bolsheviks had started in much the same fashion and proceeded in much the same way. The totalitarian disdain, even hatred, of the legal rights of individual citizens is identical whether Fascist or Communist. When the Communists began to seize power in the eastern European countries at the end of the late war their tactics followed a common pattern of perversion of the law and the authorities on which it rests:

1. A Communist in command of the Ministry of Interior which in Europe controls all branches of the police.

2. A Communist as Minister of Justice, which subjects the courts to Communist domination.

3. Communist control of the Army high command.

These co-ordinated controls took over successively in Poland, Yugoslavia, Albania, Bulgaria, Rumania, and Hungary. With the police, the courts, and the Army first purged and then flooded by Communists, the law was entirely at their mercy. Every citizen was chained by the "new legality," which suppressed all fundamental rights and liberties.

The procedure of the Reds in Czechoslovakia was perhaps most revealing because that country was more pro-

* Cf. ibid.

foundly democratic than any of its neighbors. Here Stalin's henchmen were up against people who understood parliamentary freedom and the full realities of citizens' legal rights. How did the Communists proceed in their Czech coup of February 1948?

The Czech Communists violated their country's laws from the outset. They had formed secret and illegal "action committees"—in all governmental and municipal departments, in shops and factories as well. At a given signal the Communist "action committees" took over the various ministries in the Prague government, besides the provincial and municipal administrations, and proclaimed themselves the managers of all industrial and other enterprises. In less than a month no Czech could participate in a political party of the so-called National Front without permission from the Central Action Committee. The action committees were merely another name for the soviets that were formed in cities and villages during Russia's Bolshevik revolution. The Czech parliament, suddenly become a puppet of the Communists, promptly passed legislation legalizing the action committees. That was one of the first steps in the destruction of law in Czechoslovakia and its replacement by fake totalitarian legalism.

The Czech Communists, in exact conformity with Hitler's Fascists, immediately set up Emergency People's Tribunals to purge and punish all anti-Red citizens of any influence or importance. Antonin Zapotocky, the new Communist Premier, announced a complete overhauling of the legal and judicial system "to wipe out the last traces of capitalistic law." The Communist Minister of Justice declared: "The courts will have the power to crush and destroy every center of reaction and treason without a long discussion."

From the late spring of 1947 onward the Red dictators clamped down with increasing ruthlessness in Hungary, Rumania, Bulgaria, and elsewhere. Many thousands of citizens were arrested, often on the strength of anonymous denunciations of a most questionable nature. They seldom knew what charges were made against them, yet frequently remained jailed indefinitely. Thousands of persons simply disappeared; their families were never able to discover what had happened to them. Thousands of others were given heavy sentences. Tens of thousands of men and women were deprived of all opportunity to work or practice their professions, on the ground that they were "politically unreliable" or "pro-western imperialists." All laws which might have protected such people were abolished or ignored.

In our time, then, we have had repeated and numerous demonstrations of the terrible price that perversion of the law imposes upon entire populations rendered defenseless by dictatorship. But in any nation undermining of the law exists either as a temptation or as a reality. There is always the danger that the individual citizen's basic rights and freedoms may be curbed or seriously diminished long before totalitarians can complete the process. We can best appreciate this fact by examining—

Certain violations or temptations to pervert the law in the United States.

On March 31, 1948 I happened to be in Columbus, Ohio. The *Evening Dispatch* carried an eight-column headline: RED LEADER'S HOME SMASHED BY MOB.

"Now it is happening here," I said to myself.

On the previous evening about thirty persons had invaded and plundered a frame house occupied by Frank Hashmall, a Communist organizer. They first hurled rocks through the windows. A crowd of about a thousand "cheered as the door was crashed in" while the Hashmalls were absent. "They cheered as they heard furniture being upset. There was no arrest. The invaders, presumably

warned by the sirens of approaching police cruisers, min-
gled with the crowd." The marauders had scattered after
their first attack. But the police failed to maintain a guard.
The anti-Red hoodlums returned within twenty minutes
and carried out their major destruction, again without a
single arrest.

The milling mob became so ugly that Police Captain
Tibe threatened a "riot act" if they committed further
"depredations." "This is what the Communist people
want," said Captain Tibe. Police Chief Berry later declared: "I have never condoned violence in any form and I
will not in the future. The whole incident is most regrettable." Even so, the police had failed seriously, both to prevent the mob assault and to apprehend the culprits.

The *Ohio State Journal* reported:

> Two patrolmen were heard discussing the raid after-
> wards. The first one asked:
> "They didn't catch anybody, did they?"
> "No. I don't think so," said the second policeman.
> *"Anyway, I hope not."*
> "I hope not, too." [Italics mine.]

This same attitude on the part of those entrusted to
maintain public order has paved the way for Fascism or
Communism in many different countries.

According to the *Ohio State Journal* of that date, the
sheriff and public prosecutor of Columbus were to confer
"on what steps can be taken to declare Hashmall a public
menace and compel him to leave town." Apparently that
extraordinary and illegal step was not taken. But the fact
that supposedly responsible public officials could consider
the idea is a sufficient warning. The Columbus anti-Red
riot revealed how Americans can be incited into breaking
the very laws that offer us our first protection against Communism. The ramparts we must watch above all others
are—the Law.

In Indiana a mob attacked a Wallace third-party meeting early in 1948. A different kind of policeman remarked:
"It looks to me as though the people outside are doing
what they are accusing the people inside of doing."

That is precisely where our fidelity to democratic practices either meets the acid test or is belied by our attitude
and actions. We can never successfully resist or defeat
either Communism or Fascism by acting like Reds and
Fascists. We cannot defend the law by violently and recklessly taking the lead in its destruction. A Columbus
editor assured me that "probably some seventy or eighty
per cent" of that fine city's citizens would secretly approve
of the anti-Communist mob's housebreaking assault. If
his judgment is as accurate as an experienced editor's should
be on such a local event, we must wonder how much similar sentiment might easily be whipped up in countless
cities and towns throughout the United States.

Opposition to mob violence is a first defense
of our civil liberties and democracy.

Those who assaulted Henry A. Wallace with eggs,
tomatoes, and other missiles in several different localities
during the 1948 Presidential campaign were in no sense
acting as Americans. They acted as Fascists acted in Italy
and Germany. In the Iron Curtain countries Communist
intimidators often indulge in similar gangsterism. Mobs
that seek to deny freedom of speech to others are, in fact,
much more anti-democratic than a Communist on a soap-
box in any city square. While professing to combat Communism or some viewpoint diametrically opposite to their
own they introduce totalitarian methods. We cannot participate in mob rule, nor tolerate or condone it, without
helping to destroy our own personal freedoms and the
foundations on which a free, self-governing society rests.

This is what the anti-Red rioters have done in Columbus, Houston, and other communities.

For a country of our great size and diversity, and despite occasional shameful exceptions, the United States has been remarkably free from explosions of mob violence in recent years. The South, to its great credit, has also made notable progress in reducing the occurrence of lynchings. But anti-Red sentiments have been dangerously inflamed since the war ended. Their intensity has precipitated a series of mob assaults that should serve as a sharp warning. We have a Right-wing fringe highly susceptible to Fascist ideas and actions. If such persons continue to take the law into their own hands they can poison our national life and undermine our democratic institutions more destructively than plotting Red agents can do. For Communism thrives on mob oppressions and injustices. Violence inevitably breeds counter-violence. This can never be the path toward internal security. It leads to spasmodic and increasing civil conflict throughout the nation.

The strength of our free society depends upon the continued preservation of those civil liberties which the law assures to all U.S. citizens, regardless of their personal or political convictions. Precisely because the Communist and Fascist ideologies are so challenging—and because we, the middle majority, stand in between—we need desperately to have these civil liberties reinforced and extended. To discredit and reduce them would be to expose our way of life to dominance by one form of totalitarianism or another.

This is why President Truman's civil-rights program should rightfully be regarded as a needed contribution to our national defense. It is a necessary and urgent subject for Congressional action because our democracy requires the maximum inner strength it can develop. American Negroes and other minorities have every right to expect our form of government to eliminate those grievous injustices from which they still suffer. A small but very influential number of our Negroes have already been won to Communism because it seems to offer them much greater freedom than they now enjoy. If we do not make much more practical progress in relieving all our minorities from unjust discriminations, we shall plow the field for Communist growth; in reality we may force perilous numbers among our underprivileged citizens into the ranks of the Lenin-Stalin Marxists. The Soviet Constitution sounds wonderful in many sections when you read it. But many of its most laudable "rights" exist only on paper. For too many millions of Americans this is still true of our own Constitution.

We have readily available, however, the weapons with which to make American democracy invulnerable within our borders. We need only insist upon the maintenance of law and order for all, without favor or exception. We need but defend freedom of speech, freedom of assembly, and all other civil liberties so that all citizens may remain free from intimidation and violence. For what public opinion rejects and condemns overwhelmingly in our separate communities will not long be tolerated by the police and public authorities.

It is true that our present struggle against Communist and Fascist infiltration will persist throughout our lives and probably long afterward. But we have the mighty armor of civil liberties, if we keep that armor strong and buttress it wherever we can. This is something every American can do in his own community. When basic civic rights are violated it is not a question of who the victim is—whether he is a Communist, a Republican, or a Holy Roller—nor whether we agree in the slightest with his opinions. It is a question of protecting *through him* the privileges by which alone you yourself can remain free.

There is a vital role here for Americans who are truly

liberal. And this brings up a matter to which perhaps far too few of us have yet given much consideration. The existence of a small and untrustworthy Communist minority in the United States in no sense justifies American conservatives in attacking, repudiating, or ridiculing American liberals as such. The truth is that—

Courageous and loyal American liberals are
more essential to the defense of U.S.
democracy today than ever before.

There is a necessary and important function for honest conservatives in any democratic system. Such conservatives, without being reactionary, serve as a brake and a balance wheel on many issues. They are often an influence for prudence and moderation. They sometimes keep our most ardent crusading spirits from taking us over the dam with reformist experiments.

But in a predominantly conservative-minded nation like our own we have an equally great need for the watchdogs of sincerely democratic liberalism. Such liberalism is not a monopoly of any one party. In Wendell Willkie the Republicans produced one of the great American liberals of our generation. In general, of course, a majority of liberals are to be found near the center, or to the Left of center. That does not alter their unique value to our democracy. Our liberals are the first to fight against injustices and inequities in our society. They have always been our most effective defenders of civil liberties and of a multitude of measures that preserved or improved our basic freedoms. American liberals also serve as an indispensable balancing force in our democracy. Their enlightened and progressive influence is exceptionally essential today. For the essence of true liberalism is to defend the rights and interests of the common man, the very middle men upon whom our ideology and system chiefly depend.

It is an alarming development when conservative Americans tend, as so many at present do, to denounce all liberals as "Communistic" or "fellow travelers." This attitude imitates the extremism of Fascists and Communists alike. It is not only a gross distortion of the truth. It is the emotional and demagogic device of blanketing all those who happen to disagree with you into a single convenient smear-category. In reality it is a form of political blackmail—and the totalitarians employ it unscrupulously to discredit and destroy all opposition. They also employ it knowingly to stifle a free expression of opinion.

Since the Soviet-Communist issues became clear we have had abundant proof from such American liberals as Mrs. Eleanor Roosevelt, Harold L. Ickes, Chester Bowles, and a great many others (all formerly warm supporters of the New Deal) that they cannot and do not tolerate totalitarian methods and oppression by Communists or any other extremists. As our 1948 elections demonstrated, many millions of their fellow citizens are liberals in exactly the same manner. They are convinced progressives who have defended, and continue to defend, our freedoms and our form of government at all costs. They have rendered, and continue to render, inestimable services to our country. To denounce such liberals as "Communistic" or to insinuate that they are stooges of Moscow's Marxism is more than an unpardonable calumny. It is the same type of reckless distortion that Communists and Fascists employ in order to divide a national society so deeply that it can fall a prey to their designs.

The United States needs the voice of a courageous and socially conscious liberalism today quite as much as it needs an intelligent, responsible conservatism. We need both if we are to hope to reach those compromises by which our embattled, capitalistic democracy can alone endure. If it is a badge of honor to be an enlightened and moderate conservative, it is certainly as great a badge of honor to be an unswerving and courageous liberal in the finest sense of our American tradition. Our true liberals will never be cowed into silence by irresponsible and utterly unjust accusations of being "fellow travelers." The road they travel and defend is the road of self-government, free discussion, and human rights. They serve the best interests of us all when they stick to this road of progress toward more democracy.

In the years immediately ahead we shall have exceptional need of progressive leadership in our national life, and equally of the balance wheel of moderate conservatism. We cannot find safety without respect for the opinions of others quite as much as for the privilege of expressing our own. We shall need the self-discipline of adult citizens who can disagree without resorting to vituperation and libel. More than ever we shall need free discussion and debate, with renunciation of hysteria and of indiscriminate tarring and labeling of those whose opinions differ considerably from our own. But without a firm adherence to our civil liberties and democratic freedoms these things will be impossible. We cannot contradict ourselves and suppress our basic rights without opening the door to suppression of—ourselves.

Perhaps it is from this viewpoint that we would be prudent to consider:

The various demands to outlaw the Communist Party.

The crossfires of totalitarianism have brought us to a serious and perplexing quandary. Most of us believe wholeheartedly in the broad principle of freedom of political expression in the United States. Yet we find ourselves up against a question aptly expressed by the *New York Herald Tribune*: "How can a democratic majority defend itself against a militant, ruthless minority which has no respect for democratic processes but merely takes advantage of them so that it may destroy them? . . . A legitimate and effective defense must be found, and that is one of the primary tasks of democracy today."

Certainly there can be no easy answer to this extremely complex problem. The bitterest enemies of democracy consistently exploit its privileges in order to destroy them. Yet we cannot ourselves reduce democratic freedoms to a mockery by depriving this or that category of citizens of the very principles we claim to defend.

In search of such a defense the House of Representatives first passed the much-disputed Mundt-Nixon "Communist Control" bill by 319 to 58 votes in May 1948. This marked merely the opening stage of a prolonged and bitter debate. The bill itself revealed the great complexities of the problem to which it was addressed. Without outlawing the Communist Party it would impose heavy penalties for working or conspiring for establishment of a foreign-controlled totalitarian government in the United States, bar Communists from federal jobs, and deny passports to Communists. Other provisions in the bill raised delicate questions of definition and of individual rights.

Communist organizations and "Communist front" groups would be required to register with the Attorney General, whose office would decide what groups should be so considered. Such organizations would have to report their finances, the addresses of their leaders, and, if outright Communist, to supply membership lists. But the inclusion of "Communist front" groups opened the door to possible abuses and serious injustices. On what precise basis could it be decided that this committee or that was subversive or Communist-dominated? The Attorney General was supposed to grant a hearing, but he, a single individual, would have the power to stigmatize entire groups of citizens in a manner that might be damaging to their very ability to earn a living. Control of Communists by legislation immediately raised many threats to the civic liberties of individual citizens.

This was true to such an extent that a Washington correspondent of the *New York Times* reported: "Alarm over the implications of the Mundt-Nixon bill is widespread in Washington, and without regard to party or ideological grounds. . . . The definition of subversive activity is so inclusive that a literal reign of terror against all liberal or dissident groups would become possible." * *Time* (May 31, 1948) concluded by saying: "It seemed very doubtful whether the bill was workable and enforceable—and would achieve its aim." To impose certain restrictions and registration upon definitely confirmed Communist groups that sponsored a "foreign-controlled" totalitarian regime in the United States might be made legal. (If so, why not also any political groups that might favor an "American-controlled" totalitarianism? Is dictatorship any less destructive if home-grown and home-fed?) But to grant any small group of officials the power to make their own interpretation of what is "subversive" could not fail to invite dangerous abuses. "Subversive" means whatever the person who uses the term wishes it to mean. In recent times it has been applied indiscriminately to the late Harry Hopkins, Harold L. Ickes, Miss Frances Perkins, David E. Lilienthal, and a host of New Dealers, liberals, and progressives.

J. Edgar Hoover, director of the FBI, had placed the total membership of the U.S. Communist Party at 74,000 in the same month in which the Mundt-Nixon bill was first debated. As a result Congress granted Hoover's request for $35,000,000 for FBI operations in the following fiscal year. This was certainly a sum large enough to permit an impressive amount of police surveillance of 74,000 party members. Legislation that would permit serious discriminations against far greater numbers of non-Com-

* *New York Times*, May 22, 1948.

munist liberals or possible oppression of them could not
fail to violate or undermine important American civic
liberties—a vital segment of our traditional law.

Factors such as this were the essence of a debate between
Thomas E. Dewey and Harold A. Stassen as rival candidates for the Republican Presidential nomination. Should
the Communist Party be outlawed? Governor Dewey insisted that we could not drive the Communists underground politically without violating our basic principles.
He rejected such "easy panaceas" as "nothing but the
methods of Hitler and Stalin. . . . Thought control, borrowed from the Japanese." It was encouraging that most
Americans, perturbed but thoughtful, seemed to agree
with this viewpoint. Indeed, the Canadians had already
tried to outlaw their Communist Party—and Canada's
Reds responded by taking cover under a convenient bit
of camouflage. It was called, as if foreshadowing a decision
of the campaign managers of Henry A. Wallace, the Labor
Progressive Party.

Agitation to outlaw the U.S. Communist Party continues. Under certain conditions it might seem successful.
Yet such a step would merely make it much more difficult
to keep Communists at least partially "out in the day-
light" where they can be observed, heard, and guarded
against. Meanwhile the political freedoms of all Americans
would have been reduced and violated at a considerable
risk. *No law that suppresses freedom of speech or of
thought can promote respect for law.* "I wholly disapprove
of what you say," wrote Voltaire, "and will defend to the
death your right to say it." It is this great democratic
principle that Communists and Fascists seek to destroy.
Difficult as it is to tolerate their grave abuse of that priceless privilege, it is the obligation of free men and free
societies to preserve the inexpendable law that keeps them
free.

When twelve U.S. Communist leaders were indicted, it

is important to note that this action was not taken because of their political affiliation. They were charged with having conspired to overthrow the government of the United States by force. The law covered such an offense. The central question of the ensuing trial was whether the prosecution could produce adequate evidence to substantiate its charges. This made the case of the "Red twelve" of unusual significance. But they did not go to trial because they were Communists, nor was their right of free speech challenged in any way. It was the obligation of government attorneys to prove that the Communists "conspired" to resort eventually to "force" against our system. The question remained: how much could be done, if anything, to limit the activities of Communists as a political party?

How can democracy-in-crisis defend the Law?

This depends in large measure, of course, upon the attitude of a majority of the citizens, in the United States or in any self-governing society. You might say it depends upon the collective democratic conscience, its strength or its weakness. Mass hysteria and a prevailing "witch-hunt" psychology are obvious menaces to the maintenance of normal civil rights and legal protections. Hate groups, inciting ignorant people to vengeful actions against minorities, are as treasonably anti-democratic as rabidly revolutionary Communists can be. Police who fail to afford all citizens, regardless of their politics, race, or creed, equal protection from mob violence help to destroy the very law that they are employed to serve. But it is possible for average citizens to contribute quite unconsciously to this process of disintegration.

Freedom of speech is a tremendous thing. It covers every avenue of information: the press, radio and television, motion pictures, the publication of books, and much else.

Freedom of information certainly constitutes one of the most vital aspects of that law which, until now, has kept the United States a free society. Yet this freedom is never safe from infringement and attack. We are amply justified in denouncing the censorship of totalitarian regimes, Red or Black. Even so, the tendency to suppress and to censor constantly threatens our Constitutional privileges under the law.

Within the space of a few weeks in New York City this type of pressure was manifested from quite opposite quarters. Communists picketed a theater where a film based upon the Canadian Red spy case was being shown. The Catholic War Veterans attempted to dissuade the management of a chain of theaters from exhibiting the Charles Chaplin picture *Monsieur Verdoux*. In the latter case objection was not made to the motion picture itself, but to Chaplin's failure to become a citizen of the United States. A spokesman was quoted as saying: "He calls himself a citizen of the world—a typical Communistic statement." Socrates, Seneca, and Thomas Paine had all called themselves citizens of the world, as indeed they were.

In any democratic society the law, beginning with freedom of information and speech, is first undermined by seemingly small repressions. They remind one of Huey Long's brutally cynical promise: "Hell, no. I won't censor the press. When you've got enough power the newspapers will do it themselves!" It is, in fact, *where we censor ourselves*—through one pressure group or another—that one of democracy's major defenses is slowly undermined.

Speaking at the annual conference of the American Library Association, Paul North Rice, chief of the reference department in the New York Public Library, recently warned that our intellectual freedom is being imperiled in many ways in many localities. He was concerned about instances of censorship of books in public libraries. Mr. Rice said:

Should a religious minority be allowed to keep off the shelves of a library a biography of their founder which does not depict her as they feel she should be depicted? Should copies of *The Nation* ever be removed from library shelves? Should libraries in the South fail to have current books on the race problem? Should witch hunts for subversive books persuade librarians not to stock a book because it is friendly to Russia or a Communistic idea? The answer to all these questions is, of course, an emphatic no.*

The American Library Association was so alarmed over the recent growth of censorship that it drew up a "library's bill of rights" to be acted upon by its full membership. This bill insists that "books or other reading matter should not be proscribed or removed from library shelves because of controversial or doctrinal disapproval." When the Nazis burned great heaps of books, Americans expressed their revulsion and indignation. Pressure-group censorship, of whatever origin, is merely a more insidious way of burning books or magazines.

What we need most urgently to defend and preserve in a democracy are all those manifestations of the law which Communists and Fascists always destroy as quickly as possible. These essential freedoms are so simple and ordinary, for the most part, that many of us may betray them ourselves, inadvertently or by prejudice—freedom of information, freedom of speech, freedom of assembly, freedom of political convictions, the legal sanctity of the home and of property, protection of the individual citizen from violence, the legal rights of labor, the legal rights of free enterprise, freedom of religion. These are all great privileges which totalitarians, Left-wing or Right-wing, seek consecutively to suppress and destroy. They are indispensable features of the law in free societies. For that reason they must be broken down and abolished or dictatorship cannot be imposed and maintained.

* *New York Times,* June 14, 1948.

We live in a period of intense anti-democratic offensive. What is Communist or Fascist is definitely "subversive" to our way of life. But whatever is subversive to preservation of our essential freedoms—to the Law in our American democracy—weakens our society equally, from whatever quarter it may come. That is why the American people must understand that the Law is truly their first defense. To keep it strong it must be defended by an alert, comprehending majority of our citizens in every field, on every issue, wherever the freedom of our minds and our persons threatens to be diminished or denied. This is where the issue is joined every day in countless ways, little or big. This is where the issue ultimately will be decided—whether the Law of our traditional freedoms remains uncorrupted and inviolate, or is replaced by the brutal mockery of totalitarian substitutes.

Chapter X

THE PERILS OF "SECURITY"

How can we obtain adequate physical security in the atomic age without seriously undermining our traditional individual freedoms and without destroying some of our most essential civil rights?

This is the grave and perplexing problem posed for all Americans by the existence of atomic weapons. It also constitutes an ironic paradox which cannot be sidestepped. For if the United States still enjoys a monopoly on possession and production of the bomb, we are equally the political and social victims of its consequences. The American way of life is in no slightest degree immune to its anti-libertarian effects.

The atomic bomb is not only a physical menace to the whole world, including the nation that guards it jealously. It is likewise either an immediate or a prospective menace to the legal protections and the civic liberties of every United States citizen. This is true because the bomb itself, by its very nature, is an uncompromising enemy of the ideals, institutions, and privileges of a free society. To adjust its requirements and implications to the framework and customs of our American democracy involves deep and disturbing contradictions.

Our quandary originates in the simple fact that the atomic bomb is the most perfect totalitarian instrument yet devised by man.

Even though it was produced by free men in a democratic nation, the A-bomb is pure terror and dictatorship.

Because it is so completely anti-democratic you might call
it the perfect instrument of both Communism and Fascism. Certainly it is the ideal physical expression of the
totalitarian concept. Dominance in atomic rockets and
other missiles means world dominance through terror or
through forceful intimidation. Give any police state a clear
superiority in such weapons and it will immediately be
capable of imposing a World Police State. This is what
American industrial and technical genius produced, under
the curious impression that it was defending human freedom.

The awe-inspiring mushrooms of atomic chain reaction
not only have spread fear around the rest of the world,
but have also spread hitherto unknown fears throughout
the United States. Although the productive know-how still
remains almost exclusively our own, the A-bomb dictator
has already distorted and radically altered our accustomed
procedures in federal employment, scientific research,
and some branches of industry. These changes have been
more drastic because the Communist ideology offers a
major challenge in the new atomic age. Totalitarians are
bound to have an exceptional interest in history's greatest
totalitarian weapon. But in a free society like our own, it
imposes a revolutionary change in governmental and police procedures.

Since the advent of the atomic bomb the United States
government has been compelled to seek a new definition
and revised interpretations of national and federal security. But we cannot redefine security and revise security
precautions without creating new pressures upon the individual rights—in other words, the *personal* security—of
ordinary citizens. This is where the inauguration of loyalty
tests has great significance for each of us. If you have any
interest in voting as you please, in reading whatever publications you desire, in having whatever associations may
suit your taste or curiosity, or in voicing your political

opinions without fear or reservation, then our current experiment with loyalty check-ups has a personal meaning for you. It impinges or threatens to impinge upon your civil rights and interests, as upon those of every individual American. How, indeed, can we get more security in a period of competition in atomic armaments and Communist or Fascist espionage without paying for it an exorbitant and dangerous price in the reduction of our personal freedoms?

We have rapidly become obliged to recognize that—

Loyalty tests are a serious, long-term challenge to democratic American liberties.

Since the tests were instituted, the Federal Bureau of Investigation has fingerprinted and checked more than 2,100,000 federal employees. A full screening was decided upon for 6,344 of them. By September 1948 five sixths of these cases had been completed, and during the investigations 619 employees had resigned. The percentage of possibly disloyal persons in our federal civil service had been found, gratifyingly, to be extremely small. But some of the early procedures and decisions of the loyalty boards in various federal agencies had raised grave questions about adequate protection of the civil liberties and Constitutional rights of free American citizens. It was certainly not intended that those who work for our government agencies should be penalized and deprived of certain basic privileges that all other Americans enjoy under the Bill of Rights. Yet this is what was allowed to happen, and has continued to happen in many instances since then.

We rightfully repudiate and frequently denounce many specific practices and abuses that are common under Communist or Fascist systems of totalitarianism. Any Soviet employee, for instance, can be dismissed on the basis of unspecified charges the exact nature of which he is not permitted to know. If he is brought before an examining board or given a hearing of some kind, it may happen that he is not allowed to have legal counsel or even to question witnesses who testify against him. As a Soviet citizen he may also be denied the right to appeal his case to higher authorities. In a totalitarian system, Communist or Fascist, either most of these vital protective rights are at the discretion of some suspicious party bureaucrat or they do not exist. That is part of what it means to live in a police state.

Yet each of these individual rights, long established in the United States, was denied in various cases when ten State Department employees were dismissed summarily in 1947. None of the ten was informed of the nature of the charges made against them. None of the ten was granted the right to appeal, or provided with the alleged facts upon which he might have based an appeal. They were victims of the same type of anonymous denunciation that was rampant in Mussolini's Italy and Hitler's Germany and is still rampant in the Soviet Union and in the satellite countries under Communist control.

Although they had no means of defending their record and reputations, only three of the State Department's dismissed ten were at first permitted to resign "without prejudice." Had it not been for alert and courageous newspaper reporters, the remaining seven would have been seriously handicapped in gaining employment because of a permanent black mark for alleged, although completely unproved, disloyalty. Bert Andrews, Washington correspondent of the *New York Herald Tribune,* rendered a national service that won him a merited Pulitzer award by putting the facts of the State Department's anti-democratic procedure in public print. The remaining seven employees were finally allowed to resign "without prejudice," but the State Department's first attempt to apply a yardstick of loyalty had disclosed shocking abuses of fundamental legal rights presumably enjoyed by all United States citizens.

The Loyalty Review Board, under Seth W. Richardson as chairman, made a commendable attempt to prevent repetition of the most flagrant abuses revealed in the case of the State Department ten. It ruled that a "detailed identification of the facts" on which loyalty was being questioned would be given each suspected employee; that a "proper hearing" would be required, with counsel and witnesses available to the employee; and his right of appeal was thereafter established. But there were certain glaring and dangerous omissions. In the "great majority of cases" an accused employee would not be allowed to see the alleged evidence or accusations in the FBI file of his case. He would still be denied the right of confrontation, and so could not face his anonymous accusers. He could not cross-examine them. All this, of course, is contrary to the universal privileges of citizens in any U.S. court.

These serious limitations aroused great anxiety among members of the Loyalty Review Board, particularly the denial of the right of cross-examination. Chairman Richardson admitted that the FBI had insisted that its sources of information must be kept "entirely confidential"; that it could not function if the identity of its informants were not protected. This viewpoint of the FBI, however typical of secret-police organizations, can be argued lengthily pro and con; but the consequences of the FBI restrictions cannot be argued. For the first time a large and important portion of American citizens is exposed to the irresponsibility and injustice of secret denunciations. Secret denunciations of any one among more than 2,100,000 federal employees could occur thereafter as readily as in Soviet Russia, in Franco's Spain, or in any other police state.

When those who go to the secret police to denounce and

accuse know they will be protected by complete anonymity they usually feel free to make the most sweeping charges, often farfetched and based on hearsay. Crackpots, fanatics, and persons with private grudges are much more likely to write letters to the FBI than responsible citizens with a scrupulous regard for facts. Yet the positions of countless patriotic and reliable federal employees can be endangered, their reputations damaged, and in some cases their livelihood menaced. This has already happened to a regrettable number of federal employees and of scientists on atomic projects simply because they have been deprived of certain basic civic rights. These are the rights that assure us full protection under due process of the law. *Wherever due process is denied, the door has been opened to totalitarian discrimination and repression.*

We are in this critical and risky situation because of the necessity for atomic secrecy and because of the dangers of Communist infiltration in governmental agencies and of Communist spying. These dangers would be equally great if either a foreign or a native Fascism ever develops a fanatical following, even though small, among our population. As for the present and immediate future, however, the Communists' methods have been established far too definitely and clearly to be overlooked. This raises two closely related questions:

How much security does the average American want? And how much can he afford to sacrifice in the name of increased national security?

As a nation we are strongly united in our rejection of totalitarian ideologies and concepts. We do not trust dictatorships or persons who defend or give their allegiance to dictatorial systems. We are overwhelmingly in agreement that our governmental departments, our federal agencies, our atomic projects, and our armed services must be kept free of Communists or near Communists—and of Fascists or near Fascists. The Red spy case in Canada and the Red spy testimony in Washington have made us acutely aware of the problem of infiltration and fifth-columnists. Consequently we approve emphatically of Washington's objective of reinforcing all sections of the government against subversive activities. We want the security of knowing that effective, legal and tolerable precautions are being taken to prevent espionage or betrayals inside our government. We want the security of a federal system, operated and staffed by dependable and loyal personnel— for tomorrow quite as much as for today.

Quite probably the average American is willing to leave it at that and say that the rest is up to Washington. But we have already had numerous sharp reminders that the means of achieving internal security, in a time of atomic weapons and totalitarian conspiracy, are infinitely more complex than the end itself. Apparently the ordinary citizen cannot get greater security in his government without making certain contributions and certain sacrifices of his own. Loyalty tests have been established and laws that attempt to deal with Communist subversion are very likely to be adopted. More specific legal definitions of treason are also to be expected. In each case the traditional rights and privileges of all Americans are involved. It then becomes a matter of how much the average American is asked to sacrifice—and how much he can *afford* to sacrifice —of his personal protection under the law and of those individual freedoms and privileges that have remained inalienably his until now.

We are confronted by a security dilemma, which expresses itself in difficult ways. Can we get a treason-proof and infiltration-proof governmental personnel without undermining or destroying some of the most essential rights of citizens? Can we find means to keep the necessary role of our secret police within assured democratic limits and controls? Can we devise more effective protections against espionage and totalitarian movements without falling into some of the most notorious abuses of the totalitarian police states? How can loyalty-test procedures be safely confined within the vital principles of our Bill of Rights?

All this might be summed up by saying that our dilemma of internal security is a dilemma—and a formidable one—precisely because it involves values that are directly opposed to each other and in many respects highly contradictory. In an ideologically warring world how can we reconcile public security with the individual's democratic freedoms? Even if it were possible to obtain absolute public security, at how great a price would it have to be bought? At how drastic a diminution of the average citizen's freedom of association and his right to dissent? There is a profound conflict here between opposing aspirations. For our desire for internal security conflicts with many of our most cherished individual rights. It also conflicts with our conception of justice for the common man and our firm belief in every citizen's right to a fair trial.

In the past year or two we have seen many instances of this conflict between security and justice, and between security and the civil rights of individuals. In its vigorous probing of Red spy activities, both real and rumored, the House Committee on Un-American Activities provided the opportunity for slanderous and unsubstantiated accusations against officials with distinguished records as public servants, as well as against many minor employees who had much less possibility of defending their reputations. Miss Elizabeth Bentley, a self-confessed agent for a wartime Communist spy ring, was, for headline purposes, a sensational witness. She failed completely to link Lauchlin Currie, an aide to President Roosevelt, or Harry White, of the Treasury Department, to the espionage contact men whom she glibly described. Under the procedures of the

Thomas committee these able and widely esteemed officials had no fair and reasonable means of defending themselves from reckless insinuations and defamation. Currie was well within his Constitutional rights when he declared: "I am outraged that my reputation, built upon many years of public service, should be attacked by this apparently neurotic woman who has no shred of evidence to support her irresponsible charges. I deny emphatically each and all of her charges." White died from a heart condition which was aggravated fatally by the strain of the hearings to which he had been subjected.

The efforts of the House Un-American Activities Committee to uncover Communist espionage activities were entirely laudable in their objective, but they degenerated again and again into character assassination and violation of basic rights of United States citizens. *When any individual American is deprived of the fullest opportunity to defend himself, what kind of "security" is taking shape in our land?*

The experience of the noted and widely respected atomic scientist Dr. Edward U. Condon demonstrated that this question is posed for all of us. In the late spring of 1947 the Un-American Activities Committee released a report making serious insinuations against the loyalty of Dr. Condon. It conducted a bitter campaign to prevent his continuing in his position as director of the National Bureau of Standards. He was accused of being, "knowingly or unknowingly," an associate of "alleged Soviet espionage agents." All the charges made against him were based upon nothing more specific than association. It was said that Dr. Condon occasionally saw one or two persons among his wide circle of acquaintances who might be "politically unreliable" or "Communistic"; that he had once served among the sponsors of a Southern Conference for Human Welfare dinner, an organization described as "Red"; that his wife was "foreign born" (which was untrue); that his name had been used in a letter soliciting members for the American-Soviet Science Society, which specialized in furnishing translations of Russian scientific papers to American research workers.

During the war Dr. Condon had known a great number of our top atomic secrets and had never divulged an inkling of them. This was fact rather than assumption. But the House Committee chose to ignore his distinguished wartime record, and it disregarded the unanimous character endorsement of Dr. Condon by leading scientists who worked closely with him during the war. In addition its members committed a flagrant and indefensible injustice. When he appealed for an opportunity to appear before the committee and to "help in any way to answer any questions they might have," the Un-American specialists—in a most un-American manner—ignored his appeal. In July 1948 the Atomic Energy Commission ruled that Dr. Condon's loyalty was "unquestionable" on the basis of two extremely detailed FBI investigations. But even after a full year this eminent scientist, who had contributed much to the success of the bomb, was still denied the right to defend his reputation before the Congressional group that had pilloried and slandered him.

The *Bulletin of the Atomic Scientists* acidly remarked in the August 1948 issue: "We seem to recall that this House Committee has *the practice of never stating clearly that a man they have investigated has proved his innocence;* but drops the investigation if it becomes 'unprofitable,' leaving lingering suspicions. But what of younger and less prominent scientists . . . in a similar predicament? . . . The civil rights of American scientists will not be assured until not only a man as prominent as Dr. Condon but also the youngest graduate . . . will be certain he will not be subject to defamation and threatened in his livelihood *without evidence other than malicious gossip or hearsay.*" (Italics mine.)

Because the FBI refused to reveal the identity of its informers except in minor cases, and because the Loyalty Review Board against its better judgment accepted this stipulation, our government's search for public security has greatly increased the *individual insecurity* of many Americans. In particular a serious situation was provoked in regard to atomic scientists. Owing to the methods on which they are based—

Loyalty probes threaten, unnecessarily, to undermine the progress and over-all success of U.S. atomic projects.

Exposure to secret denunciations, often based on nothing more than malicious gossip and hearsay, have driven large numbers of virtually irreplaceable atomic specialists from government projects concerned with military weapons and defense. By May 1948 one third of the sixty senior physicists and chemists at the Oak Ridge atomic plants had resigned, and others planned to do so. Two atomic scientists had been suspended at Oak Ridge, three others had been called before a loyalty board, and nearly thirty other cases were scheduled to be heard. The charges consisted of *"anonymous* accusations of Communist leanings." The *New York Herald Tribune* reported (May 18, 19, and 29, 1948) "a state of acute apprehension," causing many to fear "that the outcome is likely to be the annihilation of Oak Ridge as a major contributor to atomic energy research." This situation could scarcely be called an advance in America's atomic security.

The Oak Ridge scientists had simply reacted as all Americans whose professional standing and reputation are indiscriminately attacked would react. They had accepted real financial sacrifices to serve their government. Many had declined brilliant opportunities in universities or industry to do so. Now they themselves or associates whom they respected and trusted were branded as unreliable for such reasons as these: "A neighbor has stated that she believes a close relative by marriage is a Communist." A landlord says that certain magazines "which may have been left on the premises by you may have included a copy of the [Communist] *New Masses*." A close relative by marriage was the editor of a newspaper "which has been reported to have had pro-Communist leanings." It was not surprising that only eleven per cent of 576 U.S. scientists, in answer to a questionnaire, stated that they preferred work in the federal government. But if only some eleven per cent of our scientists (and these certainly considerably below the general average) should hereafter accept such posts, how much additional "atomic security" will the United States be getting as a dividend from loyalty tests?

President Truman was fully justified in warning that scientific work "indispensable" for our national security "may be made impossible by the creation of an atmosphere in which no man feels safe against the public airing of unfounded rumors, gossip and vilification. Such an atmosphere is Un-American, the most Un-American thing we have to contend with today. It is the climate of a totalitarian country in which scientists are expected to change their theories to match changes in the police state's propaganda line."

The root of the trouble had originated in the FBI-imposed secrecy of the denunciations used in the loyalty-test program—a program adopted under the Truman administration by a board appointed by the President himself. A critical situation had been provoked by depriving two important categories of Americans of Constitutional rights. A double standard of civic rights and privileges always exists in a Fascist or Communist state, since party members and leaders always benefit by being above the general law. In a democracy any introduction of a double standard under the law becomes intolerable and an eventual menace to every citizen.

If the average American did not yet see this clearly, he might suddenly grasp its import in a period of internal turmoil or of extreme international crisis. For the police states have already demonstrated there is no end to where loyalty investigations and security precautions may lead. In a time of pronounced tension both radio and press could become subjects for security measures. So could all the members of the teaching profession. So could all workers in any industry remotely connected with national defense. If our present loyalty tests were extended to several of these professions or occupations the entire United States would become a happy hunting ground for anonymous denouncers, often motivated by aims far less commendable than patriotism.

The abuses under the loyalty program are but one aspect of the crisis mentality that has agitated Americans increasingly since the war ended and the "cold war" began. In reality our sudden exposure to a prolonged international crisis, that with Soviet Russia, has transformed the crisis mentality into a witch-hunt psychology and anti-Red hysteria on the part of many Americans. Here, too, our justified desire for greater internal security has come into conflict with basic rights that must be maintained if our democratic freedoms are to be preserved. The American way, above all, is a middle way. When any considerable proportion of our people yield to angry and violent extremism, we no longer rely upon legal protections and objective justice. Instead, millions of our citizens are caught in between and lashed by emotionalism, prejudice, and mounting fear. Perhaps there is yet time to ask a pertinent question:

*How much security have Red witch-hunts
provided? What other consequences
do they have?*

The declared objective of the Un-American Activities Committee's investigation of Hollywood was to purge our films of alleged Communist propaganda. The supernationalist *Chicago Tribune* jubilantly promised a "sizzling report." Presumably the committee would unearth "scenes skillfully interpolated in certain motion pictures" calculated "to stimulate disrespect, contempt, even hatred for the American capitalistic system." Also scenes "to arouse ill-feeling against *nationalists* [italics mine] and those expressing doubt in the efficacy of the United Nations or in the good faith of Soviet Russia."

But what the "Un-American" specialists failed notoriously to do was to produce any factual and valid examples of either pro-Communist or anti-capitalist propaganda in Hollywood's products. Most Americans were not ready to be convinced that such an outstanding film as *The Best Years of Our Lives* tended to "undermine respect for the American system." Meanwhile ten screen writers, actors, and directors were charged with contempt of Congress when they refused to admit whether or not they belonged to the Communist Party. In any event the committee found no evidence of Red propaganda in the films on which these men had worked, and that was what the Congressional hubbub was presumably all about.

Although no evidence of Communist infiltration was produced, the ten Hollywood executives and writers were suspended or dismissed through a decision of the Motion Picture Association of America. The Hollywood witch-hunt set aside the procedures of law and justice and enthroned intimidation. When cancellations and boycott demonstrations threatened the loss of millions of dollars in business, the movie magnates weakened, beginning with the industry's chief representative, Eric Johnston.

The result of the Un-American Activities Committee's publicity-making foray was not at all greater ideological security in Hollywood productions. They were proved to be already ideologically secure. The results were chiefly negative, aside from the inflaming of public anti-Red emotionalism; and they were all destructive of American democratic practices. Ten citizens were deprived of an opportunity to earn their living in a very specialized profession. They were pilloried for what they *might* believe politically—not for any actions they had taken. It was demonstrated that not all Americans, in civilian employment, have a right to think as they please. They were treated as anti-Nazis were treated under Hitler, and as anti-Communists are treated in the Soviet film industry. In addition, some thirty thousand Hollywood employees became subjected to extreme intimidation of prolonged effect.

Without any procedure that could stand in our courts Congressional witch-hunters had coerced the entire motion-picture industry into self-censorship. But this was also a kind of censorship utterly foreign to American law and practices. As the Authors League of America promptly pointed out, this was censorship of the man himself, not merely of his works. It amounted to "thought-control" as the Japanese war lords practiced it.

Another reprehensible result of the filmland witch-hunt was a "reign of fear" that immediately dominated Hollywood. All film people with a sense of social awareness and responsibility were silenced, quite as much as a few possible Reds or fellow travelers. Gladwin Hill of the *New York Times* reported that the Congressional investigation "has thrown the motion picture industry into a panic, the effects of which will be felt for years." Films containing any social significance would be shelved lest they be considered "Red." Rather than gaining something in ideological security, the vast American movie-going public would be smothered in still greater doses of froth and triviality.

Throughout its 1948 Red spy inquiries in Washington the Un-American Activities Committee seriously discredited its major purpose by its restrictions on the rights of witnesses, by the publicity-seeking actions of some of its members, and by its toleration of irresponsible, character-smearing denunciations of public officials and private citizens. These abuses became so shocking that they boomeranged on the committee itself. One of the first acts of the new Eighty-first Congress in 1949 was to propose new rules governing the conduct of all Congressional committees having the power of subpoena. In large part this trend toward reform and self-discipline was due to the sharp citicism of the most responsible section of the U.S. press and radio, backed by an aroused minority of public opinion.

Despite its damaging and questionable procedures the committee's investigation finally managed to produce real evidence of a prewar Communist espionage ring through the revelations of the case of Whittaker Chambers and Alger Hiss. The microfilms from Chambers's pumpkin were much more than loose talk. The Un-American Activities Committee at last offered something of constructive value for future improvement of governmental and national security. But this development did more than prove that greater protective measures are needed against spy infiltration by Communists or others. It also demonstrated the necessity for the most responsible and judicious investigatory procedures, within Congress or without.

True security cannot be promoted through extremism, the spreading of an atmosphere of suspicion and fear, and the violation of the civil rights of large numbers of citizens. The achievement of security, like the defense of democracy, must come through legal processes and respect for the law. The average American has shown no signs of wanting more security on such an autocratic basis that he cannot hold whatever political opinions he prefers—and still keep his job. Certainly he does not want many of our ablest scientists driven from federal work and our atomic projects jeopardized through extreme measures of this kind. It is highly probable he would prefer that any American's reputation, habits of association, and political convictions be protected by due process of the law.

This raises another question:

What can the average American do about increasing threats to his civil liberties?

Let's get it straight at the outset. If the American middle class understands the dangers of witch-hunts and secret denunciation procedures, it is powerful enough to reduce or prevent them. There can also be no doubt that any Congressional committee has as great an obligation to respect the civil liberties of the people as to defend our national security. If enough of us insist upon justice with security, we can have it.

Actually we have tended to let things slide because we forget that *what we condone* in government policies or Congressional action *is what we get.* John Between, as an ordinary American, has failed to see that he cannot protect *himself* from slander unless he insists that all citizens be given just means to defend their reputations. He has failed to see that he himself cannot remain free indefinitely from secret denunciations unless he opposes the first intrusions of such totalitarian practices into our free society. He has failed to understand that the defense of all freedoms begins wherever the first cracks in the dike appear.

All excesses committed in the name of security can be reduced and corrected by normal democratic processes. The average American resents personal injustice very deeply. When it afflicts him, in his own life and where he

lives, he fights back. But the time to fight back against
violations of basic civil rights is not merely when they hit
you. In a democracy the time to fight back is when such
abusive infringements first develop as a pattern—before
they have become established habits in our national life—
before a double standard of conduct and privileges has
been imposed on different categories of citizens.

As an average American you have an instinctive sense
of justice. You believe in government *by law*. You believe
in the individual's right to read what he likes, to associate
with such persons as suit his preferences or interests, to
hold his own set of political opinions, and to express his
disagreement with others' views. You believe in the value
of civic and community organizations. You believe that
public opinion should be brought to bear upon Congress
and the administration, whether privately or through
group action. Sometimes you even believe in writing a
letter to your Congressman.

These are common beliefs that almost all of us share as
Americans. Translate these beliefs into action—into objec-
tions or recommendations made to your Congressional
representatives and to the White House—and you will
make as lasting a contribution to American security as our
recent Red witch-hunts are likely to make. Our greatest
potential weapon in defense of our civil liberties is available, waiting to be used. That weapon is political action,
and public pressure upon Congress. Senators and Congressmen will always act when an alert and enlightened electorate demands action and reform. *What we don't ask for
we seldom get*—unless it is something we don't want.

If we want a tolerable civilian life in the United States,
we shall have to combat—consciously and consistently—
the tendency to accept the conception of "guilt by association." This is one of the most vicious measuring rods that
have emerged from the loyalty-test experiment. As Lauchlin Currie pointedly observed, "To say that I was engaged

in espionage because I knew men who allegedly were, is like saying I am Chinese because I knew and worked with Chiang Kai-shek." On the presumption of "guilt by association" I suppose all foreign correspondents—and certainly myself—should be regarded as the most suspect citizens in the U.S.A. We have associated with Fascists, Nazis, Communists, and other varieties of totalitarians all over the world. We have read Communist publications as well as all other kinds. When an American scientist is suspect because he has read a Soviet physicists' magazine, we might as logically maintain that a Protestant or a Catholic has secretly embraced Mohammedanism because he read the Koran. There can be no internal security and no middle way in America if we yield to a witch-hunting psychosis such as this.

An eminent American lawyer, John Lord O'Brian, has said:

> In practical effect the result of a finding of such association is analogous to that of a criminal conviction—loss of occupation, lasting disgrace to the individual, and a continued impairment of his ability to earn a livelihood. . . . The inevitable effect of all these so-called loyalty tests *is to place some new degree of constraint upon the thought as well as upon the utterance of the individual.* . . . Surely all may agree that determination of the fate of an individual upon secret evidence constitutes *a grave departure* from our Constitutional theory of the right of the individual. . . . Our great task is to strengthen the faith of our own people, and the people of foreign lands, in our standards of justice and fair play.*

Most of us in the United States want and need a greater faith in democracy. We also want and need a greater faith "in our standards of justice and fair play." But we cannot expect to achieve such strengthened faith unless we resist hysteria and witch-hunts; unless we reject the anti-Amer-

* *Harvard Law Review,* January 1948. Italics mine.

ican idea of "guilt by association"; unless we insist that legal processes alone should assess guilt and that any and all Americans must be regarded as innocent until proved guilty.

It is true that the perils of our security program, and those of past procedures of the House Un-American Activities Committee, are serious and real. But they can be tempered, revised, or removed by legislative action, and in some cases by White House decision. These will be determined finally by what average Americans demand, or fail to demand. The decisive force lies among millions of American voters whose deep regard for justice and for the civil liberties of the individual cannot be doubted. First of all, it is up to us and whether we care enough to fight for what we really cherish. Either suspicion, increasing violation of our freedoms, disunity, and extremism—or democratic action through Congress and loyalty to the due process of our laws.

Is it possible to have more security without undermining or destroying our basic civil rights?

Of course, we can never achieve absolute security against dangers, within or without, in a world of human beings. But there seems no reason to doubt that the American system is capable of creating more security with more justice than it has yet done. Certainly it is if we learn from recent mistakes and seek to improve present practices in securing loyalty. We cannot strengthen our democratic system by giving the state more and more protection at the expense of protection for the individual. We are compelled to devise better and more precise defenses for the rights of citizens quite as much as for the security of the state.

How can the complex problem of Communists and

Communism in a democratic society be handled without destroying the things we live by? The existence of a very small but zealous Communist minority, and the perfection of totalitarian techniques of infiltration, perplex us and equally our most responsible officials in Washington. This is largely due to the fact that the loyalty-test program was a swift improvisation, in a field where improvisation can be most dangerous and damaging. Yet it is inevitable that no hurriedly improvised mechanism can be expected to be faultless or ideal. But any thoughtful citizen will be justified in asking: Have we as yet put enough specialized brain-power to work on this and related problems? Have we yet begun to use the kind of authoritative knowledge that our dilemma requires and that is available?

It has been suggested by the *New York Herald Tribune* that some better and more judicious agency should study the entire problem of Communism and infiltration. Others have been thinking similarly. Suppose the President should appoint a body of fifteen or more leading judicial authorities, men of the stature and qualifications of John Lord O'Brian? In the course of a few months such a commission of legal experts would explore a wide range of possibilities. Their recommendations would be invaluable to Congress. They would also give the average American a new assurance that his rights would be protected by legal means. Rather than continue to flounder about in a hubbub of witch-hunt accusations and hysteria, it would seem that this might be a sane and sober approach to an extremely sober problem.

In the process a commission of distinguished jurists might also consider and recommend revisions in loyalty-test procedures; and equally a method for much more careful selection of members of loyalty boards. To me it seems that the appointment of loyalty boards ought to be most rigidly controlled rather than appointed by the heads of various federal agencies. Clifford J. Durr of the Federal

Communications Commission put his finger on a great
danger. "Who," he asked, "are to be the judges of a person's loyalty or disloyalty? . . . Can we safely vest in our
secret police jurisdiction over the 'association' and 'sym-
pathetic affiliation' and thoughts of men, and be sure that
we are safe? Can men be fairly tried when their right to
face their accusers depends upon the 'discretion' of those
who accused them?"

In a period of unprecedented checking up on several
millions of private citizens, *who checks up on the checker-
uppers?* This is a tremendously important question, yet
curiously slight public or official attention has been paid
to it. It would seem that loyalty boards themselves, and
also the personnel of the FBI, should require an especially
careful scrutiny by some independent outside authority.
A general accountability to Congress and the President
does not provide adequate information or precautions. In
the interests of democratic security both the loyalty boards
and the FBI should welcome a more balanced and effective
system of checks and supervision.

Congress itself has the power to revise the procedures
of its investigating committees so that they will cease indiscriminate smearing of reputations and abuse of citizens'
Constitutional rights. Certain recommendations have been
made by members of Congress; and some of them seem
likely to be acted upon by the new Congress. A so-called
model "Fair Procedures" bill, drafted with the support of
the American Civil Liberties Union, has been available
for a considerable time.

This bill would accord persons who had been attacked
in a Congressional hearing the right to appear with four
witnesses before the committee. Such persons would also
have the right to cross-examine any accuser for one hour.
Persons called before a Congressional investigation could
also have the aid and advice of legal counsel. These are
simple democratic decrees that would strengthen the civil

rights of all Americans in one place where they seriously need strengthening—in Congress itself.

The perils of our internal security improvisations need not become a permanent menace, because they do not need to be tolerated. If we use the wealth of judicial knowledge and experience available in the United States, and if average citizens will become concerned with a problem that bears profoundly upon their personal independence, we can fortify justice for the individual while fortifying our security. As always in a democracy, it depends on ourselves.

As Americans we have a great and excusable pride in living in a free society where law prevails and where the concepts of justice and of personal freedom still have force and meaning. In our kind of world it is something big and fine and brave to have somehow preserved this kind of society in a vast and mighty country like our own. We can keep it as it is, big and free and respectful of the rights of the individual man. But we can keep it this way only by eternal vigilance; by rejecting the little betrayals, and by closing the cracks in the dike, which are forever opening or threatening to open.

What, after all, is our greatest security? Not loyalty boards. Not the Army, the Navy, and the Air Force. Not even the atomic bomb. Our greatest security lies in the fact that the overwhelming majority of 148,000,000 Americans can live securely and unmolested under the law; can associate as they please, go as they please, and read what they please; can believe politically as they see fit; can voice a dissenting opinion with any man; can stand up, anywhere in the world, and say proudly: "I am an American." That is a security that only the most fortunate still possess on this planet and in this century. It is the first security we must preserve, because it is the basis of all security for men who are free and intend to remain free.

Chapter XI

WHAT PRICE NATIONAL DEFENSE?

No people has ever spent such colossal sums in the name of national security as we Americans are now spending, and are scheduled to spend for years to come. Yet despite these enormous drains upon our personal and collective incomes we have no sense of genuine security. On the contrary, citizens of the United States have never remotely experienced such a widespread and acute feeling of insecurity as today. "National" defense has become the most fantastically expensive, yet the most flighty and uncertain gold-devourer in our nation's history.

This is not primarily the fault of generals, admirals, or politicians. It is due in part to the circumstances and incredible follies of our times. Above everything else it is caused by the existence of atomic bombs and of barbarous biological weapons. To escape devastation by atomic and biological weapons of unprecedented reach and frightful potency we resort to the self-contradictory expedient of making more and more of these doom-spreading devices. Against instruments of globe-girdling destructivity we attempt to raise a strictly "national" barrier.

It is like trying to eliminate bubonic plague by breeding more and bigger rats—supposedly for exportation only. But the plague of atomic-bacterial war can never be curbed indefinitely by creating additional plague-spreaders by the tens of thousands. In reality we are pouring out the life-blood of the American standard of living (and of American capitalism) for a short-term gamble of considerable

230

risk. The expedient cannot conceivably operate for more than a limited number of years. As a matter of fact, it will cease to provide even an illusion of security whenever the Soviet Union possesses a certain number of atomic bombs and long-range bombers. According to our foremost military and scientific experts, that situation may exist some time between 1960 and 1970, while the Soviets may have their first A-bomb between 1950 and 1957.*

These dates represent the probable maximum margin of our present highly superficial security based upon a one-nation, outdated national defense. Because it is one-nation and merely national it cannot offer adequate protection against world-reaching weapons of mass destruction. Such a defense has serious limitations of national facilities and resources, plus enormous geographical limitations. It is merely an unavoidable short-term expedient. But there are other, far greater reasons why what we are attempting to do cannot possibly work for any length of time.

In the United States "national" defense today simply attempts, desperately and at stupendous cost, to achieve the impossible. For the immediate present and future there seems no alternative. Soviet policies and Communist methods dictate the maintenance of a counterbalancing armed power for several years at least; possibly for more. But this unpleasant necessity need not blind Americans to the utter inadequacy of the expediencies into which we have been pushed. The course we are traveling is called "national" defense. That course offers us no long-term safety whatever, and no permanent solution. For a patently unsatisfactory and artificial article we are presently compelled to pay the most fabulous price in history. Is this an exaggeration? The men who made the atomic bomb know it is soberly and tragically accurate. We are building—

* Cf. Hanson W. Baldwin: *The Price of Power* (New York: Harper & Brothers; 1947), Chapter iii.

*A gigantic U.S. "national" defense against
atomic missiles, against which no real
defense exists or is faintly probable.*

The most authoritative atomic scientists insist: "There
is no defense against atomic missiles—or against smuggled
atomic bombs."

This is true for several reasons:

First, because nothing less than a hundred-per-cent defense against atomic weapons could protect some sixty
million Americans who live in two hundred or more cities.

Second, because no means of intercepting atomic rockets
—traveling much faster than sound—is today regarded as
likely or possible. And because even a future interception
average of ten or twenty per cent (through some device
that scientists cannot yet envisage) is most improbable.
Therefore our generation cannot expect anything remotely resembling protection against atomic rockets.

Third, because no combination of fighter planes, anti-
aircraft fire, and similar aerial defenses can be expected
to shoot down every plane among hundreds of attacking
bombers. One or two atomic bombs that reached their
target would cripple or destroy entire cities.

Fourth, because the Soviets already possess the deadliest
submarine in existence in important numbers. This is the
Germans' Type 21, obtained complete and in parts as
reparations at the war's end. It is the highest-speed and
longest-range submarine known, still admitted by U.S.
Navy spokesmen to be radar-proof as late as the end of
1948, and possibly so for many months or years to come.
Our intelligence representatives, in their most conservative estimates, place the total of Soviet Type 21 super-subs
at one hundred, and other long-range Red submarines,
without Schnorkel "breathing" equipment, at another

hundred. Obviously, the Type 21 submarines—still unde-tectable—can easily reach United States coasts. They can be equipped with rocket bombs (eventually with atomic heads). They can deliver bacterial weapons, spreading many sorts of epidemics among humans, livestock, and crops. Of course, they are capable of employing poison gases against coastal cities. Anything like one-hundred-per-cent defense against Type 21 submersibles is admitted by experts to be most unlikely if not impossible.

Fifth, because our vast aerial boundaries cannot be made penetration-proof against every single enemy plane. Hence terrible epidemics can be germ-sprayed and spread across the country.

Sixth, because both bacteria and atomic bombs can be smuggled in such a variety of ways and places that no re-liable or absolute defense can be built against them.

Qualified scientists could undoubtedly add to this list. Few can speak with greater authority than Dr. Philip Mor-rison, of the Los Alamos Association of Scientists, who helped assemble the bombs used against Hiroshima and Nagasaki. A group of students asked him: "Is there a defense against the atomic bomb?"

Dr. Morrison replied: "The Japs found one within a week. *It was peace.*"

Peace is the only known or discernible defense against atomic weapons. In fact, *no genuine defense against atomic, bacterial, and gaseous weapons of mass destruc-tion exists today, nor can such defenses be expected in our lifetime.* Some of these deadly instruments, and the means of delivering them, are already possessed by the Soviet Union. The Russians should also have atomic bombs within ten or twelve years at the outside.

Thus our present "national" defense is far from im-pregnable. And despite any improvements our science may manage to contrive, their practical value will still remain

limited and insufficient. In any event population centers
in the United States can enjoy their present inadequate
degree of protection only for another few years. Bacterial
weapons plus long-range bombers and Type 21 submarines
can make America's "national" defense virtually meaningless at any time. *Nationally* it has become impossible
for us to defend ourselves either completely or sufficiently.

We must not deceive ourselves about the extremely
transitory nature of such armed "security" as we are now
purchasing at an enormous price. It may prove providentially sufficient for another five years or ten, even though
it is obviously subject to imponderable incidents and accidents. But despite our billions of expenditures we are not
building foundations upon which a national fortress of
real security can be constructed in the future. In an atomic
age no such *national* fortress *can* be built. We are pushing
feverishly down a road that has a dead end.

The dead end is atomic and scientific. But it may also
be economic and financial. Have we as yet given anything
like adequate attention to—

The cost of previous wars to the United States.

The President's Air Policy Commission opened its January 1948 report by saying: "We believe that the United
States will be secure in an absolute sense only if the institution of war itself is abolished under a regime of law.
World peace and the security of the United States are now
the same thing."

The report warned that a preparedness program will be
extremely expensive. *"Eighty percent of the budget for
the fiscal year 1948 is in payment for past wars and the
maintenance of our present military establishment.* Eighty-
five percent of our total Federal budgets since 1915 have

been for war or preparation or payment for war." (Italics mine.) This is a graphic way of informing every tax-paying United States citizen where eighty per cent or more of his taxes have gone and continue to go. War and the costs of defense are the only great obstacles to an almost unimaginable health, progress, and prosperity in the United States. Merely one fifth of our standing investment in destruction and counter-destructive measures would completely transform America productively, scientifically, educationally, culturally, and in many other life-saving, life-giving, and life-enriching ways.

The National Industrial Conference estimates that total costs of World War II to the United States will reach the staggering sum of $700,000,000,000 by 1972. It also states that by 1957 veterans and their families—"all prospective applicants for government benefits"—will number approximately 62,500,000 persons.* The military aspect of our wars constitutes only a slight fraction of their long-term expense. The N.I.C. report pointed out that the military cost of the Spanish-American War was $582,000,000 —but its continuing costs had totaled $2,400,000,000 by July 1946.

During World War II the U.S. national debt increased to ten times what it had been in World War I. "Another comparable increase in our national debt is inconceivable," declared the Senate's Special War Investigating Committee. "It would amount to $2,600,000,000,000" (more than two and one half *trillion* dollars). *"More drastic and carefully considered legislation to eliminate unfair profits from war is imperative.* Confidence in the system of free enterprise can be preserved *in no other way.* Capitalism's capacity for self-discipline faces its supreme test." †

We stand today, then, at a fateful juncture where the

---

* Survey by the National Industrial Conference of New York City; *America's Resources for World Leadership,* November 1947.

† *New York Herald Tribune,* April 24, 1948.

American people have never stood before. The costs of
another war would be absolutely insupportable for our
capitalist economy. They would force our system into
bankruptcy. We have solemn reasons to consider this brutal fact at greater length. But for the moment we have imperative need to examine more closely another brutal fact
that already confronts us.

What are the present and prospective costs of U.S. "national" defense?

This has become our most acute and most difficult
domestic problem. Postwar defense expenditures have increased with such mighty and successive bounds that it is
virtually impossible to keep them up to date except in
weeklies and the daily press. In January 1948 total defense
expenditures were estimated at a record-breaking $11,-
000,000,000 for the fiscal year 1949. That meant twenty-
eight per cent of all federal income allotted to our armed
services. But before Congress adjourned, the adoption of
the new Air Force program, revived selective service, and
other related matters combined to boost defense costs for
the fiscal year 1949 by several additional billions of dollars.

Without venturing into too many harrowing details
we can say that "national" defense has become the costliest, most disturbing luxury in American life. The only
billions that can be talked about indiscriminately in the
U.S. Congress are those earmarked, suggested or envisaged
for any aspect of defense. The Air Force urged planes,
armament, and personnel at a total cost of approximately
$20,000,000,000 over a few years, and obtained initial in-
stallments on roughly that basis. Conversion of the Panama
Canal into a sea-level waterway at a cost of $2,482,000,000
was recommended to Congress as protection against pos-

sible atomic-bomb attack. After further Eniwetok tests and the breakdown of U.N. efforts at atomic control it was reported that another $2,500,000,000 or more would probably have to be spent for atomic-energy development in the United States in the next few years.* Items of one or several additional billions of dollars keep cropping out in published reports, based on official sources. The U.S. Navy seeks gigantic, 60,000-ton aircraft carriers, each of which would cost some $200,000,000—and could conceivably be destroyed or knocked out by a single atomic-torpedoed superrange submarine. The total cost of each carrier and its flotilla of escorts may reach $1,000,000,000.

Our eyes and ears have been buffeted for many months by such staggering and astronomical "items" for defense that their true meaning is extremely difficult to absorb. What do they add up to, and where do they lead?

Beardsley Ruml, a recognized authority on finance and taxation, has stated that United States defense budgets will total *$30,000,000,000* annually within a few years. In Washington Joseph and Stewart Alsop reported: "A qualified expert among the American planners has placed the minimum American defense budget in a world gone to smash at between $40,000,000,000 and $50,000,000,000 annually." † Even at or near Mr. Ruml's estimate, however, something like forty to fifty cents of every U.S. taxpayer's dollar may be expended directly for our armed services in the years immediately ahead. From a 1949–50 estimated defense budget of $15,000,000,000 (which will probably be increased by several billion dollars) to an annual budget of some $22,000,000,000 is a tremendous jump, which threatens to become an early reality. As a result a question of inestimable importance is posed for the U.S. government and the American people:

* *New York Times,* May 30, 1948.
† *New York Herald Tribune,* January 21, 1948.

How great a proportion of its income can the United States afford to spend on defense?

Curiously enough, this vital question has scarcely been investigated by the federal administration and by Congress. It has not yet been the subject of serious inquiry by prominent groups of industrialists, bankers, and other capitalists. It has not been probed by taxpayers' associations, nor even by economists and research groups to any observable degree. It has not become a prominent question of exploration and discussion in the nation's press or on the radio. Yet the net earnings or net profits—and certainly the tax expenditures—of almost all classes of citizens are directly at stake for years to come. The U.S. standard of living is seriously jeopardized by the vastly increased costs of "national" defense. If continued, important governmental controls of certain key industries will be required. An unprecedented military influence in many aspects of our national life is developing.

All these are dangerous trends which directly affect the welfare of every American. Yet there have been alarmingly few indications of perceptive concern over what extreme defense expenditures may shortly do to Americans and their way of life. It seems that we do not understand exactly what we are doing, do not know where we are going, and are even less interested in what the inevitable consequences of further haphazard and ill-considered actions may do to us.

Secretary of the Army Royall exhibited a commendable sense of public responsibility when he warned the President's Air Policy Commission: "We must realize there is a dollar limit on what this country can spend for national defense. *There is an absolute limit beyond which we cannot go without endangering the economic security of the country.*" (Italics mine.)

Coming from the chief spokesman for U.S. Army requirements, this statement has compelling force. But such organizations as the National Association of Manufacturers and the U.S. Chamber of Commerce had long functioned as self-designated defenders of our "economic security." Why had they remained silent or seemingly indifferent? Are not our defense costs vastly exceeding all the peacetime expenditures of the New Deal? Fear of Soviet Russia seemed, at least throughout 1947–8, to have paralyzed the thinking of most businessmen, bankers, editors, and members of Congress.

Among the last a notable exception was Senator Henry Cabot Lodge, Jr., of Massachusetts. Although supporting a seventy-group Air Force, he registered reservations that got down to the heart of our defense problem. Senator Lodge asked how much could be appropriated to this purpose "before economic controls became necessary." He added: "There should be a thoroughly scientific determination of what the point of public expenditures is at which we shall have to militarize our economy and go to allocation, priorities, rationing and other controls. . . . We cannot legislate wisely without having a sure and definite idea of just exactly what straw it is that breaks the camel's back." *

Nothing could appear more logical or fundamental than a "thoroughly scientific determination" of how much the United States can safely spend for defense. Senator Lodge was fully justified in his protest. Neither the Administration nor Congress had assigned experts to explore and report on this central question. The National Security Resources Board devoted its attention chiefly to planning for the contingency of war. Other groups, like the Advisory Commission on Universal Training, concerned themselves with various needs for defense. *But how much cash can the U.S.A. expend for how many categories of defense? For*

* *New York Times,* May 14, 1948.

how long? With what consequences? At this writing there still exists no authoritative group exclusively occupied with an attempt to find fundamental answers to questions such as these.

Thus, "What price 'national' defense?" remains unprobed and unanswered—even in a strictly financial sense. It is not at all surprising that Congressional debates and legislation on defense measures have been extremely confusing, and in some cases of questionable value or recklessly wasteful of public funds. Few things are so urgently needed as a survey of possible and probable defense expenditures over the next five or ten years. Creation of a Defense Costs Survey Commission could meet this need. Such a commission would include outstanding economists, bankers, and businessmen as well as military specialists. Since 1946 Washington has operated on the premise that our first question is how tremendous a defense structure the United States should build. But that is putting the cart before the horse. The first question, consistently ignored, is: how tremendous a defense structure can our American economy support? When you build a house, its size and facilities are determined uniquely by how much money you have available. In this case, too (as Samuel Grafton has ironically observed), we are building a house "for fear to live in." It is, in every sense, a terribly expensive house—but infinitely more so because it has no sober, intelligent financing behind it.

The dilemma of our strictly "national" defense has many horns. With Soviet-Western relations strained and unpredictable, Americans were presented with a devil's choice. It is to the great credit of Secretary of State Marshall that he never tried to gloss this over. Addressing a Congressional committee, Secretary Marshall frankly said: "We must not permit the free community of Europe to be extinguished. Should this occur . . . it would impose *incalculable burdens* upon this country and force *serious readjustments* in our traditional way of life." (Italics mine.)

The accuracy of this statement cannot be challenged. Without the European Recovery Program our defense expenditures, even as tremendous as they are today, would have to be doubled or tripled immediately. But even with ERP in existence, Americans already face defense costs that remain "incalculable"; and they cannot increase much more without forcing "serious readjustments" in our way of life.

What changes may a gigantic and prolonged "national" defense program impose upon our democratic, capitalistic system?

We must keep in mind that Soviet Russia is expected to produce its first atomic bomb some time in the 1950's, possibly within three years. Whenever that happens, the war fears and "Red spy" apprehensions of Americans will be very much intensified. Congressmen will be quite as susceptible to panicky reactions and hysteria as any private citizen. When the Soviets have the bomb, or we believe they have the bomb, Congress will certainly react with typical American extremism. Hasty, ill-prepared, and recklessly drastic countermeasures are likely to be enacted. It will be a most difficult period in which to maintain an adequate guard over our normal freedoms, either individual or in free enterprise. Our already huge defense costs would also be subjected to powerful upward pressures, fear-impelled.

It is possible today, however, to discern growing encroachments of national-atomic defense upon our governmental, scientific, and industrial institutions. Most notable is the pronounced increase of military influence—in the White House, in Congress, in American diplomacy, in research and industry and many other fields. In the past few years an unprecedented number of generals and admirals have been appointed as ambassadors and ministers abroad. Military men have been given executive positions in the State Department and in other departments or federal agencies. Civilian control of the Atomic Energy Commission was established after a hard battle, but a portion of the military still seeks to get direct control of atomic bombs and dominance over most aspects of atomic energy. The prestige and authority of U.S. military careerists have never been so great—aided understandably by the remarkable qualities and staunch democratic loyalties of such exceptional men as Generals Marshall, Eisenhower, Bradley, and others.

Because we blundered into an atomic arms race the government is spending several billions of dollars on atomic weapons, experiment, and scientific research. Consequently a major share of basic or pure research in the United States is subsidized by federal funds in very large amounts. American science is mobilized for war purposes on a hitherto unimagined scale. This means that hundreds of our university laboratories, and others owned by industry, are working chiefly for the Army or Navy and are dependent upon government support. For all practical purposes the military has become a controlling factor in our most important and best-equipped research laboratories. Federal intervention can be extended almost anywhere on the grounds of defense necessities. Until now this has never been the American way in matters of science. The long-term implications are disturbing and dangerous.

Atomic defense, plus the Communist problem, must continue to increase the role of the secret police in our democracy. The activities of the FBI were greatly extended by the requirements of the loyalty tests. Spy revelations and Red scares constantly add to the responsibilities of J. Edgar Hoover and his several thousand agents. Our troubled times make an efficient secret-police organization indispensable if a free society is to protect itself. But we do not know how much the secret police will be expanded, nor how far-reaching its powers may become under future threats of atom-bomb or bacterial smugglers, espionage, and the like.

In his remarkably balanced and informative book *The Price of Power* the authoritative military analyst Hanson W. Baldwin writes: "Great restraint is necessary in the use of the power entrusted to the FBI; that organization, too, should be subject to the close scrutiny of a Congressional committee or mass hysteria may force it into undemocratic, unnecessary and un-American methods. . . . The FBI must develop a greater deftness and a greater sensibility for democratic processes than it has sometimes shown." *

This is a measured and understanding statement of the problem of the secret police in any democratic nation. By the very nature and significance of its functions it requires the guidance and checks of a "close scrutiny" by the people's representatives. In the past, Congress has failed to provide this type of supervision and direct assistance. It may be that the FBI will have to be tripled or quadrupled in size over the next five years or so. Certainly its existing staff is pushed to the limit, with each spy scare piling up more responsibilities. But when some foreign power possesses an atomic bomb that can be smuggled, the FBI's present headaches will be multiplied many times over. Such complications lie somewhere ahead. Even without them, however, the role of secret police in the United States has entered an entirely new phase as part of our vastly enlarged "national" defense. This is a basic change in the American way of life.

There are other important changes in process or unavoidable. But before considering them, permit a brief digression. There has been an alarming amount of loose talk about a so-called "preventive war" against Soviet

* Op. cit., p. 217.

Russia. On a Town Hall radio program former Governor
George H. Earle urged that long-range United States
bombers be ready "to wipe out every town, city and vil-
lage in Russia." Many equally incendiary and irresponsible statements have been made over the past two years,
usually on the theme that "we should knock out Russia
before she can attack us." Here or there a pre-Neanderthal,
anthropoid specimen has recommended "annihilating
Moscow" and its three million inhabitants in a surprise
atomic attack. Apparently no twinge of conscience is experienced in proposing that the United States should resort to an inestimable crime that would place the Japs'
sneak attack on Pearl Harbor in the category of playing
post office at a Sunday-school picnic.

But aside from its Bluebeard advocates, "preventive
war" is a vicious and utterly misleading idea under any
circumstances. No fancy adjective can make modern war
anything less than what it is: a horrible and uncontrollable
plunge into mass murder and revolutionary chaos. To
invite and provoke a so-called "preventive" war would be
to hurl ourselves and many other nations into an abyss of
the unknown and unpredictable. The assumption is that
the United States could be assured of "winning" such a
war if we started it before the Soviets had atomic weapons.
The truth is that no nation can "win" in another major
war—at any time.

First of all, the United States does not possess enough
atomic bombs and cannot produce them fast enough to
be confident that so vast a country as the Soviet Union
could be "knocked out" by atomic bombardment.* Nor
could annihilation of major Russian cities prevent the
Red Army from occupying all of western Europe, and
then Americans would also have to pulverize the cities and
populations of all continental Europe. Undoubtedly that
would be the most effective way in which to drive the

* Ibid., p. 301.

great majority of surviving Europeans into Communism. In a world of famine and disease, anarchy would triumph, with democracy the first victim.

But we cannot fight the Soviets at any time without the necessity of invading and subjugating the U.S.S.R.—one sixth of the earth's surface. We would be compelled to attempt to suppress civil wars of terrible intensity throughout Europe, the Soviet Union, and much of Asia. With how many millions of American soldiers? For how many years? With how many millions of American occupational forces? Stationed in how many distant lands for how many more years? At the cost, in cash alone, of how many trillions of dollars? At a further cost of what inestimable impoverishment and immeasurable military controls and oppressions at home?

Realism of the harshest kind dictates that every American ask himself or herself the most basic and inescapable question that exists for us today:

What would another major war do to the United States?

While in Prague in October 1946 I had a confidential conversation of more than an hour with President Eduard Beneš of Czechoslovakia. In Europe only Winston Churchill and Joseph Stalin could rival Dr. Beneš in long experience. None could rival him in his between-the-crossfires knowledge of the East-West struggle or surpass him in astuteness. I had suggested deliberately that I did not want an interview for newspaper publication. In the delicate situation of his country President Beneš could only express his sincerest convictions with complete freedom if he spoke off the record. Because of his tragic death I can now quote him directly. In answer to my first question he said: "I do not believe in any early war. It is absolute folly to talk of such a war."

President Beneš summed up his reasons for saying this with this statement: *"Of course, the United States of America would be the biggest loser in a war,"* he said with great soberness. "I need not go into the details. But you have elements in your American society which would be a great menace if war came. Your free institutions could not survive. War would be your greatest calamity."

It should be obvious that the United States must inevitably be the "biggest loser" in another major war simply because we Americans have infinitely the most to lose. Far more than any other people *we have everything to lose:* the greatest national wealth and well-being per capita in the world; the greatest freedoms and privileges; the most tremendous industrial plants and the most modernized cities—everything that is and means the American way. They cannot conceivably survive a global orgy of organized mass destruction.

These are but a few of the frightening and immense unknowns that any future war, "preventive" or otherwise, must raise as an immediate specter to all Americans. Even the staggering load of our present "national" defense has important temporary advantages beside the certain price of another war to us. This defense cost *can* be kept within reason if we insist upon it. It can be controlled, revised, and adjusted to tolerable proportions. If we recognize this much, we are compelled also to understand that these things *must* be done. One way in which to begin is to consider:

The dimensions and the dangers of our present arms-production boom.

In March 1948 the headlines and financial pages of American newspapers were peculiarly revealing. The *New York Times* reported: "STOCKS UP SHARPLY AS TRADING

SPURTS. Gains on Wide Front Range Up to $5 a Share—Rearmament Regarded as a Factor." Brokers, it explained, "were inclined to attribute it to a stepping up of the rearmament program . . . the [price] breakout created a more optimistic feeling in the financial community." (As far back as November 1946 a leading financial weekly had carried the comment: "An armament boom is the only ultimate alternative now visible to a decline in business. . . . Such an armament program in the long run appears inevitable, if we don't want to commit national suicide.")

The certainty of huge production for Air Force and other defense programs inspired other pertinent headlines: "TEXTILE INDUSTRY AWAITS QUARTERMASTER BUYING. . . . CRISIS ORDERS MAY BAR SLUMP IN HEAVY GOODS. . . . DEFENSE BOOM ON IN METAL INDUSTRY. . . . ARMY OUTLINES UNDERWEAR INDUSTRY MOBILIZATION DRIVE." The *Journal of Commerce* quoted a high official as remarking (on March 23, 1948) that "only an improved international situation can dim the business outlook." Somehow the splurge of this type of reaction and comment did not inspire much confidence in the basic health of U.S. capitalism. Had it become incapable of maintaining a genuine prosperity without tremendous artificial injections of production geared for war?

In any event, the armaments boom was on in the United States. Billions upon billions in defense orders were placed, or were in sight and assured over the next few years. Big Steel was doing a record-breaking business, with record-breaking profits. The aviation industry and a great variety of war-matériel plants were booming. Net income, after taxes, of our one hundred largest corporations had increased ninety-one per cent in 1947 over similar income in 1945.* Now most of these corporations

* Cf. The National City Bank economic letter of June 1948.

were earning still greater profits. After each quarterly period financial pages in the daily press carried a succession
of reports of record sales or abnormally swollen earnings
by scores of major industries and enterprises. Defense appropriations, plus ERP, had ended most conjecture about
an early postwar "recession." Yet concern about an ultimate
depression remained significantly vivid.

The arms-production boom has affected the U.S. economy exactly as a stiff dose of heroin affects a drug addict.
For the immediate present everything becomes rosy and
stimulatingly wonderful. One is not inclined to worry
until the effects begin to wear off and one begins to wonder where the next shot is coming from—not unless the
police start snooping around. But there are also camou-
flaged policemen concerned with this massive outburst of
defense production. How could the necessary basic materials for such great quantities of planes, armament, tanks,
guns, and related equipment for war purposes be obtained
without priorities and controls?

Increased restrictions and controls are
dictated by the vast U.S. defense
program.

Although American capitalists were naturally receptive
to big profits from the boom in arms business, they were
ill-prepared—by habit and philosophy—to accept less
pleasant counterparts of their favorable situation. Sooner
or later prevailing scarcities, under excessive demands,
would necessitate governmental allocation of materials in
key industries. The requirements of defense, of aid and
arms to western Europe, would have to be placed ahead of
a large variety of consumers' goods for American customers. Steel would have to go predominantly into planes,
arms, and ERP (to help restore Europe's plant) rather
than into uncurbed production of motor cars, refriger-

ators, electric washing-machines, and many other products still greatly in demand by American citizens.

Washington hesitated long about establishing priorities and allocations of key materials, but it could not keep hands off indefinitely. Neither the Marshall Plan nor defense requirements could be jeopardized. If the American people wanted much more "security" than they now had, a great many of them would have to go without new automobiles and other conveniences in order to get it. If industrialists and businessmen enjoyed a booming business, they would have to accept some governmental regulation for the boom to produce what it was supposed to produce.

There was also the question of restoring an excess-profits tax to fifty per cent of wartime levels, as strongly urged by Bernard M. Baruch. An excess-profits tax proved much too strong medicine for the ballot-conscious special session of the Eightieth Congress to touch in midsummer of 1948. Nevertheless, like other anti-inflationary bitters, it could not be avoided for long. With corporation profits setting or maintaining all-time highs, who could logically deny that an excess-profits tax was necessary in the face of our enormously swollen federal expenditures? Without this and other important "balance-restoring" measures the great arms boom threatened to zoom out of control—into a major depression, which would then be inevitable.

It is evident, then, that part of the price of our great defense program is a seriously accentuated inflationary menace. Part of the price is a greatly increased influence of the military in American life. Part of the price is an extension of governmental controls and regulation in industry and sections of business. Still another part is federal domination and control over a major portion of scientific research. A still unestimated part of the price is exactly how stupendous the costs of "national" defense will ultimately be in scores of billions of dollars—and resultant increased taxes. Nothing so extraordinarily and excessively expensive has ever happened to the United States government and people in peacetime.

Will U.S. capitalism strangle itself in the name of "national defense"?

It has occurred to me more than once that perhaps the most diabolically clever "Red plot" would be for Stalin and the Politburo to conspire deliberately to do one thing. Not to prepare to attack the United States. Simply to keep the United States so alarmed over possible war that its defense expenditures would cripple and eventually ruin our national economy.

Senator Lodge expressed the same thought to his Senate colleagues. He hoped, he said, that history would not record that the Russians merely sat back and "angered" the United States into appropriating so largely and unintelligently for defense that we "bled our own economy to death."

Discussing the disastrous consequences to ourselves of any universal anti-Communist crusade by force of American arms, Walter Lippmann has written: "If . . . we entangle ourselves in such a commitment, history will say that we encompassed our own ruin—a thing which no external foe was capable of doing."

The essential problem should be plain enough, if we would face it squarely. At what point will the expenditures of U.S. capitalism for self-defense become self-destructive?

Evidently neither our staunchest capitalists, nor Congress, nor most American citizens are particularly interested in finding out—not until we are smashed, collectively, on the head by it. But this time is fast approaching. Our present defense costs are already highly destructive. Present and prospective defense expenditures make increased federal taxes of many kinds inescapable over the next several years at least. Serious deficits in the federal budget also threaten. American capitalism, in actual fact, is "bleeding itself" in a perilous fashion when it pours a serious portion of the national income into defense channels and devices that are predominantly nonproductive. We cannot siphon off twenty billion dollars—or much more—per year for such sterile purposes for more than a very limited period without grave consequences. Such a radical disruption and distortion of our national economy almost certainly would end either in another great depression or in another war.

Because our enormous defense outlays are incompatible with a sound and balanced economy, Americans of all classes are due for a rude and painful awakening. The profits system is doomed to yield less and less profits to more and more people over a prolonged period. Just as excess-profits taxes are unavoidable, all taxes must become heavier and heavier if expenditures for defense continue to mount. Big business and enterprises of every kind will be condemned to get along with radically diminished margins of profits. The abnormal, lopsided, record-breaking profits of 1946–8 are in the process of vanishing for an unpredictably long time. "National" defense has reached the point where it dictates tightened belts for everyone, even the giant corporations.

In a remarkably thoughtful speech General Omar Bradley said: "I am afraid that war loses some of its fear to those people who fight it on an over-time paycheck or a cost-plus contract. *The immoral companionship of prosperity and war* may have blinded some of us to the realization that all war ultimately is a process of destruction. War destroys wealth. It does not produce it." (Italics mine.)

Exorbitant defense expenditures also destroy wealth; and in proportion to destruction of U.S. wealth, U.S. capitalism must become anemic and exposed to fatal illness.

Let our present defense costs continue to run rampant and they may well be capable of killing the goose that has laid the golden eggs for capitalists of all sizes in the United States. That so many of our leading industrialists, bankers, and businessmen have appeared, until now, to be among the least concerned must be indicative of something—let us hope, not of the degree of their perception.

We Americans have a pronounced dislike for tightened belts, but an even greater antipathy for self-discipline. We are born worshippers of laissez-faire, and "the devil take the hindmost." But suppose we laissez-faire ourselves into a situation where the devil gobbles up everybody, including Big Steel and Big Motors? What we obviously yearn for, however secretly, is an easy way out. Is there, or can there be, any easy way out?

It seems to me that General Bradley merits a Distinguished Service Medal of an exceptionally distinguished sort for courageously employing that single phrase: "the immoral companionship of prosperity and war." The chief executives of U.S. industry and the great minds of U.S. capitalism, save for a very few and notable exceptions, do not possess the moral stamina to discuss this subject. Nor do most of our organized religious bodies, our ministers and priests. It is much easier to dwell chiefly on the sins of the Soviets and the Communists while blithely assuming that our own hands are clean.

Yet virtually all of us in the United States profited directly—in better food, more cash, more luxuries, more diversions or more dividends—from the mass murder of World War II. It may be that no Christian nation should indulge in war. But how can any so-called Christian nation accept profits and prosperity *from* war? Especially from a modern war of mass annihilation. If all the churches in the United States would face this question boldly, and demand legislation *now* to freeze all prices, wages, and profits at the immediate outset of any future war, they would make a real contribution toward world peace. For if there is any immorality on earth, certainly the immorality of accepting profits and prosperity from the mass murder of tens of millions of people must be one of its most abhorrent manifestations. Of this we are collectively all guilty.

Neither Congress nor American public opinion possessed even sufficient fortitude (and sound common sense) to insist that Americans devote a really important percentage of their swollen wartime incomes toward paying for our tremendous war effort as we go. In January 1944 President Roosevelt asked for at least $10,500,000,000 in new taxes, rather than some $2,275,000,000 then proposed in a bill before Congress. Unless taxes were increased at least this much, President Roosevelt warned, we would be "treating unfairly those who must face the accumulated bill after the war." Under existing conditions his recommendation was modest. The British, under bombs, footed their war bill far more heroically than we throughout five and one half years of hostilities. Our Congress in 1944 did not possess sufficient stamina even to vote an additional tax levy of some $8,000,000,000 when incomes of all categories were abnormally high. U.S. war profits were well-nigh sacrosanct.

Short of an intervening depression, or even because of it, the "easy out" to crushing American defense expenditures would be another war. Under our existing lethargy we would again indulge in "the immoral companionship of prosperity and war"—at least until our cities were atomized. There would be no drastic and airtight curbs on war profits of all kinds; and those profiteers, petty or prodigious, who were so inclined could continue to go piously to worship on Sundays, for a little while perhaps or in some places.

From building a colossal war machine, through an arms-production boom and national militarization, to employ-

ing that machine for its only logical purpose is a simple
step. Adolf Hitler condensed the entire process into six
and one half years. Do not a great and free people have as
great a responsibility to protect their souls as to protect
their bodies?

Bernard M. Baruch is very much in a class by himself
among U.S. capitalists. As a citizen of outstanding prestige
and influence he has been almost alone in urging "taxation
to take the profit out of war" as part of a broad legislative
program for mobilization in wartime. If such a statute were
in vigor when war came, prices, salaries, wages, rents, *and*
profits would be frozen. For the first time in history an
entire people would renounce "the immoral companionship of prosperity and war." For the first time also we
should be compelled to pay as we go, on an unprecedented
scale, throughout the period of hostilities rather than leave
it to our children and grandchildren to pay the major
financial price for our folly. At last there would be something approaching an equal sacrifice for the objectives of
a great conflict. At last, too, every citizen might serve with
hands untarnished by blood-money.

More than a year after Mr. Baruch's proposal, however,
there exists no discernible or emphatic demand to take the
profits out of war. The Marxists would say that capitalists,
by their very nature, will never tolerate such a reform.
Cynics would say that the greediness of human beings
prohibits it. They may be right. So far as American democracy and American capitalists are concerned, they may
never have another chance. It is virtually impossible to
conceive that our way of life can survive one more major
war.

A few Senators (of the Special War Investigating Committee) have insisted that "legislation to eliminate unfair
profits from war is imperative." Congress has character-
istically ignored the subject ever since. Yet the Senators
were profoundly justified in declaring: "Capitalism's ca-

pacity for self-discipline faces its supreme test." It would be clearer, perhaps, and even more accurate, to say that the American people's capacity for self-discipline is at stake. From huge profits in an arms-production boom to renewed vast profits *in war* is only a step. Defense expenditures are already devouring the accustomed prewar profit margins in the U.S. economy. If permitted to continue, they cannot fail to devour a greater portion of our already diminishing profit margins. This way lies the ultimate self-strangulation of free enterprise as we have known it.

A second question commands equally serious consideration:

*Will our democracy gradually suppress some
of its most vital practices through extreme
defense preparedness and precautions?*

Because our massive defense program is based upon tremendous industrial production, governmental controls are almost as unavoidable as in wartime. In key industries federal regulation is an absolute necessity. Without centralized authority the requirements of our armed services and international commitments cannot be met. Military efficiency, therefore, becomes of greater importance than various democratic practices or the normal privileges of free enterprise. The longer defense dominates our economy, in dollar volume and in political importance, the more it must intrude upon the normally free and little-disturbed areas of the nation's life.

Existing impingements are already considerable, but must be expected to expand as vast defense expenditures become entrenched and also expand. Through loyalty tests the civil liberties of individual citizens are already threatened. More than ever before, the necessity of maintaining civilian control over all aspects of military activity is evident. In another sector our traditional freedom of basic scientific research is jeopardized by governmental subsidies and military supervision. We are also confronted with the steadily increasing power and scope of the FBI, without any system of Congressional supervision having been established as yet. In these and other ways new strains and pressures are brought to bear against our normal democratic processes.

Secretary of State Marshall has warned that, in the event of Communism dominating Europe, Americans would be compelled "to live in an armed camp, regulated and controlled." But whenever the Soviet Union possesses a few dozen atomic bombs, much the same result must be anticipated. For whenever the United States must exist in a constant state of preparedness against a possible atomic aggression very drastic curbs must inevitably be placed upon many of our traditional liberties. A "national-atomic" defense will not tolerate half measures. Eventually it must dictate to Americans where they cannot go—even inside their own country; where they cannot live; what they cannot say; and, to several millions in all probability, where they must work.

This is the dead end toward which our defense program is headed by the very nature of its national limitations, in our kind of world. Freedom of individuals cannot be reconciled with it in the long run. The greater the crisis, the less democracy we can have. Thus, in today's world and for any democracy, a strictly "national" defense becomes self-contradictory. It cannot and does not provide real security for the citizens who foot its stupendous bills. General Eisenhower recognized this implicitly when he said: "My plea is, let us realize there can be no absolute security for us alone. It must be for the whole world." Being a military specialist of exceptional intelligence and perception, General Eisenhower sees our defense program for what it is: an expedient; perhaps an unavoidable temporary expedient, but in no sense either a guarantee or a solution.

We live today in a vicious circle—on borrowed time. The plight of the world with its international crisis is a vicious circle. Chief reliance upon national strength and national weapons for safety is equally a vicious circle. At some point the vicious circle of armaments boom and ever mounting defense expenditures must be broken. For despite astronomic billions spent in its name, a strictly "national" defense is a myth. It has not yet produced, and it cannot produce, genuine security. It threatens to undermine our economy and pervert our democratic system unless a substitute is found in time.

Fortunately there is an alternative—another defense—if Americans in sufficient numbers grasp its meaning and are willing to work to make it work.

Chapter XII

THE OTHER DEFENSE—WORLD GOVERNMENT
THROUGH WORLD LAW

Do you believe in policemen?

Since you undoubtedly do, the next question is: But what makes a policeman?

Why, policemen are appointed, of course. That is, the mayor or somebody appoints the chief of police, and the chief selects any new men he needs on the force. You might say the city or municipal government does it.

But where does the mayor, or the municipal government, get the right to recruit policemen?

Well, there must be a law—

Of course, that is it. The law really creates the policeman—and his whole job is to enforce the law. Behind the cop on his beat are the courts and the laws that the courts apply. Without legal institutions the police could not exist. There could be no controls on robbery, assault, murder, arson, or gangsterism. Policemen are only important because they represent the Law.

So we have municipal police, state police, and federal police—and we take them all for granted. Because town or city police have limited functions, state or provincial police have been set up all over the world. Because state police are also limited by the political and geographical unit they serve, a federal or national police system also became necessary. Different kinds of police for different types of work, reporting and responsible to different kinds of courts. When you think about it at all, it makes a great deal of sense.

But if cities, states, and nations all need policemen, why shouldn't the world need policemen, too?

The only available answer is that the world's peoples, until very recently, haven't been thinking about that. Until quite recently it simply hadn't occurred to most of us that police—and the Law—might have to be extended beyond, much beyond, purely local or national functions. But when the whole world is in danger of chaos through a universal breakdown of law and order, you cannot attack the problem of peace intelligently without considering how to extend law above and beyond national boundaries. The shrinking globe, modern science, and the horrible scourge of modern warfare have combined to jar our dormant imaginations into new awareness. If we want protection from war, if we ardently desire a world-wide peace, how can we longer dissociate World Peace from World Law? If laws plus police enforcement provide us with great and vital protections in our home, state, and nation why should not a similar system provide new protections on a global scale?

Of course, our national defense forces are also a type of standing police—the police that guard our borders, our sea and air lanes. But when we speak of "national" defense we are also speaking of a cardinal aspect of national sovereignty. What is "sovereignty"? The dictionary says it is the "authority in which the political power, as of the state, is vested." When we find ourselves at war, our armed forces are defending our national sovereignty—the privileges, powers, prerogatives, and security of the state. Since the armed forces are the only official, qualified defenders of the nation-state, their unique function is to defend the national sovereignty. It is a costly, bloody business, but the only means human beings have yet created whereby a nation's rights and existence can be immediately protected.

But in this twentieth century a curious, unfamiliar

thing has happened. Like so much else in this fantastic century, it is highly revolutionary. *No nation on earth today can afford weapons and armed forces that might give it relative security from attack.* Only two governments in our present world, the United States and the Soviet Union, even *think* they can afford armed equipment of such enormous dimensions. Soviet Russia can only compete in an armaments race of unprecedented costliness because it is a dictatorship, with iron controls over a vast region of the earth's surface. The United States can continue this bankrupting expedient only because it possesses a temporary monopoly of wealth, plus a fabulous industrial plant.

Look around among the other nations and you see a strange spectacle indeed. In Europe and Asia most of them are either half or outrightly bankrupt from two world conflicts that were fought in the name, and by the methods, of national defense. Within a matter of thirty years national defense, in operation, has so impoverished a long list of countries that they no longer possess sufficient means to defend themselves. Even if they could regain most of the means they had in 1938, these would still be of scarcely any use. The atomic bomb, bacterial weapons, rockets, and long-range bombing planes have rendered all previously normal, *national* defense methods utterly futile.

As a consequence even Great Britain, still the world's third largest power, finds herself incapable of creating a highly dubious atomic-age "defense." As an atomic target the British Isles are most critically exposed. Whatever Britain still manages to spend for her defense forces comes out of the food, clothing, and livelihood of her citizens, yet it is inadequate to supply a half-reliable defense, even if such a thing could be bought today. The British Isles can be defended from attack only by immediate and powerful help from the United States—if then.

On the European continent there is no nation, combatant in the recent war, that can afford defense forces consistent with atomic-age requirements. Neither France nor Italy can rearm without vast amounts of U.S. cash in the form of gifts, veiled or outright. No former combatant country can provide, by its own efforts, a defense system that would protect it from aggression. China is far more bankrupt and equally exposed. Throughout Latin America there is not a single nation, including Argentina, that can create adequate aerial defenses against even World War II bombers—without considering rockets or atomic bombs.

Such is the extraordinary, paradoxical situation in which the world's nations find themselves today. "National" defense not only provides no real protection whatever. It has become such an extreme luxury that no governments, save the Big Two, can even make an impressive bid for it. A worker might as well attempt to buy a Morgan yacht on forty dollars a week.

What is the meaning of these cold, demonstrable facts in terms of national sovereignty? Of course, the backbone of any country's sovereignty is national defense. But when national defense becomes impossible, both physically and financially, a nation's traditional sovereignty is reduced to tissue paper on a hoop. It is at the mercy of the first big stick thrust at it. It persists only as an illusion, without relation to the new realities. What nations cannot protect, by their own laws and their own strength, no longer belongs to them. It can only be held on sufferance, until the big bully of atomic aggression comes along. Thus, in the heart-zone of defense, national sovereignty is no longer workable or preservable for virtually any nation today.

This is so for several reasons: Because national sovereignty—regardless of Colonel McCormick and other American isolationists—cannot provide real protection against atomic and bacterial weapons. Because its gigantic costs destroy the very economy it professes to defend. Because such extensive militarization forces any nation into increasingly anti-democratic controls and totalitarian practices. Because no single country possesses the globe-circling reach and bases with which to build an adequate "national" defense by itself. Finally, because it requires any nation that relies upon it to defend itself alone or without assured and sufficient allies. Consequently *national sovereignty is incapable of creating a permanent preponderance of armed power in the world; and without that preponderance it must remain forever subject to attack and possible defeat.*

At this point we might well ask ourselves:

Are the governments and peoples of today's world all insane?

After two devastating global wars the world is no nearer peace and security, law and order, than it was in 1914. "National" defense and sovereignty have proved utterly incapable of preventing greater and greater bloodshed, revolution, and social anarchy. We have had repeated demonstrations through many generations that national preparedness, of itself, cannot ensure peace. We have had successive proofs that national armed forces, as such, are unable to assure nations against aggressive attack. In scores of vivid examples, in our lifetime, we have seen that nationalism alone provides such flimsy protection that it has no dependable relationship to security.

Yet the governments and peoples of our planet continue to worship the same false gods which have betrayed them again and again. They still prostrate themselves before Nationalism, "national" defense and "national" sovereignty. Hunger, impoverishment, disease, and illiteracy still afflict some four fifths of the world's 2,100,000,000 population. Even in the United States about one tenth of its citizens live in deplorable conditions of undernourishment and want; vast slum areas in our cities remain intolerable; our educational and soil-conservation facilities are notoriously inadequate, deprived of even a paltry few billion dollars a year in federal support. Yet the governments and taxpayers of the world continue to pour scores of billions of dollars yearly into national armaments and instruments of self-destruction. The way that has never worked to prevent war is the only method we persistently pursue, presumably to escape war. Could the inmates of our insane asylums conceivably adopt a policy of greater madness?

National sovereignty and defense have had more than one hundred years in which to perfect some reasonably effective means of preventing catastrophic wars. Instead these long-revered institutions have demonstrated their complete incapacity to provide peace and security. Has it not become urgently necessary, then, to create a new instrument and a new method? When single tribes could no longer adequately defend themselves they merged, at least for limited purposes of defense, with other tribes. When duchies and principalities found themselves constantly exposed to attack and conquest they merged with other principalities and duchies. Step by step little kingdoms became larger kingdoms until nations became the predominant political unit in most parts of the world. And in each step the radius of a single organization of law was extended and then re-extended. Without a common system of law and its enforcement there could be no tribe or city; finally no nation.

If there is any central meaning to the long, slow evolution of mankind, it must lie in large measure in the steady outward and upward progression of the application of a common law. Although imposed by force, every empire has been based upon legal concepts and authority. In the age of nationalism both sovereignty and defense forces became foremost expressions of each nation's laws. In our present world revolution, we have reached the point where another step—a further progression—has become inevitable. For the preservation of an organized, durable, and livable society in an atomic age nothing remains to be tried except the one thing that has never yet been attempted. The way cannot be back. It cannot be "along" —along the same course that has brought repeated wars and disasters. It can only be *up*. The only other defense and the only remaining alternative is:

World Government through World Law.

The second global war multiplied the bloodshed and destruction of the first many times over. It also culminated in the first experiments with the chain reaction of atomic fission—with Hiroshima and then Nagasaki. By some miracle, men and governments were permitted to pause on the very brink of the final abyss.

But these recent developments have created a great historical certainty. *In the long term a world government under World Law will inevitably be established.* It will be a limited world government under limited laws. It may not come until after the white man's civilization has largely destroyed itself in a catastrophe of almost inestimable proportions. It may not come until another generation, possibly not until the next century, is compelled to resort to it. Nevertheless, world government is historically certain. It is dictated both by man's compulsion to save himself and by civilization's compulsion to be renewed.

The entire course of human history indicates clearly that some form of world government will ultimately be established—either by the free choice of peoples and nations, *or* by dictatorship. If our generation lacks the vision, intelligence, and wisdom to carry through this crowning evolution of law, we need not doubt that we shall make a final and truly supreme sacrifice on the altar of impotent Nationalism. Just one major and full-scale atomic war would wreck the world's house so utterly that foundations for a new structure could not possibly be postponed much longer. Either under an atomic, armed totalitarianism or under the enlightened efforts of free men *the world will be governed.* It will be governed because it is precipitately reaching a point where it must become governable. It is an organism that cannot remain indefinitely at war with itself and continue to retain great entities of human life. For mankind's safety and survival, in the longer term, we have nowhere to go but *up.* If we, now living, prefer first to go down in order to make universal recognition of this fact inescapable, of course we can offer a final and desperate demonstration of the folly of national defense. Those who may survive are unlikely to require a further demonstration.

As we look back, the drafting and adoption of the United States Constitution by the thirteen colonies was a simple action of elemental common sense. But the people of the thirteen separate colonies were extremely reluctant to unite themselves in a federal government under federal laws. As Carl Van Doren has so eloquently reminded us in his book *The Great Rehearsal,* the thirteen colonies were only united under a tremendous compulsion. For the sake of survival they were compelled to choose the lesser of two great gambles and two grave dangers: either a greater law in a much larger political federation that might become too centralized and powerful, or a divided and vague "association" of colonies which would remain so permanently weak as to be open to outside aggression and conquest at all times. Either a greater law in a greater unity, or an unpreventable continuation of strife and bloodshed. It required less than one hundred and sixty years for the same choice to be thrust upon the peoples and nation-states of the entire world.

To isolationists the idea of world government is "foreign-inspired," impractical, repulsive, and intolerable.

Yet in essence it is simply the next logical step in the evolution of man and of organized society. The isolationists insist that in American union there is strength and virtue—but that in world union there could be neither virtue nor strength. They insist that what has proved of exceptional benefit to inhabitants of the United States could not benefit all peoples to any worth-while degree, if applied by and for all. In reality isolationists employ the identical arguments that citizens of Rhode Island and other colonials made against the establishment of our federal government. The most simple and most obvious solution is what human nature most fears. Men denounce world government as something radically new and dangerously different when, in fact, it can only be *an extension on a higher level of what we already practice and believe.* If there is any strength in union under law, then there must be greater strength in greater union under law.

There is a vast amount of sober, compact truth in these observations by C. G. Paulding of the *Commonweal:*

> There can be no trusting the generals to save us. The scientists already have said emphatically that science cannot save us. In turn the statesmen cannot save us because they are busy saving America, or saving Russia, or saving the Republic of San Marino. They are thinking in terms of national sovereignties and interests, and that means they are incapable of thinking in terms of world government. World government alone, representing mankind and not governments, can save mankind from a last and totally disastrous civil war.

It is not surprising that our much shrunken world remains perpetually at war with itself. After all, it still possesses no common policeman for even a few commonly accepted, universal laws. Instead there are some seventy or more separate sources of law, dressed up in seventy or more separate national sovereignties, fiercely competing and conflicting with each other on hundreds of points and issues. Even a modestly limited World Law, applying only to a few specific and vital matters, would remove the most aggravating and dangerous of these conflicting issues.

As Emery Reves has concisely pointed out, it is not at all a question of "surrendering" national sovereignty. "The problem is not negative and does not involve giving up something we already have. The problem is positive—creating something we lack . . . but that we imperatively need." *

This is what hundreds of atomic scientists in the United States, Britain, and other countries were among the first to understand clearly and emphatically. Profoundly thoughtful and gifted men, like Dr. Albert Einstein and Dr. Harold C. Urey, see no defense whatever in an atomic age except through the establishment of a world law and the beginning of world government. The United World Federalists, under the leadership of Cord Meyer, Jr., and many other prominent Americans, are dedicated to this single objective. The Committee to Frame a World Constitution, headed by Chancellor Robert M. Hutchins of the University of Chicago, works to provide a preliminary draft that can serve as a basis of discussion. A remarkable number of organizations concerned with regional or world federation and peace enforcement exists today, with steadily widening influence and support.†

In the turmoil of East-West controversies and international crises one most encouraging fact is repeatedly befogged and too generally ignored. Even though the world's powers appear to be making little or no immediate progress toward peace, there does exist—

---

* Emery Reves: *The Anatomy of Peace* (New York: Harper & Brothers; 1945), p. 137.

† For an authoritative summary of various proposals for world government, together with a complete list of organizations and educational materials available, Harry H. Moore: *Survival or Suicide* (New York: Harper & Brothers; 1948).

*A world-wide trend toward greater federa-
tions and toward a supernational unity.*

Unquestionably World War II was an immense calamity. Yet strong influences toward regional or world
unification have emerged from this frightfully costly conflict. If mankind *can* only learn thoroughly through the
experience of bloodshed and barbarism, contemporary
peoples have experienced enough of it to have begun to
learn some things—even against their will.

We think of a Europe divided in half—with the eastern
half dominated by Soviet Russia and Communists—as
both a menace and a retrogression. The Red-ruled half of
Europe does constitute a menace in this particular pin-
point of time. But it need not necessarily prove to be a
retrogression. Actually, although our fears prevent us from
seeing it, even the present Communist control of satellite
Europe may finally prove to be a progressive step in the
evolution of that continent. In the long view this may be
a positive gain despite police-state dictatorships, terror,
and oppression.

For something has happened in eastern Europe which
had never happened before throughout its centuries of
tribal and national conflicts. For the first time there exists,
to all intents and purposes, a great and broad federation of
eastern Europe, which includes six different nations and
some one hundred million people. It's true, this is an
involuntary federation, imposed by Communist dictators.
It has not yet been officially proclaimed either a Danubian, a Balkan, or a Pan-Slav federation, and possibly
it may never be. But the economies of these satellite
countries are being co-ordinated as never before. For the
first time in their turbulent, war-studded history Bulgari-
ans, Rumanians, Hungarians, Czechs, and Poles find it
impossible to fight each other, or to create armies designed

primarily to combat one another. Despite their deep
national antagonisms they are compelled to merge their
productive aims, their trade interests and their defense
activities.

All this is embarrassing to the western democracies, and
cruelly repressive to the eastern European peoples caught
in the Red vise. Nevertheless, the Red-ruled half of
Europe has become federated and unified as never before.
If these nations continue to co-operate economically and
politically for any period of time, will they dare to revert
to their former weak and exposed nationalism? Will they
not, more probably, strive to preserve the obvious advantages of closer co-operation while struggling to establish
much greater and wider political freedoms than they enjoy today? In any event the march of mankind has been
toward ever larger political units and unity. It may be
that Communist domination, like Napoleon's surges across
Europe, will teach lessons of other connotations than those
dreamed of in the Kremlin. Where dictatorship cannot
endure indefinitely, the seeds of federation may survive
and grow.

In western Europe this is already happening as a matter
of free choice rather than police compulsion. There, too,
the stern compulsion of circumstance plays an important
role. But the governments and the people are recognizing
that their security and prosperity reside only in "Western
Union" or a Federation of Western Europe; ultimately,
in a United States of Europe. When I heard Aristide
Briand movingly champion a United States of Europe in
Geneva in the late 1920's, he was generally regarded as a
nobly intentioned but impractical visionary. No European
government then in existence would seriously consider
the idea.

The contrast between Geneva in 1928 and The Hague
in 1948 was startling. Without waiting for official action
by their governments, a distinguished group of western

Europe's parliamentarians and private citizens assembled at The Hague in the "first Congress of Europe." They convened on their own initiative, impelled by a common feeling of urgency. Addressing their opening session, Winston Churchill urged "the gradual assumption by all the nations concerned of that *larger sovereignty*" which alone could offer them protection.

> We aim [declared Churchill] at the eventual participation of all peoples throughout the Continent, whose society and way of life are not in disaccord with a charter of human rights and the sincere expression of free democracy. We welcome any country where the people own the government, and not the government the people. . . . We must do our best to create and combine the great regional unities . . . to prepare for the day when there will be an effective world government resting upon the main groupings of mankind.

Already, in the previous March, a five-power agreement had been signed in Brussels by Britain, France, Belgium, the Netherlands, and Luxemburg. The Brussels Pact was a first step toward a Western European Union. It was a protective alliance, inspired by fear both of the Soviet Union and of a restored Germany. A permanent committee of the five nations' defense ministers was set up. But the Brussels Pact went far beyond prewar practices. Its goal was also unprecedented economic co-operation between the five powers, and an eventual customs union, radically reducing tariff walls between them. It contemplates a "partial merger of the national sovereignties" of the five nations concerned.

Delegates to the first "Congress of Europe" greatly developed and expanded the main ideas of the Five-Power Pact. They agreed: "It is the urgent duty of the nations of Europe to create a political and economic union so as to secure security and social progress to their peoples." Their resolution demanded "the convening, as a matter of real urgency, of a European Assembly chosen by the parliaments of the participating nations from among their members and others."

The conception of a European Assembly has grown notably since World War II. It is intimately linked, of course, with much-increased recognition of the necessity for a federation or a United States of Europe. In Briand's day no such influential and widespread support for this objective existed. But since the war 190 members of Parliament in Britain signed a motion urging the government to support a European federation. A large group of French deputies are committed to the same endeavor. The movement has gathered strength throughout western Europe—wherever the peoples' hunger for greater security could express itself.

The practical difficulties that confront any regional federation, whether a strictly western or all-European union, are tremendous. Even progress toward a three-power, Benelux * customs union has been slow and painful. Years of effort may be required before so much as a western European Federation can be established in some impressive form. But here we are concerned uniquely with a distinctly new and vigorous trend—the trend toward regional federations, whether in Europe or Indonesia. *Regional federations have powerful new champions and a new meaning simply because people can no longer find real security in national defense, and because most nations no longer can hope for restored prosperity without pooling many of their resources in much larger economic units. To remain free or to hope to achieve freedom most of the earth's peoples must seek a Greater Union.*

By a curious and persistent evolution of circumstances the security of the American people is inextricably linked to the security of all free European nations. Thanks to the obstructionism, suspicions, and policies of Soviet Communism—and perhaps to its secret ambitions as well—we

* Belgium, the Netherlands, and Luxemburg.

are not only forced to defend western Europe. In order to hope to make such a defense adequately powerful we are also compelled to join in organizing a western European defense force. Such a force cannot be organized without the participation and guidance of the United States. It can be given the reality of vast amounts of weapons and matériel only if the United States supplies them. And this Western European Defense Force requires definite guarantees of immediate American support if any of its members become victims of aggression. That is probably the only guarantee with sufficient weight and power behind it to give serious and effective pause to any present or future Soviet policy-makers who might be tempted by ideas of military expansion across Europe.

Thus there is already taking shape in the preliminary stages something much bigger than a strictly Western European Defense Force. There is taking shape an Inter-Atlantic Defense Force, which amounts to an alliance between European and U.S. democracy. In a sense it marks the first faint stirrings of *an Inter-Atlantic federation*. For military co-operation cannot become pronounced without increasing political and economic co-operation. But this common military necessity has already given great impetus to efforts toward a Western European Federation. Foreign Minister Bevin of Great Britain frankly declared to the United Nations Assembly in Paris in late September 1948: "I can assure you that it is decided to build a union —a Western Union—which can stand on its own feet and rally its own people against any aggression."

Mr. Bevin's assurance was based upon the fact that Britain, France, and Benelux had already agreed upon a common defense policy and formation of a permanent, joint military staff and command. But it was based even more upon recognition by American leaders that true security for the United States depends upon creation of an enlarged sovereignty. Lacking a U.N. or a world police force, a Western European Union has become an absolute minimum of what we require for our own protection, for the immediate future, until a wider law can be established.

The United States cannot escape larger and shared responsibilities any more than we can fail to continue to strive toward an enlarged world sovereignty. Thomas E. Dewey made a tremendously important contribution to public understanding of this fact in his Salt Lake City declaration on U.S. foreign policy during the Presidential campaign. We shall use European aid, he stated, "as the means for pushing, prodding and encouraging the nations of Western Europe toward the goal of European Union. . . . What is needed is a third great, peaceful power which will be so strong that no despotic ruler of a totalitarian nation will think the cause of freedom so weak that he dares to wage war. . . . What is needed is a United States of Europe."

There, in sober truth, is an objective great enough and challenging enough to match the finest ideals and to electrify the imaginations of the American people. Governor Dewey had the vision to express it in such terms. "A federation of Western Europe's 270,000,000 people into one strong economic, political union," he said, "would be the greatest triumph of statesmanship in history. It would be the firmest guaranty of peace in all history." Would Americans remain content to be palsied by fear of Communism and a feeling of frustrated impotence? Or would the American people prefer to be up and doing, bending their efforts toward a great and constructive objective? What would be more fitting than that the United States of the New World should devote its enormous influence and power toward the establishment of the United States of the Old World? Even by furthering the Union of Western Europe we should be refortifying the walls of our own democracy. And this dedication to enlarged federation has already become both a practical and an inspiring part of American postwar leadership.

This is far more than an anti-Communist improvisation or the negativism of "block the Communists." It is a specific commitment to do something positive and to build in the direction of the higher level of the world community. It is in harmony with the aspirations of the free peoples of Europe—and it happens also to harmonize completely with the best self-interests of the American people. In this direction we shall only be practicing those things which have made our own union great and strong.

When groups of nations turn toward regional federations, they are groping, in reality, toward One World and a World Law. They are repudiating the lie of national self-sufficiency and national safety in the modern, technological age of atomic fission. They are realizing that the Maginot lines of our very recent past are a delusion and a betrayal. It may be, as often seems probable, that enough of the world's people of our generation will not reach this awareness and act upon it—in time. It may be that another and much more terrible catastrophe will be necessary before sufficient people understand and work toward the great objective. Nevertheless, one must deny the testimony of mankind's entire laborious and excruciating upward march if one is to assume that this much intensified new trend toward a world sovereignty will fail to make notable progress in the next two or three decades. The trend may suffer many setbacks, or even appear to have been submerged in destruction. But because it is a trend of great hope and ultimate promise for mankind, it can never be destroyed or permanently abandoned. Man can abandon almost anything save the promise of life, and of a better life.

The tremendous hopes that the masses of the world's peoples have placed in the United Nations strikingly demonstrate their profound instinctive impetus toward some universal law. However much their governments may fumble and bungle in early U.N. endeavors, the peoples' faces are turned forward—and also upward. To date the United Nations may have proved a sharp disappointment to a majority of people in many lands. Yet the fact remains that they have nowhere else to turn. They can only remain faced toward regional federation and co-operation; toward the United Nations and world co-operation. Nothing less than these can possibly offer them what they seek most—some real hope of peace and better livelihood. Although a relatively tiny minority may as yet be conscious of it—

The United Nations constitutes an early-stage foundation for the creation of a World Government.

We have become fairly familiar with rising demands for drastic reforms of the U.N. charter, especially of its much abused veto privilege. We are more aware of the early stalemates and failures in the Security Council than of U.N. achievements in other fields, such as the considerable progress toward a peaceful settlement in Palestine. Perhaps, as almost invariably we do, we expected too much of a new and vast experiment still in the process of finding itself through trial and error.

Yet the fact remains that the United Nations has been compelled to develop peace-enforcing machinery in a world that is far from having established peace. Its efforts continually founder upon the rocks of controversy between the Soviet East and the democratic West. Its instruments, even if experimental and often inadequate, can seldom get an opportunity to function fully. There is much more blueprint of a world organization than structure. Yet the U.N. Charter is as open to amendment as was our original Constitution. And because there is much more blueprint than structure, the foundations of the United Nations can still be greatly enlarged, revised—and then built upon. Amendments and reforms are bound to come.

Perhaps the most serious liability of the United Nations, as it currently exists, is that it is an organization of sovereign states. It does not yet possess any real world sovereignty—any supra-national laws—of its own. The U.N. is forced to attempt to reconcile the irreconcilable; to reconcile some sixty *national* sovereignties of as many nation-states. But whenever vital issues like the enforcement of peace are concerned, national sovereignties cannot be restrained or contained unless all member states accept and are bound by a common superior law. Not until at least a few universal laws are adopted can the U.N. be in a position to curb the present struggle of power politics in its activities, especially on the part of the big powers. But the important thing to recognize is that this change *can* be brought about inside the U.N. under its Charter; and that this change *must* come. Under the pressure of public opinion it could begin to make itself evident, constructively and hopefully, within the next few years.

Even a relatively small and limited union between Britain, France, and the Benelux countries has forced these five governments to sacrifice certain elements of traditional *national* sovereignty in matters of defense. More accurately, these nations have been compelled to create a common, five-power, *super*-sovereignty for defense purposes. This is also true in limited aspects of production, trade, and finance. The same process is being dictated, interestingly enough, in the application of the Marshall Plan. European nations that benefit by ERP do so by accepting common rules for all. The greater gains promised western Europe as a whole can be had only by subordination of certain strictly national interests or privileges. Through ERP certain practical foundations for a Western European Union may well be laid. The lesson is that regional planning through a regional sovereignty can pay greater dividends, economically and defensively, than the anarchy of national cross-purposes ever can. Without a common and superior legal framework ERP, with its billions of expenditures and commitments, could not be administered.

From ERP or a Western European Federation, or from any sizable regional federation, it is but one more step up to the international organization of the United Nations. Obviously, the U.N. cannot enforce peace—which we all say we want it to do—without creating a law and a sovereignty of its own. It has already taken a first step, even though modest, in this direction. The U.N. has created an International Law Commission. By electing the fifteen members of this commission the 1948 General Assembly authorized a new codification of international law. It has also submitted a draft convention on genocide (racial mass extermination as practiced by the Nazis against the Jews). In the words of Secretary General Trygve Lie, "The object in view is to make international law apply to individuals as well as to states."

People have talked for centuries about this or that "crime against humanity"; but there has been no universal law under which any individual, regardless of nationality, could be held punishable for such crimes. Planned racial extermination is certainly such a crime, yet scores of thousands of those who contributed to it or practiced it under Hitler will never be punished. If the U.N. under a world law succeeds in making individuals directly responsible for genocide or other varieties of mass murder, it will have made a tremendous contribution toward an orderly, decent world.

The whole problem of the United Nations is to create

a minimum of universal laws within the framework of a new, *supra*-national sovereignty. For this to happen, a U.N. or World Supreme Court will be necessary. Whether in a new structure or through an extension of the International Court of Justice, the laws that will make the U.N. truly "peace-enforcing" will eventually require a universal supreme court on an expanded scale. For without a Supreme Law, universally applicable, world aggression cannot be restrained or punished effectively.

So we come back to the policeman, and especially to what he represents. This is why the U.N. Charter contains provisions for the creation of special armed units that would actually constitute a U.N. World Police Force. Establishment of this vital body has been blocked, thus far, by disagreements in the U.N. Military Staff Committee—yet there is little, if anything, that this war-fearing, defense-bankrupting world needs so urgently as a true world police force. We do not have it simply because nationalism and national sovereignties are so incredibly, suicidally upheld. Nations and governments, and apparently most individuals, would rather destroy one another than create a higher, universal, law-enforcing organization that could be made strong enough to prevent them from indulging in self-destruction.

Reconsider for a moment what we are now doing—and consider what we might do.

The United States and the Soviet Union are wasting vast fortunes for armed defense each year. They are eating up their national wealth and thereby destroying their long-term security, internal and external. Other nations, in great majority, are spending on defense many times what they can really afford. As Trygve Lie sharply warned, "There has never been any effective monopoly of bacteriological and chemical weapons . . . *but not a single proposal has been made by any of the [U.N] member nations for any system of preventing or controlling*

their manufacture." * Thus even a third-rate power remains free to menace hundreds of millions of human
beings with destruction from germicidal weapons—and
our governments quibble over whether to transfer a major
portion of their national forces into a common U.N. police
organization for world defense.

A relatively minor part of any nation's armed forces is
undoubtedly necessary for emergency use to defend the
government and maintain internal order. But when
strictly *national* defense forces have become utterly inadequate to provide a real, workable defense against atomic
and germicidal weapons, why not turn to something that
at least promises to be a great deal more effective? Why
pour good billions after bad?

What inspired United States support of a Western European Defense Force and what inspired Governor Dewey's
statesmanlike pledge of the fullest American support for
European Union was recognition of an unpleasant but
inescapable fact:

*There no longer exists such a thing as security
for any nation alone, not even for the U.S.A.*

Solitary security for single nations disappeared in the
gigantic columns of smoke above Hiroshima. The solitary
quest for national security as such is self-defeating as well
as self-bankrupting. We can no longer be self-sufficient for
self-protection. Although we may spend $25,000,000,000
per year to this end—or much more—even the United
States still depends upon the stability and strength of
western Europe today, and perhaps of India and Japan
tomorrow. In our much narrowed world it is futile to seek
adequate security alone, because no nation possesses sufficient power and wealth to be able to attain it, or to sub-

* Cf. *Annual Report* of the Secretary General to the U.N. General
Assembly, August 1948.

sidize it for any considerable number of years even if it could be attained.

In its essentials strictly "national" defense is a weak policy, offering no reliable assurance for the future. But in our radically shriveled world nationalism itself has become a perilous form of weakness. Nationalism itself cannot provide sufficient strength for its self-protection, nor adequate economic strength for its own durable prosperity. Nationalists, American or foreign, talk shrilly because the very remedy they propose cannot produce what they promise. Nationalism is too narrow, too limited, too restricted in its resources and too small at its base to offer a successful barrier against this century's revolutionary tides of change. Nationalism attempts to substitute one country's growth for the world's progress and growth. But Europe, Asia, Africa, and the Americas are all swept by similar social, political, and economic forces. *Nationalism is fatally and intolerably weak because it is an insular expedient based upon an insular state of mind— on a planet where islands no longer exist in reality.* Even our continents and oceans are fast becoming illusions. Otherwise why should Americans worry about being atom-bombed? Of and by ourselves we have no security. Nationalism can give us no more than the weakest and most questionable defense, at the greatest price and the highest risk.

Because there is no longer such a thing as national or solitary security our own government's chief efforts are now based upon building as great a degree of collective security as we can immediately achieve. A North Atlantic regional agreement and defense pact fits into that enlarged endeavor. The safety of the United States and Canada depends on Europe. From a collective security with western Europe we can reasonably hope to move on to a still larger collective security, and within the framework of the United Nations. Our nostalgia for the "good old days" of isolationism cannot blind most of us to the realities. If it were to do so we should have no security whatever, and no hope whatever of avoiding the calamity of war. For there is no aloneness left in this world save for such nations as may wish to commit suicide.

Those who still insist that we can stand alone are contradicted by all the major evidence since 1918; by a great depression and a second great war—and equally by the "cold war" of the present. Every power move of the Soviet Union and every critical development in Europe or Asia underscore the fact that collective security is the only possible kind of security which may be painfully created in an atomic age.

Most of us have accepted this fact subconsciously without analyzing it. Suddenly, as Americans, we want allies and friends. Until very recently that was the least worry of the average United States citizen. He had always felt he could rely on American might alone. Now he becomes deeply concerned about the outcome of elections in Italy or France, or about Communist encroachments in Korea. Somehow our billions upon billions for national defense have not proved enough. We are aware, however dimly, that we can no longer rely exclusively on our own defense organization. That being true, we can no longer rely upon our own national sovereignty. It is a solitary thing. It can only reach so far, and its reach falls far short of security for any of us.

But other means do exist and are available.

Why not move to a higher level where great possibilities exist for creating a defense under world law, which would be unquestionably more effective since it could not conceivably be less so? In any event its risks could not be greater than those we now endure. Its costs would assuredly be much less, especially in the long run.

If this cannot be done with the co-operation of Soviet Russia under its present leadership and policies, it could still be done leaving the door open for future participation of the Soviets and their satellites. This is true because a *preponderance* of the world's armed power already exists *outside* the Soviet-controlled nations. Consider this fact. The nations of western Europe, the British Commonwealth, North and Latin America, and India possess an overwhelming preponderance of the world's armed forces, manpower, industry, and other resources. Through the U.N. Military Staff Committee most of these governments could insist that a U.N. World Police Force be established; that their individual quota contributions should be in accord with each nation's size and military resources; that their home defense forces be reduced to a minimum as a result; that the newly constituted World Police Force, acting under World Law, would thereafter defend any and all of them from outside aggression—in the name of the United Nations.

What would be the result of such a decision? First of all, the Soviet Union and its satellites would be compelled either to accept an accomplished fact or to invite war with a formidable preponderance of the world's armed forces. They could not choose war without seeking inevitable defeat and the certain overthrow of the Communist dictatorships. They would be faced at last with a devil's choice —participate or withdraw. But if they elected to quit the United Nations, they would merely lock themselves up in a prolonged and extremely costly isolation. There would still exist a majority of United Nations, a supra-national organization, a new sovereignty above national sovereignties, and a new law common to most of the globe.

A U.N. police force might originally be drawn from no more than half of its present membership; or it might be based upon two thirds or possibly more. But even if based on approximately half, beginning with the United States, the British Commonwealth, France, Latin America, and India, such an organization would constitute by far the mightiest all-round armed power in the world. Automatically a considerable portion of each contributing nation's home forces could be reduced. Since the United States is best equipped to supply air and naval units, immediate reductions would logically be made first in its standing army. Cut even fifty or sixty per cent from the U.S. Army's appropriations and a very important saving would be made. Over a period of years, as the U.N. police force became efficient and accepted, greater and greater economies would result for every participating nation. It is impossible to calculate how many tens of billions of dollars might be saved or diverted to socially useful purposes annually.

Is this a pacifist's pipe-dream? It only seems so, I believe, because we lack the logic, vision, and courage to tear the scales of outmoded "national defense" worship from our eyes. The only thing that prevents the free nations from moving now into a U.N. Defense Force is our individual and collective lack of a will for peace—and *the will for peace is will for a common Supreme Law*. If by chance we cannot begin with a truly world law, we can at least begin with law that is more nearly universal than it has ever been in the past. That, of itself, would be a monumental step toward world government. Again quoting Emery Reves, "Collective security without collective sovereignty is meaningless." But to achieve collective sovereignty, and therefore collective security, some preponderant and impressive portion of the world's nations *must act collectively*. The first place to act is in establishing collective law, enforceable by collective police.

At every turn we come to the central problem of what to do about the Soviets, or whether to risk doing this or that without them. Is that risk, however, nearly so great as the long-term risk of failing to do something that is big and vital and strikes to the heart of the world's present nationalist anarchy?

With or without the Russians the United Nations will

have to be reformed and amended or it cannot fulfill its essential purposes. With or without the Russians the United Nations must create the first instruments of a new World Law. With or without the Russians a majority of the world's peoples are compelled to make a start at laying the foundations for a future world government. With or without the Soviets and Communists a majority of the world's population must be freed from the crushing, impoverishing burden of ever mounting "national" defense costs. With or without the approval of the Kremlin a preponderant and superior common force capable of enforcing peace and subduing aggressors must be created. If the free governments and free peoples insist upon attempting these things within the framework of the United Nations, ways to proceed will be found. A beginning will be made. The will for peace and the will for law alone can be decisive.

Dr. Albert Einstein has much support when he urges that the door should be left open for the Soviet Union in every possible way. It is one thing, of course, to leave the door plainly open; another thing to say: "But we wouldn't dare enter the room unless you come in with us, right away." Yet, necessary and urgent as One World is, we cannot reasonably expect it to be achieved in the lifetime of this generation. Desirable and logical as One Europe is, we cannot pretend that half of Europe free is worse than none. In the same fashion half the world, or two thirds of the present world, free and united under some common sovereignty, under a common law and backed by a common-purpose defense force, would mark a tremendous progress over our present predicament under uncurbed nationalisms.

In his valuable and perceptive book *Peace or Anarchy* Cord Meyer, Jr., says: "If patriotism is an active concern for the freedom, welfare and survival of one's people, there is no patriotic duty more immediate than the abolition of war as a national right and institution." * But of course we cannot abolish war as a "national right" so long as we pour a major portion of our wealth into "national" defense. It cannot be necessary to wait until the Soviet Union, or every nation's government, sees the light. It is merely necessary that the free, western peoples see the light and demand that the first steps be taken—to transform the United Nations into an instrument of supranational law, and to lay the first foundations on which world government can eventually be built. Whenever we end the supreme folly and waste of relying upon strictly national armed forces for security, we in the West will have placed half or more of the world on the march—toward safety, on the upper level.

Here I have not intended to underestimate the enormous difficulties involved. But my chief concern has been to emphasize that "the other defense" already exists in the minds of people who are fully aware; that the trends toward regional federation and the impetus toward world government through world law are already significant realities; and that the choice between alternatives cannot be long delayed by a majority of citizens in every free country.

What do these questions of a world law, a U.N. police force, and ultimate world government have to do with United States citizens? With the great American middle class?

It should be evident that either another big depression or another war would have disastrous and irreparable effects upon all Americans; and the most destructive effects would fall upon those scores of millions who are in the middle in our exposed society. Through a depression we who are America's middle men would be rendered economically desperate. We would be driven toward extremes of Communism or Fascism; our freedoms would be grave-

* Op. cit., p. 190.

ly threatened and almost certainly much reduced. These consequences would be multiplied by an atomic war, unpredictably and immeasurably. But so long as from thirty to fifty cents out of every dollar we pay in taxes is devoured by national defense, our nation will deplete its defenses against depression. The steady dissipation of our wealth and reserves will also serve to increase our eventual exposure to outside aggression and war. Under such strains, if prolonged, our internal disunity will grow rather than diminish.

It would be a calamity for all free peoples quite as much as ourselves if any considerable proportion of the United States middle class should be forced into the ranks of the disinherited and the impoverished. For the strength of our middle men also stands on economic foundations. And it is because the middle class constitutes the great American majority that its collective influence, or the absence of its collective influence, must be decisive.

There are various ways in which the influence of America's middle men can be decisive. It will be decisive in demanding and supporting prudent measures to prevent a depression, or in assuring an eventual depression through their political indifference. It can be decisive in keeping defense expenditures within reason before one more straw breaks the back of our capitalistic camel. Above all, it *can* be decisive in demanding that "the other defense" be tried, both with vigor and with a will for peace. But this, especially, can offer safety and security only if the American middle class and the United States government act in time.

We are not likely to have much more than a possible margin of about ten years in which to begin to build effectively a house of World Law. Nor much more than this brief margin in which to begin to create a sovereignty above individual nations; in which to begin to transform the United Nations into an instrument capable of defending peace.

In all these issues our lives and welfare and progress, our security and future opportunities, are at stake. In all these issues the United States of America must be the determining balance in the scales. And inside the United States of America the average middle-class citizen—the man between —is himself the determining balance and finally decisive influence.

You may take the pessimistic or the more hopeful view, according to how much you are aware and how much you care and how much thinking you are willing to do.

If there is reason for pessimism about depression or war tomorrow, no citizen of any other country can be so much to blame as America's John Between. For he alone is the giant, drowsing or not. In these recent years he has had ample time in which to become informed, to study his own situation and that of the world, and to draw intelligent conclusions. He has had unique opportunities to inform himself and to do his thinking in comfort and on a full stomach, greater opportunities than the peoples of Europe and Asia. He has had every opportunity to throw his influence toward intelligent self-defense, both domestically and internationally.

For the self-defense of the U.S. middle men is, in reality, the defense of free men and free minds and free societies everywhere. *Freedom, too, is a collective security, which cannot be preserved without collective action and collective sovereignty.* We are average Americans and therefore we are the common men of our nation. If we cannot understand these things, and act upon them in an emphatic majority, then the crossfires of totalitarianism and of ultimate war cannot fail to mow us down. *It is we, the men between, who make our own fate.*

But if there is reason for hope—even for a restrained and

sober hope—it lies in the qualities and above all in the demonstrated capacities of the average American. He can be big indeed when he chooses to be big. He can serve great objectives and ideals with devotion and an exulting heart. It is within his capacity and power to comprehend the essential nature of the forces that are ganged up on him. It is within his educational training to perceive that he, and he alone, guards the key sectors of freedom's front. And it is equally within *his* possibility to choose, and then to support, those representatives and leaders who also know how to choose. Because he has the strength of his convictions, a deep regard for justice and a great deal of common sense this average American has the unquestioned capacity to resist extremism and hysteria; to assert himself for sound actions; to build a middle way that is better, more equitable, and finer than anything in his past.

If there is reason for hope it is because America's middle men have both the capacities and the power to achieve what they most desire to achieve; because they can still *make tomorrow,* if once they catch the vision of its possibilities and the realization of its needs—the sense that *tomorrow is ours to shape.* For there is only one livable and endurable tomorrow that any person living today can hope to have: a tomorrow in which an entirely new measure of collective security has been established through World Law on the upper highway toward World Government.

Index

Advisory Commission on Universal Training, 239
A.F.L., 26, 55, 158
agrarian reform, *see* land feudalism
Aikman: *The Turning Stream,* 49 n.
Albania, 190
Allyn, S. C., 177
Alsop, Joseph and Stewart, 237
America First Committee, 143
America First Party, 151
American Civil Liberties Union, 228
American Library Association, 204–5
American Newspaper Guild, 159
American Veterans Committee, 159
American-Soviet Science Society, 216
Americans for Democratic Action, 159
Americans and Europeans: differences, 38–58; common interests, 58–64
Americans United for World Government, 145
Andrews, Bert, 210
anti-Red riots, 192–5
Argentina, 186, 261
armament-makers, European, 67–68
arms-production boom, 169, 176, 246–8
atomic bombs, 11, 185, 207–8, 216, 230–3, 241, 244, 260, 264

atomic control, 237
atomic project and research, 215–18, 223, 237, 242
atomic scientists, 267
Attlee, Clement, 100
Australia, 16–17, 34
Austria, 50, 68, 85, 87
Austria-Hungary, 46
Authors League of America, 221
automobile industry, 171

Baldwin, Hanson W.: *The Price of Power,* 231 n., 243
Baldwin, Stanley, 142
Balogh, Father, 51
Baruch, Bernard M., 176–7, 182, 183, 249, 254
Belgium, 46, 84, 95, 144
Benelux customs union, 271, 272
Beneš, President Eduard, 245–6
Bentley, Elizabeth, 214
Berry, Police Chief, 193
Best Years of Our Lives, The, 220
Bevin, Ernest, 272
biological warfare, 230, 233–4, 279
Bowles, Chester, 32, 135, 198; "Challenge to the Business Man," 179 n.
Bradley, General Omar, 242, 251, 252
Briand, Aristide, 269
British Commonwealth, 4, 282
British government, *see* Great Britain
Brussels Pact, 270

i

Bulgaria, 102, 190, 191
Bulletin of the Atomic Scientists,
    216
Byrd, Senator Harry F., 135

Canada: Communist Party in,
    202; spy case, 204, 213
Canby, Henry Seidel, 145
capitalism and capitalists, 27, 31,
    35, 94, 99–101, 114, 115, 122–3,
    153, 166–8, 170, 180, 235–6
capitalists' support of Nazism and
    Fascism, 77–9, 81, 97–8, 157
cartels, 67–8, 115
Catholic Church in U.S., attitude
    toward Communism and Fas-
    cism, 26, 157–8
Catholic Church properties in
    Hungary, 103
Catholic hierarchy in Italy, 112–
    13
Catholic People's Party in Czecho-
    slovakia, 50
Catholic War Veterans, 204
CCC, 179
Chamberlain, Neville, 90, 142
Chambers, Whittaker, 222
Chaplin, Charles, in *Monsieur
    Verdoux,* 204
Chiang Kai-shek, 186
Chicago Tribune, 145–6, 220
China, 45, 61, 63, 103, 130, 186,
    261
Christian Democratic Party in
    Italy, 113, 114
Christian Front, 150
Christian Nationalists, 151, 158
Christian Socialist Party in Aus-
    tria, 50
church and state, 49–51
Churchill, Winston, 108, 245, 270
C.I.O., 26, 55–6, 135, 158, 159
Citroen, André, 40
civil liberties, 186–206, 223–4
civil-rights program, 195–6

clericalism and anticlericalism,
    49–51, 53
collaborators, 97–8, 110
Columbia River floods, 130
Columbians, Incorporated, 148
Columbus (Ohio) anti-Red riot,
    192–4
Cominform, 104
Comité des Forges, 68
Committee to Frame a World
    Constitution, 267
Commonweal, 266
Communism and Communists: in
    Europe, 23, 59, 67, 94–5, 98,
    102–7, 111–12, 114, 117, 118,
    124, 190–2, 274; in U.S., 26–7,
    54, 140–1, 146–8, 150, 153, 154,
    156–7, 199
Communism, fear of, 20, 23, 25–7,
    70, 192–4, 274
Communist Party in U.S., 197–
    203, 226–8
Condon, Dr. Edward U., 215–16
"Congress of Europe," 270
conservatives, U.S., 126–8, 131–2,
    151, 158, 160, 190 (*see also*
    Right-wing groups)
Coolidge, President Calvin, 33,
    39
cost of living, 32, 169, 172–8, 182
Council of Economic Advisers,
    President Truman's, 178 n.
Cousins, Norman, 145
"crisis mentality," 84-90
Currie, Lauchlin, 214–15, 224
Czechoslovakia, 50, 62, 94, 190–1

Daily Worker, 140
Daniels, Jonathan, 145
Davenport, Russell, 145
Dawes Plan, 71
defense program: costs of, 236–41,
    250–1, 286; restrictions entailed
    by, 248–50; possible democratic
    losses due to, 255–6
de Gaulle, Charles, 117

de Gaullists, 119
Democratic Party, 127, 134, 135
depression: in Europe, 67–72, 180; in U.S., 26, 27, 33, 70–1, 165, 168–9, 179, 181
Dewey, Governor Thomas E., 127, 135, 160, 202, 273, 279
Dollfuss, Engelbert, 71
Douglas, William O., 135
Durr, Clifford J., 227–8

Earle, George H., 244
Eccles, Marriner S., 171–2
Edison, Thomas A., 28
Einstein, Dr. Albert, 145, 185, 267, 284
Eisenhower, General Dwight D., 242, 256
emigration from U.S., 16–17
ERP, *see* Marshall Plan
Euro-American civilization, 58–64
Europe: eastern, 268–9; western, 61–4, 119, 124, 269
European Assembly, 270–1
Europeans and Americans: differences, 38–58; similarities, 58–64
Evening Dispatch (Columbus, O.), 192

Fadiman, Clifton, 145
Fairbanks, Douglas, Jr., 145
"Fair Procedures" bill, model, 228
FBI, 26, 150, 201, 209, 211, 212, 216, 217, 218, 228, 242–3
fears, Americans', 20–7
Federal Communications Commission, 228
Federal Reserve Board, 171; Report, 7 n.
Field, Marshall, Jr., 145
Finletter, Thomas K., 145
Foster, William Z., 135
France, 4, 46, 51, 52, 68–9, 72, 78–9, 84, 85, 92, 94, 96, 97 100, 101, 116–17, 119, 261, 272, 282
Franco, Francisco, 154, 186

Frank, Hans, 149
freedom of speech, thought, press, 186–206 (*see also* civil liberties)
French under Nazi occupation, 92

gas warfare, 233
Gasperi, Alcide de, 112, 114
General Electric, 171, 177
General Motors, 171, 182
genocide, 277
German-American Bund, 151
German industrialists, 76–8
German Labor Front, 80
Germany, 46, 66, 67, 68, 72–9, 85, 87, 117
Goebbels, Joseph, 73, 74, 79, 82
gold standard, 71
Gore, Representative Albert, 129
Göring, Hermann, 78, 149
Grafton, Samuel, 240
Great Britain and the British, 46, 53, 55, 68, 84, 85, 95, 99–100, 107–13, 118, 142–3, 144, 253, 260, 272
Greece, 108–9
Grzesinski: *Inside Germany*, 80 n., 189 n.
guilt by association, 215, 224–6, 228

Harding, President Warren G., 33
Harriman, Mrs. J. Borden, 145
Hart, Merwin K., 153–5, 160
Harvard Law Review, 225 n.
Hashmall, Frank, 192–3
Hearst press, 142, 151, 152, 160
Henderson, Leon, 135
Hill, Gladwin, 221
Himmler, Heinrich, 79
Hiss, Alger, 222
Hitler, Adolf, 71, 73, 74, 76, 77, 87, 93, 140, 188–9, 254
Hlinka, Father, 50
Hoare, Sir Samuel, 147

Hollywood writers, investigation of, 220–1
Homestead Act, 48–9
Hoover, President Herbert, 33
Hoover, J. Edgar, 201, 242
Hopkins, Harry, 201
Hungary, 45, 51, 66, 85, 96, 102, 103–6, 132, 190, 191
Hutchins, Chancellor Robert M., 267

Ickes, Harold L., 198, 201
ideologies, conflicting, 53, 133, 137–9
I. G. Farben, 68
India, 61, 63, 282
Indo-China, 108
Indonesia, 108
industrialists under Nazism, 76–8, 97–8
inflation: in Europe, 67–70, 96–7; in U.S., 32, 69, 170–2, 175
Institute of World Economics and World Politics, Moscow, 167
Inter-Atlantic Defense Force, 272
isolationism, 142–6, 261, 265–6
Italy and the Italians, 51, 67, 72, 75, 83, 85, 94, 108, 109–14, 144; elections (1948), 112, 114, 116
Izvestia, 139

Jefferson, Thomas, 61
Johnston, Eric, 221
Journal of Commerce, 247

Károlyi, Count, 103
Kelley, Dr. Douglas M., 149
Krupp von Bohlen, 67, 68, 79
Ku Klux Klan, 148, 161
Kun, Béla, 66

labor and labor unions, 26, 30, 55, 68, 99, 110, 111, 113, 114, 122, 141, 146, 147, 175, 176
Labour Party in Britain, 95, 99, 100

Lamont, Thomas W., 78
land feudalism, 43–9, 99, 102–5, 107, 111
land-holding in U.S., 48–9
Latin America, 261, 282
la Touche de Pellerin, Baron de, 69
Laval, Pierre, 97
League of Nations, 18, 269
Left, non-Communist, in U.S., 158–60, 197–9
Leftist trends in Europe, 67, 70, 94–9
Ley, Robert, 149
liberals, U.S., 197–9
libraries, censorship in public, 204–5
Lie, Trygve, 277, 278
Lilienthal, David E., 130, 201; *TVA: Democracy on the March*, 130 n.
Lippmann, Walter, 118, 250
Lodge, Henry Cabot, Jr., 239, 250
Long, Huey, 135, 151, 204
Los Alamos Association of Scientists, 233
Loyalty Review Board, 211, 217
loyalty tests, 209–22, 224, 226–8

Macy, R. H., & Company, 177
Maertz, Homer, 151
Mallon, Paul, 151–2
Marshall, Secretary George C., 139, 240, 242, 256
Marshall Plan, 6, 31, 47, 59, 100, 118, 120 140, 144, 168, 169, 176, 241, 248, 276–7
McCormick, Colonel Robert R., 144–5, 160, 261
McDowell, Representative John, 148–9, 150
McGurn, dispatch from Rome, 113 n.
Meyer, Cord, Jr., 267; *Peace or Anarchy*, 284
middle class in U.S., 3–15, 285–8

military men's support of reactionary movements, 158
minority racial groups in U.S., 146, 147, 195–6
mob violence in U.S., anti-Communist, 192–5
monopolies and trusts, 122–3 (*see also* cartels)
Moore: *Survival or Suicide*, 267 n.
Morrison, Dr. Philip, 233
Motion Picture Association of America, 220
Mowrer, Paul Scott, 24
Mundt-Nixon bill, 200–1
Munich crisis, 90
Murray, Philip, 135, 159
Mussolini, Benito, 71, 75, 76, 87, 88, 93, 110

Nation, The, 205
National Association of Manufacturers, 32, 173, 174, 176, 239
National Bureau of Standards, 215
National Cash Register Company, 177
National City Bank, 247 n.
National Economic Council, Inc., 153–5
National Industrial Conference, 235
National Planning Association, 177, 182
National Security Resources Board, 239
national sovereignty, 259, 261–2, 266–7, 269–70, 276, 281
nationalism, 163, 262, 263, 264, 280 (*see also* isolationism)
Nazi Ministry of Economics, 81
Nazi-occupied countries, 91–3
Nazi puppet governments, 102, 105–6
Nazi-Soviet nonaggression pact, 93, 140
Nazi Winter Help Fund, 82

Nazis and law, 188–90
Nazism: coming of, 72–84; and industrialists, 76–8, 97; middle class under, 73–6, 80–2, 88
Netherlands, the, 46
New Deal, 55, 101, 119, 124–31, 146, 179, 198, 239
New York Daily News, 142–3, 160
New York Herald Tribune, 80, 199, 210, 217, 227, 235 n., 237 n.
New York Post, 144 n., 169
New York Times, 7 n., 20 n., 118, 143, 167 n., 171 n., 178 n., 201, 205 n., 221, 237 n., 239 n., 246
Norway, 91
NRA, 125, 179

Oak Ridge atomic plants, 129, 217
O'Brian, John Lord, 225, 227
Ohio State Journal, 193
OPA, 32, 69, 172–3

Panama Canal, 236
party systems in U.S. and Europe, 51–4, 134–5
Paulding, C. G., 266
Perkins, Frances, 201
Perón, Juan D., 186
Pilsudski, Józef, 72
Pinchot, Mrs. Gifford, 145
Pirellis, the, 68
Pius XII, Pope, 113
planned economy, 166, 182–3
Poland, 45, 62, 72, 85, 95, 102, 104, 132, 190
Politburo, 24, 25, 140, 165, 166–8, 250
Popular Republican Movement in France, 96
population densities, 41–2
Porter, Paul, 32, 173
Porter, Sylvia F., 169–70
Portugal, 44, 52, 103
Pravda, 139, 168
"preventive war," 243
price controls, 172–3, 174, 176–7

Progressive Party, 158–9, 160, 194
Prussia, East, 45, 102, 104, 132

R.A.F., 91
Reconstruction Finance Corporation, 128, 179
religion in politics, 49–51
Republican Party, 127, 128, 134, 135, 160, 197
Resistance movements, 93
Reston, James, 118
Reuther, Walter, 159–60
Reves: *The Anatomy of Peace*, 267, 283
Ribbentrop, Joachim von, 149
Rice, Paul North, 204
Richardson, Seth W., 211
Right-wing groups in U.S., 142–5, 148–58, 160–1
Roosevelt, Eleanor, 198
Roosevelt, President Franklin D., 21, 33, 55, 70, 101, 119, 124, 125, 128, 253
Royall, Secretary Kenneth C., 238–9
Rumania, 102, 106, 190, 191
Ruml, Beardsley, 177, 237
Russell, Senator Richard B., 135
Russia, Czarist, 46, 132

Scandinavia, 4, 46, 53, 55, 85, 95
Schacht, Hjalmar, 77, 78
Schlesinger, Professor Arthur M., Jr., 134, 135
Schneider-Creusot, 67
Schultz, Rabbi Benjamin, 151
Seipel, Ignaz, 50
Senate Foreign Relations Committee, 176
Sherwood, Robert, 145
Sieburg, Dr. Friedrich, 74
Silver Shirts, 151, 160–1
Smith, Gerald L. K., 148, 151
Social Democratic Party in Germany, 68
Social Security Act, 146

Socialism and Socialists, 35, 53, 55–6, 67, 94, 99–101, 114–15, 124; distinguished from Communism and Fascism, 126, 130–1
Socialist parties, 50, 67, 70, 95–6, 98, 114
Southern Conference for Human Welfare, 215
Soviet collective farms, 104
Soviet propaganda about U.S., 138–41
Soviet satellites, 52, 62, 97, 102–9, 268–9, 282
Soviet Union, 23–6, 61, 167, 231–3, 241, 244–5, 250, 260, 268–9, 272, 278, 281–2, 283–4, 285
space-poverty in Europe, 41–9
Spain, 44, 45, 51, 52, 87, 103, 186
Special War Investigating Committee, Senate's, 235, 254
Stalin, Joseph, 3, 24, 77, 245, 250
Stassen, Harold A., 202
state religion, 49–51
steel industry, 100, 170–1, 247
Sternberg: *The Coming Crisis*, 179 n.
Stettinius, Edward R., 145
Stinnes, Hugo, 68, 79
Stowe, Leland: "Hungary's Agrarian Revolution," 104 n.; *While Time Remains*, 108 n.
Streicher, Julius, 149
submarines, Soviets', 232–3, 234
"subversive," the term, 201
subversive activities, 209–19
Sweden, 66, 95
Swing, Raymond, 145
Switzerland, 66
syndicalism, 53, 55

taxes, 176, 235, 238, 249, 250, 253, 286
Tennessee Valley Authority, 128–30
Thomas, Representative J. Parnell, 148

Thyssen, Fritz, 68, 79, 80, 81
Tibe, Police Captain, 193
Time, 171 n., 201
Tito, Marshal, 104, 117, 140
Togliatti, Palmiro, 111
Toynbee, Professor Arnold J., 133
Truman, President Harry S., 35, 109, 127, 139, 143, 165, 171, 175, 178, 195, 218
Type 21 submarines, 232–3, 234

Un-American Activities Committee, 148, 150, 151, 214–22, 226
unemployment, 179–80
Union League Club, N.Y.C., 155
United Automobile Workers, 159
United Nations, 144, 154, 155, 272, 273, 274–8, 281, 282, 285, 287; *Annual Report,* 279 n.; Charter, 275–6, 278; International Court of Justice, 278; International Law Commission, 277; Military Staff Committee, 278, 282; World Police Force, 259, 278–9, 282–3, 285; World Supreme Court, 278
U.S. Air Force, 236, 239
U.S. Air Policy Commission, 234, 238
U.S. Army, 283
U.S. Atomic Energy Commission, 216, 242
U.S. Bureau of Labor Statistics, 173
U.S. Chamber of Commerce, 30, 174, 239
U.S. Congress, 29, 34, 59, 131, 172, 174, 175, 178, 195, 220, 222, 224, 227, 228–9, 236, 240, 241, 243, 249, 253, 254
U.S. government, 107–13, 116, 118
U.S. parties, 51–2, 134–5
U.S. State Department employees, 210–11
U.S. Steel, 170, 182

"United States of Europe," 269, 278
United World Federalists, 30, 145, 267
Urey, Dr. Harold C., 145, 267

Van Doren: *The Great Rehearsal,* 265
Varga, Eugene S., 167–8, 177
Vögler, Albert, 77, 78, 79
Voltaire, 202

Wagner Labor Relations Law, 146
Wallace, Henry, 51, 54, 159, 160, 194, 202
war: cost of, 234–6, 245–6; possible future, 19, 23–5, 236, 241, 243–6, 250; profits due to, 251–3, 254
Warburg, James P., 145
Ward, Barbara, 20–1
Werth, Alexander, 168
Western European Defense Force, 272, 279
Western European Union, 269–70, 273, 276–7
"Western Union," 269
White, Harry, 214–15
Willkie, Wendell, 197
Wilson, Charles E., 177
Wilson, President Woodrow, 107
Wood, Brigadier General Robert E., 143, 144
World Supreme Court, 278
WPA, 125, 179

Young, Owen D., 78
Young Plan, 77
Yugoslavia, 95, 102, 104, 117, 140, 190

Zapotocky, Antonin, 191
Zaslavsky, David, 139

A NOTE ON THE TYPE

The text of this book was set on the Linotype in Baskerville. Linotype Baskerville is a facsimile cutting from type cast from the original matrices of a face designed by John Baskerville. The original face was the forerunner of the "modern" group of type faces.

John Baskerville (1706–75), of Birmingham, England, a writing-master, with a special renown for cutting inscriptions in stone, began experimenting about 1750 with punch-cutting and making typographical material. It was not until 1757 that he published his first work, a Virgil in royal quarto, with great-primer letters. This was followed by his famous editions of Milton, the Bible, the Book of Common Prayer, and several Latin classic authors. His types, at first criticized as unnecessarily slender, delicate, and feminine, in time were recognized as both distinct and elegant, and his types as well as his printing were greatly admired. Four years after his death Baskerville's widow sold all his punches and matrices to the Société Littéraire-typographique, which used some of the types for the sumptuous Kehl edition of Voltaire's works in seventy volumes.

COMPOSED, PRINTED, AND BOUND BY H. WOLFF, NEW YORK